Dr Michelle Tempest worked as a hospital doctor, psychiatrist and cognitive analytical therapist for over a decade. Now she is a partner in a healthcare strategy consultancy company, Candesic, working globally. She personally invests in AI early stage companies and advises firms interested in emerging digital technology. Michelle ran for parliament in the 2010 UK General Election and teaches ethics and law at Cambridge University. She is an advocate of making learning fun, lifelong and accessible to all.

Dedications

My mother, for being a role-model and loving parent and my father for having his feet on the ground.
All those that have helped on this book journey: heartfelt thanks, gratitude and blessings.

Dr Michelle Tempest

BIG BRAIN REVOLUTION

Artificial Intelligence – Spy or Saviour?

AUSTIN MACAULEY PUBLISHERS™

LONDON • CAMBRIDGE • NEW YORK • SHARJAH

A CIP catalogue record for this title is available from the British Library.

ISBN 9781528985413 (Paperback)
ISBN 9781528985420 (Hardback)
ISBN 9781528985444 (ePub e-book)

www.austinmacauley.com

First Published (2019)
Austin Macauley Publishers Ltd
25 Canada Square
Canary Wharf
London
E14 5LQ

Table of Contents

Preface

'If a machine can think, it might think more intelligently than we do and then where should we be? Even if we could keep the machines in a subservient position…we should, as a species, feel greatly humbled.'
Alan Turing, 1951

These are exciting times for human brain evolution. Modern life is fast. Information is delivered at high speed. The emergence of artificial intelligence (AI) has meant that computers may soon become capable of mimicking the brain, and brains are increasingly reliant on machines. A critical crossroads has been reached where psychology and technology are starting to coincide.

The amalgamation of these two great disciplines has opened up exciting global opportunities, to be seized upon with open arms. But important questions loom. Will cerebral networks shrivel as an increasing number of tasks are done by AI, just as unused muscles atrophy? Will new connections spring up, different from their precursors? Will the brain evolve a new way of thinking? Will AI help humans become increasingly intelligent? Or will AI manipulate humanity and cause cataclysmic chaos?

To date, there are no clear answers. This book does not advocate any halt in advancement – quite the opposite. Instead, passionate inquisitiveness is encouraged to understand if minds may be moulded by digital forces. The joy in being part of AI's mesmerising journey is to find a constructive common path. History will not forgive us if we have a head-in-the-sand mentality. But what will be bequeathed?

The time has come to think ahead of the curve and ask the difficult questions. So, read on if you want to demystify AI and ensure the power of choice remains with its rightful owner – you!

Introduction
Wake Up Call

The human brain and digital technology are intertwining. The pace of change in computing and artificial intelligence (AI) is fast. There is little time to consciously clock consequences. Change may happen by stealth. We are living through a decade in which technology is tapping into human psychology. The time has come to acknowledge the partnership as lifelong. But remember that any binding marriage vows – 'till death do us part'[1]– only apply to the human half. AI is immortal.

In the wild, you'll frequently see stunning symbiotic relationships. The African oxpecker bird feasts on insects hidden within the stripy fur of zebras, and prevents tick bites in a harmonious fashion. The clematis and crab apple plants thrive together, and during spring produce a double whammy of blossom beauty. However, there are also examples of toxic partnerships. Climbing vine shoots can rapidly outgrow their host, and many garden hedgerows have succumbed to such strangulation. The biological boundaries of the brain are increasingly blurring with digital technology. The Big Brain Revolution provides a wake-up call about this questionable partnership.

Thankfully, there is no prerequisite for in-depth knowledge of computer sciences, physics, mathematics, electronics, engineering or economics to digest this book. No doctorate-level knowledge of philosophy, neurology, psychology, psychiatry or neuroscience is necessary. Complex technological jargon is avoided, and all that's needed is an open mind. The future isn't about minuscule details of long mathematical algorithms, software, hardware or code. Nor, though, is it a spectator sport to be observed from the sidelines while eating popcorn. The revolution is happening right here, right now, as our collective acceptance of technological innovation embeds itself deeply into society. It's imperative for everyone to be emotionally engaged in the future – otherwise the journey of digital advancement may be destined to outpace Darwinian human evolution.

It's indisputable that in the space of just twenty years, life has changed. Today, young people marvel at how the baby boom generation managed to survive without the use of mobile devices or access to wireless internet. Regular everyday activities were unimaginable less than twenty years ago. A few things now taken for granted include:

- waking up to mobile phone alarm clocks
- checking emails on phones, iPads and laptops
- making calls via mobile, Skype, Zoom or FaceTime
- shopping through Amazon, eBay or Alibaba
- instant messaging over text, WhatsApp, Viber or WeChat
- news streamed live via social media such as Twitter, Instagram or Facebook
- ordering a car from Uber or Lyft
- booking a place to stay through Airbnb
- home food delivery from Deliveroo, Uber Eats or Ocado
- health monitoring via Fitbit or Apple Watch.

The list of online platforms is proliferating and the number of apps is almost endless. Parents are advised to limit their children's screen time[2] and some adults, too, opt for a digital detox.[3] In 2012, a survey of over 2,000 US secondary school teachers showed 87% believed 'digital technologies are creating an easily distracted generation with short attention spans'.[4] A study, in 2019, scanned the brains of children three to five-year-olds and found those who used screens more than one hour a day without parental involvement had lower levels of development in the brain's white matter – meaning the connections in the brain were more disorganised with slower processing speed. This was significantly associated with poorer emerging literacy skills and the ability to rapidly name objects. 'The average screen time in these kids was a little over two hours a day,' said Dr John Hutton, who ran the study, 'the range was anywhere from about an hour to a little over five hours.'[5] Technology is being implicated in stunting development, causing conduct disorders and creating digital junkies.[6]

Yet the evidence is not robust. The rapid pace of change has not allowed for studies to be done over a long time period, nor have results been easy to replicate. In 2009, for example, researchers found that young adults who engaged frequently in media multitasking performed less well at filtering out distractions and switching tasks.[7] However, when the same relationship was explored in 2014,[8] no such deficits were found. Instead, researchers found that adolescents who engaged more in media multitasking were slightly better at ignoring irrelevant distractions. Conclusive evidence is hard to come by, due to the very nature of how fast technology and software develop. Digital today is different from digital tomorrow.

In the past five years, paediatricians and teachers have spotted that some children have not developed the fine motor skills required to hold a pencil by the time they arrive at school.[9] Instead, they are well-versed in logging on to and swiping across an iPad, and can easily gain access to the multi-billion pound industry of online games. Over 75 million children per month play Minecraft, which was bought by Microsoft in 2015 for $2.5 billion, far more than the cost of its development.[10]

To date, little money has been spent on researching the impact of gaming on childhood development. Nicholas Carr, author of *The Shallows: What the Internet Is Doing to Our Brains*, believes thinking has moved away from traditional information processing and contemplation towards a new form of distracted attention.[11] The focus has shifted from scholarly reading to skimming. The internet offers both immediate information and distractions to the user, and Carr suggests this could tinker with the brain, remap neural circuits, and in some cases, even reprogramme memory.

'Healthy thinking' as a concept is fundamentally overlooked by society, despite the fact that 'healthy eating' so easily trips off the tongue and shapes lifestyles. People carefully choose what food to ingest into their bodies, yet few think about how their brains are passively exposed to a constant stream of adverts, and to a barrage of pings, rings and dings of digital updates. Healthy thinking requires the brain to be put centre stage and nourished, just as the body deserves more than junk food.

My motivation for this book bubbled up from a desire to share my knowledge about the brain and digital, collated during my eclectic personal experience. I qualified as a medical doctor and went on to practise as a hospital psychiatrist for over thirteen years. I have seen human frailty and fragility first-hand, and remain overwhelmed by the beauty of the brain.

I trained as a psychologist in the discipline of cognitive analytical therapy (CAT) and treated medically unexplained symptoms. I found that the human mind can always surprise, and learned to expect the unexpected. Despite science textbooks and academic papers, in practice I found that few clear-cut answers could be found, unlike the neat solutions portrayed in medical television dramas such as *House*.[12]

I teach medical law and ethics, with a focus on how case law understandably lags behind the rapid pace of change brought about by technological developments. As a partner of a strategy consultancy business, I evaluate companies all over the world, many heavily invested in digital technology. It's imperative to appreciate the power of big data and AI, and focus on how to prepare for digital disruption.

Full disclosure – I love digital technology. Love is known to be able to deactivate the parts of the brain critical for logical thinking, and for a predisposition to subjectively ignore faults.[13] However, I hope any love blindness on my part will be trumped by the protective and powerful force of insight, which is held so dear by psychiatrists. The combination of all these skills and life experiences form the foundations of this book, and the premise for why I believe everyone should be mindful of their internal musings, and vigilant about omnipresent digital distractions.

The first section discusses how the brain works, respecting that no two brains are the same; each is as unique as a snowflake. It reviews brain functions such as memory, emotion and decision-making, and the growing integration between brains and computers.

The second section offers a run-down on computers, big data and AI, including machine learning and robots. The third and final section combines all this knowledge to question whether the mind can be manipulated, and how this can be avoided. It considers examples of populist trends, and the potential risks of mega-manipulation in politics and marketing, and evaluates whether brain change may impact international security.

Overall, this book takes a positive outlook regarding the amazing power of the mind. I don't currently believe that computers and technology are the all-powerful answer to everything, ready to turn individuals into nothing more than passive spectators and steal around 50% of jobs.[14] AI is still in its infancy and has not had the time required to evolve into something better than the human brain. Fundamentally, I question whether something better than a human brain can ever be made.

We live in an era in which almost everyone has had their personal data collected by someone. Billions have used Google to look up their own names, and many job recruiters have viewed Facebook profiles. In some ways, the world is already an Orwellian state, and common home comforts such as singing in the shower or dancing naked in the bedroom may no longer be entirely solo ventures. Home devices like Amazon's virtual assistant, Alexa, have allegedly recorded sound even when turned off, and in one reported instance sent audio files to contacts extracted from a smartphone.[15]

In 2014, many celebrities spoke out about how their mobile phones and iCloud accounts had been hacked. Jessica Alba, Justin Timberlake, Jennifer Lawrence and Rihanna all had personal data and images leaked online.[16] Yet the magnitude of such online stalking and privacy invasion is no longer reserved for the realms of those with celebrity status. It's happening all around us.

Modern day living means everyone is in constant digital communication, with US teenagers in 2018 reported to prefer interacting via text message than face to face.[17] This has coincided with an increase in cyberbullying and identity theft.

Today, one in twelve women have suffered from physical stalking, and cyberstalking is far more frequent.[18] The internet can be used by perpetrators as a portal to harass with false accusations, defamation, slander and libel, motivated by a desire to control, intimidate or influence the victim. Perhaps the time is right to try and turn such negatives into positives, and learn from the experiences of every man, woman or child that has been stalked, trolled or cyberbullied.

The risk that 'free will' and 'free thought' are sucked into a vortex of mega-manipulation increases exponentially as AI learns more about the human brain. This brave new world needs to observe change and define the direction of travel. I want to stimulate a sense of urgency and encourage an impassioned debate to ensure the human mind will victoriously master the uncharted and unexplored territory of new digital frontiers. It remains to be determined how AI will change or even control human thought and behaviour and impact society as a whole. Now is the key time to be open minded about both risks and benefits.

Section 1 The Brain

Chapter 1
Cerebrally Exciting Times

While explorers travel to far-flung parts of the globe to glimpse natural beauty and astronauts rocket into space, each and every one of us already owns the most precious and complex system known anywhere in the solar system – our brains. The brain weighs approximately 1.4kg, and has more convolutions and wrinkles than a bulldog's face. It contains around 100 billion neuron cells and nerve fibres that help connect the brain together.[19] If the nerve fibres were stretched out end to end, they would wrap around the world twice. Most connect to nearby cells, but around one in every twenty-five nerve fibres connects to a distant part of the brain. A picture of brain connectivity is a complex web, a little like mapping every Facebook friend connection in the world, only far more complex. In fact, there are more connections inside the brain than there are stars in the universe.

How the brain develops and grows its superhighway of connections is of paramount importance. Intelligence is not about the size of the brain but about how it is interconnected. Einstein may have developed the theory of relativity and introduced the concepts of time and space into modern-day physics, but he had a brain that was smaller than the human average.[20]

Perhaps Einstein's brain personified efficiency, focusing on the development of connections to encourage fast flow around the brain. Today, neuroscientists believe such coordinated brain function is key for high intelligence.[21] An analogy favoured by Oxford University neuroscientist Dr Joe Taylor states:

> Michelangelo created monuments by chipping away at a slab of marble, bit by bit, to reveal David. Similarly, the brain starts with a hyper-connected unorganised network that has to be refined and organised by learning. The result is the sculpture of fast functioning networks.[22]

The brain is the boss of the entire body and controls everything, even when asleep. It's made up of two halves, the right and left hemispheres. They are married together by the largest nerve tract in the brain, known as the corpus callosum. The corpus callosum is a central C-shaped, soft, rubber-like structure, about ten centimetres long, with over three hundred million nerve cell axons passing through it.

The corpus callosum is fundamental for all brain functions and connects the two hemispheres by sharing information between them. In epilepsy, this area contributes to seizures traversing from one side of the brain to the other. Historically, in extreme cases, the corpus callosum was cut to prevent seizure spread. In 1910, a cigarette smoker had his corpus callosum severed as part of treatment plan for his epilepsy.[23]

However, instead of his condition being cured, anecdotal evidence suggests that when he reached for a cigarette with his right hand, his left hand would immediately snatch it up and throw it away, perhaps caused by the disconnection of his two brain halves. This alien hand syndrome was first identified in a 56-year-old patient identified as JC whose stroke had damaged the left frontal lobe and connecting corpus callosum fibres.[24] Four weeks later, his right hand seemed to become possessed. When JC tucked his shirt into his trousers with his left hand; his right hand untucked it. He could not tame his right hand and had to restrain it. When it comes to movement, the left brain hemisphere controls the right side of the body and vice versa. Disconnecting the two halves causes severe consequences.

It's believed the right side of the brain is the more creative side, with a good intuitive grasp of what's going on in the world, and more active whilst sad.[25] It's reported the idea for Harry Potter and a school for wizards popped into J.K. Rowling's head whilst she sat on a delayed train.[26] Perhaps when her Manchester to London journey suffered a signal failure, frustration activated the right side of her brain, setting the wheels in motion for wizardry success, and a longing to reach that hidden Platform 9 ¾ at King's Cross railway station.

The left side of the brain, meanwhile, is associated with logic and with happiness.[27] That being said, a review of brain scans shows no clear-cut right-left distinction. For example, when rappers' brains are scanned during freestyle lyrics, multiple parts of their brain are active. Hot spots of high-oxygen demand are reported scattered across the scans, highlighting electrical activity involving both right and left sides of the brain.[28] It's clear that creativity is neither simple nor unidimensional, and requires neural connections linking up both hemispheres.

The biggest part of the brain, the cerebrum, makes up 85% of the brain's weight.[29] It is the thinking and reasoning part, and controls voluntary movement, such as kicking a ball. Other parts of the brain include the cerebellum, brain stem, pituitary gland and hypothalamus.[30] The cerebellum is located at the back of the brain. It controls balance, movement and coordination and is required, for example, for the core stability of any yoga pose.

A smaller portion, called the brain stem, nestles beneath the cerebrum, and in front of the cerebellum. It connects the brain to the spinal cord and is in charge of the bodily functions required to stay alive. It controls the involuntary muscles, the ones that work automatically without thinking, such as those responsible for breathing, heart rate and digestion. The pituitary gland is an even smaller part of the brain – as small as a pea. It has a pivotal role in the production and release of hormones and in maintaining metabolism. Finally, the hypothalamus is the temperature control system, and can activate shivering and sweating, to ensure a constant healthy temperature of about 98.6F or 37C.[31]

The brain is permanently busy, and on an average day consumes around a fifth of the body's fuel.[32] Even when asleep, it's bursting with electrical connectivity. Around one third of life is spent sleeping, and daily slumber is imperative to the functioning of a healthy brain. Long-term sleep deprivation can lead to cognitive impairment, memory lapses, clumsiness, low moods and decreased immune function.[33] In extreme cases, it can even lead to psychotic hallucinations.[34]

The brain requires sleep in order to get organised, process information, get rid of toxins, and have time to reshape and rewire. It's easy to relate to the foggy feeling of sleep deprivation; everyone has experienced it, be it the result of an all-night party, a restless night, or working a long overnight shift. The effect of sleep on the brain is analogous to a gardener pruning a plant, guiding growth of new shoots, and this in turn helps lay down strong root foundations.

Dreaming is also considered to be important for creative insights – and likewise so is daydreaming. Scientists, in fact, recommend indulging in unfocused thinking by carrying out tasks that are not mentally taxing, like walking or household chores, to help generate those insightful 'aha' moments.[35]

In modern life, it is increasingly difficult to disconnect, especially considering digital data downloads twenty-four seven. As a result, it's by far the most cerebrally exciting time to be alive. Until recently, data reaching the brain was constrained and shaped by the local environment and by knowledge gathered from trusted elders in the same community. Information transfer was restricted by location and speed of communication. Hand-written letters – snail-mail correspondence – would take days or even weeks to arrive, with the timeframe doubling for a single reply. Now, brains have global access to anything and everything almost in real time, thanks to fingertips being constantly connected to smartphones and the worldwide web.

However, today's brain rarely has a chance to stop. It's repeatedly distracted by updates, pressured for instant responses, and constantly expected to process emotions. In fact, electronic expressions of emotion (emojis) are now far more common than the traditional handshake.[36] With so much stimulation, the key question is: can this change the brain? The simple answer is yes.

Yes, because the brain develops and changes when learning to walk or ride a bike. Yes, because the brain develops and changes when revising for school exams or driving tests. Yes, because the brain develops and changes when discovering how to cope with the emotional loss of a first love. Brains are defined as 'plastic' by neuroscientists because they are moulded and shaped throughout life like plasticine clay.[37]

In essence, the brain self-wires in direct response to the inputs it is fed. It's the only organ of the body to have this peculiar characteristic. This gives it an amazing capacity to change over time, reorganising itself by forming new connections between different brain cells. The journey of life with all its twists and turns, and ups and downs, directly impacts the brain. It affects how brain cells connect, and ultimately how life experiences are processed and laid down as memory. The best-known neurological saying of all time states: 'things that fire together wire together'.[38]

A commonly-cited example of change in the adult brain comes from research carried out on London black cab drivers. In order to obtain their taxi licences, they have to pass an exam known as 'The Knowledge' which involves the memorisation of over 2500 London streets.[39] Some parts of these cabbies' brains have been scientifically studied, and it's been validated that change occurred whilst learning 'The Knowledge'.[40] Scans of their brains revealed the posterior hippocampus, the part of the brain associated with memory and navigation, is larger and has more interconnections than that of the normal population. Their training led brain cells in that region to fire up to such an extent that it expanded that part of the brain beyond the average size.

It's taken for granted that the brain develops in childhood but it's often forgotten that the brain is continually moulded and added to throughout adult life. Every day, it gets bombarded with sensory information: smell, taste, touch, sound, balance and sight. It's permanently busy processing information and emotions, with only the tip of the iceberg ever reaching consciousness and human awareness. Churning away underneath conscious awareness is the bulk of the iceberg, where an unfathomable amount of data is being constantly filtered, processed and prioritised by the unconscious.

Despite the phenomenal power of the brain – or perhaps because of it – humans have become amazingly adept at inventing shortcuts: calculators for calculations, satellite navigators for directions, and apps like Tinder to make finding a date easier. After all, why would the brain expend energy on thinking when a task can be outsourced? Famously, when Einstein was asked by a reporter for his telephone number, he picked up a phone directory to look it up. Dumbfounded, the reporter asked, 'How come the smartest man in the world can't remember his own number?' Einstein responded, 'Why would I memorise something when I know where to find it?'[41]

Outsourcing still requires a certain level of common sense, however. Take the example of Robert Jones.[42] He put blind faith in his car's satnav system when returning home from a friend's dinner party in rural Yorkshire. His petrol warning light had been on for a while, so he used his GPS to find the fastest route to a petrol station. He followed its directions all the way up a dirt track, which became steeper and narrower. He didn't find petrol at the end of the track, but crashed straight into a wooden fence. Miraculously, the car stopped just in time, as beyond the flimsy fence was a hundred-foot cliff drop. It took a friendly farmer and his tractor to bring Robert and his car safely back from the brink. He had not even considered overruling the machine and had instead driven on in blind faith. By way of justification, he explained, 'I just trusted it.'[43]

What will happen to the human brain if it increasingly outsources its thinking in this way? It's far too early for any cause-and-effect analysis, and perhaps impossible to disentangle. One thing trackable over time is the Intelligent Quotient (IQ) scores, an intelligence measure developed by Alfred Binet in 1904.[44]

Around the world, IQs have largely increased since the 1930s, thanks to better living conditions, and improved nutrition and education. However, since 1998, IQ scores have been on a downward trend, and the average has fallen by 1.5 points. This is consistent across large data sets, such as the measurement of 25,000 to 30,000 men per year in Denmark who have taken the same IQ test since the 1950s as part of a pre-requisite for obligatory military service.[45] Since 2004, a similar drop has also been noted in Australia, Finland, the Netherlands, Norway, Sweden and the UK.[46]

Perhaps IQ scores should not always be expected to rise. Some believe human genetic potential has peaked,[47] with brains spending far more time connected to technology. Or perhaps brain networks have wired up in new ways that are not evaluated by traditional IQ measurements. Results can be affected by many things, including cultural differences. Critics question if traditional IQ scores massively oversimplify the spectrum of human cognitive ability to such an extent that they may soon be an outdated mode of testing, to be superseded by continuous monitoring rather than milestone spot checks.

Psychologists are trying to broaden the scope of intelligence tests. Nadeen Kaufman, a lecturer at the Yale School of Medicine, believes future tests will be more influenced by the education sector, which is keen to shift the focus to identify learning issues more accurately, and to individualise teaching strategies.[48] More holistic measures include the Emotional Intelligence Quotient (EQ), which tests how emotional information guides thinking.[49]

Research is also ongoing into the possibility of using a very simple measure of the speed of brain connections. How brain signals travel is reflected in reaction times – the gap between when something is perceived and when it is responded to.[50] There are two different types of reactions that can be measured: simple and choice. A simple reaction is instinctive – immediately retracting a muscle away from a burning hot stove, for example. This happens at the level of the brain stem. A choice reaction requires the brain to perceive, process and decide how to respond to a stimulus. Shrinking the time between the sound of the starting gun at the beginning of a running race and the movement of feet off the starting block can make a big difference to professional athletes. Jamaican-born Usain Bolt, who has nine Olympic gold medals to his name, must have lightning-fast reaction times.

At the other end of the spectrum, suffering slower than average reaction times are people with neurodegenerative disorders such as Alzheimer's, Parkinson's, multiple sclerosis, Huntington's, or those who have suffered a stroke. All delay brain processing. Clinical evidence suggests that measuring choice reaction times can be a quick, cheap and non-invasive way to monitor neurodegenerative disorder progression and track any improvement from medication.[51 52]

It's worth noting that everyone's reaction times can be affected by many things such as sleep, mood and anxiety levels. Measuring variation in reaction times has started to be used in the automotive industry, and some elite cars have begun to monitor braking time. This can then be fed back to drivers as a suggestion to take a break when reaction times slow.

The importance of feedback information should not come as a great surprise. Back in 100AD, Epictetus, a Greek philosopher, stated, 'We have two ears and one mouth so that we can listen twice as much as we speak'.[53] Consider the ability to stand still. In this simple act, three feedback sources of information to the brain are required to maintain posture: the eyes, the vestibular system (inner ear) and the support areas down to the feet.[54] Standing still is immediately impaired by loss of just one of these functions.

Most people sway when they close their eyes, especially if standing on something soft. Vestibular impairment can result in falling to the ground after spinning a pirouette or having an ear infection, and information from the stretch receptors provides feedback that the limbs are in the right place, without which posture would be lost.

Whilst all this is going on, the brain is also predicting what may happen next. This is called feed-forward information. It helps keep balance and can let the body know to begin compensating for disruptions even before a change has been sensed. A striking example of this kind of learnt postural response is in the transient jolt that can be felt when stepping onto an escalator that has been turned off. The jolt represents a temporary failure to suppress the normal, learnt reaction of the movement of the feet that would occur if the escalator were actually operating. This highlights how the brain uses both feed-forward and feedback information. This concept is considered later in the book with respect to AI, so keep in mind how the brain balances information from the present frame alongside best guess inputs predicting the next frame. Professor Cox, a neuroscientist at Harvard, uses the example of tennis to explain:

> It can take 170 to 200 milliseconds to go from light hitting the retina through all the levels of processing up to consciousness. In that time, Serena Williams's tennis serve travels nine metres...so anyone who manages to return a serve must be swinging the racket on a prediction...if you are continually trying to predict the future, then when the real future arrives, you can just adjust to make your next prediction better.[55]

The tracking of human performance, measured and quantified using physical actions, only tells a fraction of the brain story. Around 95% of brain activity remains unconscious and relies on rulesets that, to date, cannot be adequately articulated, expressed or codified. The fascinating internal working of the unconscious mind involves billions of brain cells chattering amongst themselves, whilst the conscious mind remains blissfully unaware.

The three main areas of the brain implicated in consciousness are the thalamus, the prefrontal cortex and the posterior parietal cortex. What these regions have in common is that they have more connections to each other, and to elsewhere in the brain, than any other region. Such dense connections are, therefore, logistically best placed to receive, combine and analyse information coming from the rest of the brain.

How the mind solves problems can be compared across species. A famous story about the powers of the mind told some 2,500 years ago is about how a bird can solve complex problems. A desperately thirsty crow on a hot day happened upon a pot containing a small amount of water. It flew away, but returned with stones and dropped them into the container, one by one, raising the water level little by little. The crow continued to do this until the water level was high enough to permit it to drink.

Modern-day wild crows continue to be creative and have been reported to drop encased nuts from the sky onto roads next to traffic lights.[56] They then wait for passing cars to break the hard shells as their wheels drive over them, releasing the nuts inside. The crows even use their beaks to press the pedestrian crossing sign, to stop the traffic so they can safely retrieve their food! These tiny bird brains can solve difficult tasks.

Before machines can mimic minds, the mystery about cerebral processing will have to be better understood. Although brain anatomy is well-documented, little is known about how it all pieces together to create the complex connections required for human insight, critical reasoning, problem solving and judgement.

'We know much less about how the brain works than we do about the heart, liver or kidneys…and we have not had the tools we have needed to be able to study the brain in the kind of detail that we'd like,' said Thomas Insel, a psychiatrist at the National Institute of Mental Health in the US.[57]

Grand-scale cross-disciplinary working will be required to rocket-boost understanding, in a similar way to the collaborative working that got man to the moon in the 1960s. It will also take money. The US government spent $100 million in the first year of the 'Brain Research through Advancing Innovative Neurotechnologies' (BRAIN) initiative, a stock-taking exercise designed to catalogue different cells in the brain and understand how they connect in real time.[58]

Another $100 million has been spent on 'Machine Intelligence from Cortical Networks' (MICrONS), which attempts to chart the function and structure of every detail of the brain starting from a rodent's cortex.[59] The European Union (EU), meanwhile, is funding the Human Connectome Project, a research effort to map brain connections that aims for similar outcomes to the Human Genome Project, which helped unravel genetics.[60, 61]

Much soul-searching will be required to think through the ethical implications of AI trying to emulate the human brain. Technology advancements aim to delve into how brain networks are formed and such knowledge will change every facet of human existence, irreversibly and irrevocably.

Chapter 2
Building a Brain Outside the Skull

The famous neurosurgeon and author of *Do No Harm: Stories of Life, Death and Brain Surgery*, Dr Henry Marsh, described a conversation whilst operating on a patient's brain under local anaesthetic. The computer monitor in theatre showed a view from the operating microscope.

'This is the part of your brain which is talking to me at the moment,' said Dr Marsh pointing to the patient's speech area in the left cerebral hemisphere.

The patient was silent for a while, as he peered at his own brain and then replied, 'It's crazy.'[62]

Brains are not isolated entities like computers; they are an integral part of a connected body interfacing with the world. Asking the brain to understand itself is like 'trying to cut through butter with a knife made out of butter'.[63]

Since time began, people have pondered how the brain functions and what is consciousness. In the 4th century BC, Aristotle reasoned that since the heart is vital for life, consciousness must originate there.[64] The first person to identify the head as key for thinking was Galen, a Greek physician, surgeon and philosopher who lived in Roman times. He believed it was the shock-absorbing cerebrospinal fluid surrounding the brain that contained magical powers or 'psychic pneuma'.[65]

Today, both scientists and philosophers alike accept that a brain is a prerequisite for consciousness. Neuroscientist Dr Hannah Critchlow from Cambridge University describes consciousness as 'to be aware of our surroundings, hold a subjective view of the world, and then interact with the environment with our own perspective'.[66]

Critchlow continues:

> As we understand more precisely how the brain operates, it would seem inevitable that we should get closer to a straightforward explanation of consciousness. Yet, paradoxically, for many this knowledge increases the allure and mystique of the phenomenon, challenging our current definition of consciousness as perhaps too simplistic.

The quest to address the eternal debate around consciousness continues. As computing advances, key ethical questions arise, such as: will machines develop consciousness? And, if so, will it possible to invoke a shared collective consciousness?

To tackle such existential quandaries, philosophers break down seemingly unanswerable questions into bite-sized chunks of knowledge and then connect them in a logical manner. One skillset, the 'Theory of Mind', helps us reflect upon the opinion of others who may have different beliefs, desires, intentions and perspectives.[67] In a way, philosophers and scientists sit as two bookends on a shelf containing all the schools of thought about consciousness.

The scientific community, confident that consciousness will eventually be explained by physics and physiology, is considered to be made up of reductionists. Doctors assess consciousness by observing a patient's arousal and responsiveness. This continuum of states ranges from 'full alertness and comprehension to disorientation, delirium, loss of meaningful communication and finally loss of movement in response to painful stimuli'.[68]

Philosophers, by contrast, consider consciousness the most mysterious aspect of life, set in an array of complex adaptive systems with awareness being more than the sum of its parts.[69] No matter where anyone sits on the scale between these two bookends, there is no right or wrong answer, as nobody knows for sure.

What is known is that the brain is the most complex organ in the body. Canadian neuroscientist Dr Chris Eliasmith, Canada Research Chair in Theoretical Neuroscience at the University of Washington, addressed this issue in his book *How to Build a Brain*.[70] He discusses the possibility of building a brain through the use of things found in a boffin's equipment set, such as wires, transistors and electrodes. If the brain could be reduced to a circuit board, he says, it would employ the power of electricity to send signals via nerve cells which are connected together in neural networks.[71]

A thought could be considered a fizz of electricity passing through the circuit board, with inhibitory signals acting as an intelligent, dynamic, synchronised traffic-light system (although logarithmically more complicated) to prevent activity past certain junctions. To dismantle the brain down into its basic building blocks of neuron cells would be an unfeasible feat, as there are around 10,000 nerve cells within each sugar-grain segment of tissue.[72]

Building an exact brain replica is currently impossible. Neuron connections are not easy to replace. As a point of comparison, damaged skin cells repair over a couple of weeks, eye corneal cells repair in a single day, liver cells can take anywhere between 150 and 500 days, and bone cells renew around every ten years.[73] It can take between fifteen and 254 days to rewire brain-cell circuitry, which is why learning new skills and breaking bad habits take time.[74]

Thankfully, it may not be necessary to replicate the biological make-up of the brain to produce similar outputs. After all, although aviation experts studied how birds fly, air travel was invented without the need to replicate wing flapping. The brain's copy-cat capabilities remain inspirational for computers scientists, robotic engineers and AI experts. Therefore, it's worth running through how neurons communicate up there in the skull, and briefly considering how information flows from one neuron to the next.[75]

Neurons communicate with one another via a sequence of events:

- Little branches of neurons, called dendrites, bring information to the neuron cell in the form of a current.
- Neurons have many such dendritic inputs, but only when sufficient current gathers within the cell body will an electrical spike called an 'action potential' be triggered.
- The action potential spike travels down a long, slender projection of a nerve cell called an axon. It travels in a wave-like fashion, until it reaches the end of the axon.
- Tiny packets of chemicals are released at the end of the axon in the area called the bouton region. These chemicals are neurotransmitters.
- The released neurotransmitters then bind to receptors on the membrane of receiving dendrites of the next neuron and as a result change the electrical current of the cell. The entire process then starts all over again.

The number of dendrite inputs can be over 200,000, and the length of axons can be minuscule or over five metres long. It's an extremely heterogeneous environment, and although there is no need to remember the details, it's important to keep the multitude of variables in mind. Neurotransmitters, response thresholds, response magnitudes, response-to-peak times and response-to-recovery times all vary. Overall, the basic building blocks communicating inside the brain are far more complex than computers that use an on-off system of binary code.

In 1943, computational neuroscientists Warren McCulloch and Walter Pitts built what was to become known as the first external man-made brain cell.[76] It was little more than an on-off switch. This was upgraded in 1957 by Frank Rosenblatt, an American psychologist from Cornell University, who added multiple and variable inputs and then connected dimmer switches to them to create what he called the 'Perceptron'.[77]

Consequently, inputs could be weighted and then summed together to allow a non-linear activation output. This was a bit closer to the brain neuron, which can dampen or enhance a value by nonlinear rescaling, following a sigmoidal curve (also called the 'Yerkes-Dodson response'). This smooth curve is one of the reasons people have the ability to dance in a fluid motion, rather than being confined to stiff and jerky 'robot dance' moves.

In short, computers are digital, using 1s and 0s, and linking together trillions of basic transistors may not be enough to come even close to the brain's analogue system, with an almost infinite amount of variability. Cutting-edge cognitive computing adds together electronic 'neural networks' that experts have designated as 'impressive large-scale' simulations of the way brain cells are linked.[78]

Neural networks link up many small artificial neurons which take inputs from their neighbours, and generate an output depending on the numeric weights associated with those inputs. The output, in turn, influences the artificial neuron's neighbour and the system can be made to learn associations between inputs and outputs.[79] This is termed deep learning, which is a type of machine learning, a subset of AI (discussed in Chapter 9).

Neural networks were inspired by the microstructure of the brain, but a key problem is that what the networks learn and then embody is usually opaque. For example, a neural network that has been trained to recognise cancerous growths on X-rays cannot explain its decisions. The expertise the system has is hidden in numeric weights associated with each neuron, and there is no easy way to extract the knowledge that these weights implicitly carry. Sarah Woodward, a fellow at Cambridge University, states:

> At the base of the architecture of a machine learning systems are the 'neurons': mathematical functions containing 'weights' and 'biases'. Weights are the numbers the neural network learns in order to generalise a problem. Biases are the number the network concludes it should add after multiplying the weights with the data. When neurons receive data, they perform computations and then apply the weights and biases. Usually, these are initially wrong, but the network then trains itself to learn the optimal biases, gaining complexity. However, while the earliest systems had just two layers – input and output – most current systems have more layers and so the network is known as 'deep'. And as deep learning effectively takes place in a multi-layered black box, where algorithms evolve and self-learn, scientists often do not know how the system arrives at its results. So, while virtual neural networks have been around for a long time, combine them with deep learning and you get a game-changer that can still baffle scientists.[80]

One aim is for machines to have the ability to understand 'Theory of Mind' concepts and be able to see things from another person's perspective. To see how external neural networks fared against the human mind, scientists tasked machines with 'The Marble Test' – a well-known psychological experiment that evaluates the ability to reason about another person's beliefs and understandings.

This classic experiment was originally designed for children and is also known as the 'Sally Anne task'.[81][82] In it, a child is presented with two dolls, Sally (who has a basket) and Anne (who has a box). Sally puts a marble in her basket and leaves the room. Whilst Sally is out of the room, Anne takes the marble from the basket and hides it in her box. Finally, Sally returns to the room and the child is asked three questions:

- Where will Sally look for her marble? (The 'belief' question – in the basket)
- Where is the marble really? (The 'reality' question – in the box)
- Where was the marble at the beginning? (The 'memory' question – in the basket)

The critical question is the belief question; if the child answers by pointing to the basket, then they have shown an appreciation that Sally's understanding of the world doesn't reflect the actual state of affairs. If they instead point to the box, then they fail the task because they haven't taken into account that they possess knowledge that Sally doesn't have access to. The reality and memory questions essentially serve as control conditions; if either of these are answered incorrectly, then it might suggest the child has not grasped or listened to the task.

Passing this marble test revolves around identifying both first- and second-order beliefs. A first-order belief is working out what someone else thinks – for example, 'Where does Sally think the marble is?' A second-order belief is what someone thinks someone else is thinking, for example, 'Where does Anne think Sally thinks the marble is?' Children can usually correctly identify first-order beliefs by about age three, but take until the age of six or seven before they can correctly understand second-order beliefs.

Computer scientist Aida Nematzadeh, who worked at Google's AI lab at DeepMind, led the work on testing thousands of AI variants about first- and second-order beliefs using the Sally Anne test. However, AI never managed to beat the 100% score of an average seven-year-old child. The highest AI achiever, RelNet, achieved 95% accuracy.[83]

But before humans get too cocky and overconfident regarding their prowess over computers, it's worth considering another human variable: chemical hormones. Teenagers are known for hormonally-induced higher risk-taking during puberty. In adults, there is also some evidence that endogenous hormone levels of testosterone and cortisol influence decisions.

One study determined that hormones impacted financial decisions more than the share price values during a trading-floor simulation experiment.[84] Traders appear to take significantly higher risks on days when their testosterone levels are above their daily average. This in turn increases variability and uncertainty in profit and loss.

Other studies suggest profit margins are better correlated to levels of cortisol than to the underlying trading numbers.[85] [86] It's one of the reasons why it's believed that a diversity of hormones on trading floors, mixing men with women, could shift the balance books towards more stability.[87] In the future, mixing humans with a second opinion from dispassionate computers that religiously stick to running the numbers may help shift away from extreme bear and bull market trading results, and smooth out the high-risk trades that generate big peaks and troughs.

Another chemical called dopamine is involved in reward-seeking behaviour and a desire to explore, inspect and make sense of the environment. Rats learn their way around a maze faster when cheese is offered, triggering a dopamine release as a reward every time they make a correct turn. In humans, dopamine delivers the reward or sense of pleasure when a problem is solved. Dopamine-induced euphoria has also been found to be present in the seeking action, hence the oft-used saying 'the thrill of the chase'.[88]

Internet searching is a form of seeking behaviour, and so can also offer dopaminergic-energised arousal. Dopamine is the brain chemical implicated in both drug addiction and compulsive gambling.[89] A 2018 report based on a UK Ipsos Mori study of 2,865 eleven to sixteen year-olds raised concerns that close to a million young people had been exposed to gambling via video games or on smartphone apps.[90] The Gambling Commission study found that 450,000 children aged eleven to sixteen bet regularly, more than those who had taken drugs, smoked or drunk alcohol.[91] Nobody yet knows the long-term impact on young brains seeking the thrill of dopamine. Dr Timothy Fong, a psychiatrist and addiction expert at the University of California, said:

> The past idea was that you need to ingest a drug that changes neurochemistry in the brain to get addicted, but we now know that just about anything we do alters the brain…it makes sense that some highly rewarding behaviours, like gambling, can cause dramatic changes, too.[92]

Neuropsychologists measure risk-taking behaviour via an internationally-recognised and academically validated game known as the Iowa Gambling Task (IGT).[93] It's basically a computerised card game used to assess risky decision-making. Some choices within the game have low loss and low reward outcomes, and others high loss and high reward ones.[94] But future risk-taking behaviour is not easy to pre-emptively measure.

Another famous measure of self-discipline and self-control is known as the 'Marshmallow Test'.[95] It was designed for pre-school children by psychologist Walter Mischel, a professor at Stanford University in the early 1970s. The test involves a child being offered a choice between one marshmallow immediately or two marshmallows if they wait for a short period, approximately fifteen minutes. In Mischel's publication, for which he tested over six hundred children, only a third deferred gratification long enough to get the second marshmallow. The children who waited for two marshmallows were correlated to be higher achievers ten years later.[96]

Although there are multiple variables on such a decision, from mood to temperature – opting for a hot chocolate on a freezing cold day may be seen as a wise choice rather than succumbing to temptation. The only thing that is clear is that the brain is a delicate ecosystem, mixing biology, chemistry and electricity. No two brains are the same, and balance is key. The same chemical neurotransmitter does not even produce the same result uniformly across all brain cells. In some cases, they are excitatory to brain activity, in others inhibitory. The brain is precious, complex, beautiful and diverse; AI will have to develop to be extremely clever and canny to be able to replicate such vast human variation.

Chapter 3
Hacking Thoughts and Memories

'We are what we think. All that we are arises with our thoughts. With our thoughts we make the world.' These three sentences about thinking and thought are the opening lines of *Dhammapada: The sayings of Buddha* (as translated by Thomas Byrom).[97] Thinking, however, takes effort. Even though the brain is naturally curious, it's not designed to be thinking all the time. It likes to reduce effort when possible.

Henry Ford, the man who led the global success of Ford cars, summed this up when he said, 'Thinking is the hardest work there is, which is the probable reason why so few engage in it.'[98] Consider a well-known thought experiment.[99] Imagine you are in an empty room which has a candle, some matches, and a box of tacks. Your task is to have the lit candle about five feet off the ground. You've tried melting some of the wax on the bottom of the candle and sticking it to the wall, but that wasn't effective. So how can you get the lit candle five feet off the ground without holding it there?

Even after about twenty minutes, few people solve this problem, despite the solution not being particularly tricky – dump the tacks out of the box, tack the box to the wall and use it as a platform for the candle. Thinking about it in an 'out of the box' way requires effort; instead the brain prefers to spend a lot of time on 'autopilot'. It's a little like making spaghetti Bolognese. After being taught how to make it, the same dish gets served up again and again. It would take effort to deviate from this tried-and-tested tasty recipe to make a novel dish.

For the same reason, travelling can be tiring, especially to a country in which you are not a native language speaker. Mundane tasks, such as paying a bill at a restaurant, can't be done on autopilot. Thinking is involved, and vigilance and visibility over line items and currency conversion is required.

Despite the effort needed for thinking, the human mind remains naturally curious, and likes to explore new ideas. A key difference between the human brain and a computer calculation is that the human brain takes a broad-brush approach and roughly evaluates how much mental effort it will take to solve a problem upfront. Most readers probably did not even bother to solve the candle thought experiment at the start of the chapter, but instead took the shortcut and read straight onto the answer. A computer, by contrast, never contemplates effort. It unquestioningly gets on with any laborious, time-consuming task that humans may find mind-numbingly boring.

During thinking, the brain also accesses its memory bank. Human memory can be divided into working memory, also called short-term memory, and long-term memory. Short-term memory can be used, for example, to capture a telephone number long enough to write it down or input it into a phone. Long-term memory is more of a permanent record of what has penetrated the human mind and is laid down more comparatively than exactly. For memory to successfully store information, it's imperative that information can be:

- encoded,
- stored
- retrieved.

Corruption in any one of these tripartite functions may lead to a memory lapse or error. So, let's consider each in turn.

Encoding into long-term memory

Memory is a product of thoughts as the brain encodes, or lays down, concepts. The brain does not store verbatim all inputs minute-by-minute, or frame-by-frame, like the camera feed of CCTV. That would be impractical as it would require an enormous 'hard disk' inside the brain. Instead, information is processed and encoded in a comparative way, relating to already-remembered concepts and patterns of thinking and reality. This processing and encoding requires thinking, exactly because it's not a mere data dump, but a complex processed and conceptualised thought stream. Human encoding is more sophisticated than mere computer replication and duplication.

Perhaps encoding could be considered to be the management consultant of the brain. That job involves doing more than the well-known joke: 'Management consultants borrow your watch to tell you the time.'[100] They take a massive, messy set of raw data, such as accounting statements, inventory logs and sales orders, and clean, sift and bucket it into ordered chunks.

The 'so what?' or meaning of the data has to be understood and recorded, all in a limited amount of time, to produce a useful final report. They prioritise what's important, using the '80:20 rule'. The product should be an insightful view, getting directly to the nub of the issue. It's a process that avoids the issue of 'junk data in, junk conclusions out' as it sorts information at source to make sense of it all.

Encoding could also be seen as a bridge into long-term storage. It's a bottleneck, where not everything can or will pass over. Therefore, what makes it across the bridge will have gaps. Another analogy of encoding is to say it's like a good author. A storyteller sifts the wheat from the chaff and writes down a story in a way as to be remembered. Writers are experts at knowing what information in a story they can leave out for it to come out stronger and still make sense. A formula frequently used by novelists and scriptwriters can be summarised with the '4 Cs':[101]

- Causality: events in the narrative relate to another, maybe in terms of chronological order or knock-on effects.
- Conflict: events are often depicted as a struggle, where there is an obstacle to overcome.
- Complications: events may have sub-problems that need to be solved, before the main goal can be achieved.
- Character: stories are built around strong and interesting characters and their actions are consistent with the character's core values.

Narrative storytelling tricks are used to help the brain encode information and are the reason why so many novels and films have passed into memory storage without any need for effort beyond reading or watching.

Storage in the long-term memory

The storage area of the brain is called the hippocampus, located in the medial temporal lobe.[102] Humans no longer even attempt to compete against digital memory banks, as computer hard drives or digital clouds win hands down. Take the example of the unique 46-chromosome DNA code, made up of three billion base pairs – basically the genetic instruction manual. No human is able to memorise their own DNA genetic instruction code, let alone other peoples'. Yet a computer can upload and replicate DNA code data in perfect sequence with ease.

An entire human DNA sequence amounts to several gigabytes of data storage, comparable to a movie download. Such large digital capability has led the paradigm shift in the way science can now use and manipulate data. For example, the Human Genome Project,[103] which stores DNA sequences at a population level, has aided the development of personalised medicine, by which drugs are developed to be tailored to individuals with specific DNA codes, rather than non-personalised drugs that will not work on everyone and are prescribed on a 'hope and see' basis.

Retrieval from the long-term memory

Retrieval of data from storage requires extracting information from the hippocampus. Computers and human brains retrieve memories in very different ways. Computers are dependent on where data has been stored. They work in a similar way to the old paper catalogues in large libraries. Each book is catalogued according to its location in the library; the code records which floor, which bookshelf and whereabouts on the shelf the specific book has been placed. Humans, meanwhile, retrieve memories dependent on what is stored. Again, that's the reason storytelling has traditionally been the way to pass on knowledge down the generations.

Overall, what is needed for good human memory is a plethora of brain network connections. These cerebral links are constructed during the development of the brain, and continually honed and significantly updated throughout life. Hence, new memories can be formed at any age. In a sense, an old dog really can learn new tricks, as long as 'encoding, storage and retrieval' functions remain intact. However, memory errors occur when any one of the tripartite functions are corrupted.

A well-known form of dementia is Alzheimer's disease, which globally affects around one in fourteen people over the age of 65 and around 50% of people by the age of 85 years.[104] Sufferers are left living in a form of a 'time warp' as they are unable to lay down new memories. A well-known study into Alzheimer's was based around Sister Mary and 677 nuns, from the Sisters of Notre Dame convent.[105] They all underwent yearly memory tests as part of a longitudinal thirty-year research partnership. The nuns donated their brains after death for the sake of science. It became a wonderfully rich data bank, as they all lived similar lifestyles, had no children, had never smoked and had rarely drunk alcohol.

They had also all written letters when they were aged twenty-two, explaining why they had decided to take up a religious vocation. It transpired that the nuns who had penned more complex essays were less likely to suffer from dementia symptoms.[106] But perhaps the most interesting take-home message was the importance of continuing to remain intellectually active, to use the mind, to teach and to learn.

Sister Mary passed her memory tests with aplomb, and remained an active teacher until her death at 102 years, when her brain was found to be riddled with the pathological and histological hallmarks of Alzheimer's. Dr Bennett, the neurologist who led the Religious Orders Study, said, 'The brain is an ultimate high rent district…it's not like an extra kidney or an extra lung…the brain reserve is basically its plasticity…the ability to take a piece of brain and fundamentally teach it to do something else.'[107]

Hence, even if Alzheimer's causes abnormal knots of protein and kills healthy nerve cells, it's a game of chance. It's only when a critical point has been reached that the symptoms affecting activities of daily living can be spotted. Dementia researcher Professor Michele Vendruscolo said:

> As we age, the brain becomes less able to get rid of the dangerous deposits, leading to disease. It is like a household recycling system, if you have an efficient system in place then the clutter gets disposed of in a timely manner. If not, over time, you slowly but steadily accumulate junk that you don't need. It is the same in the brain.[108]

Hence, the most important lesson is never to give up, as with enough cognitive reserve and an active mind, brain cells can form new networks and reroute. In a similar way to building a bypass, it just becomes a different way of getting there.

Neurologists often talk of memory as an informational processing system with explicit and implicit functioning.[109] Consciously-recalled events are called explicit memories, whereas implicit memories can influence feelings or behaviour without actively recollecting the exact events or facts.

A good example of how emotion aids memory is to ask yourself where were you when you heard the news that Princess Diana had died. Most people remember that fixed point in time, yet remember little about the rest of that day. Despite the fact her fatal car crash in Paris was over twenty years ago, the event affected the world emotionally. Nearly everyone remembers the moment at which they were shocked by the news. Once that memory has been retrieved, it is often part of a broader storyline, such as wanting and willing Queen Elizabeth to lower the flag to fly it at half-mast above Buckingham Palace, and the lingering smell of flowers that engulfed London until the state funeral.

In the time since Diana's passing in 1997, computer memory has made gigantic leaps forward, exponentially increasing information storage. Some futurists predict there will soon be ways to upload data direct into the human brain, side-stepping the thinking effort, emotional overlay and practice required to lay down memory.[110] School pupils, in particular, would be wide-eyed at the possibility of implanting coursework directly into their heads instead of having to endure the drag of school lessons, homework and revision. But perhaps best not to play truant from school just yet! Cracking that conundrum is still a very long way off.

Research is ongoing into restoring lost memory. There is a computer chip already in existence, MIMO, which stands for 'Multi-Input Multi-Output'.[111] This helps detect meaningful brain signals by picking them out from the background noise of millions of firing neurons. MIMO serves a function similar to singling out the needle in a haystack.

Through MIMO, researchers have managed to isolate signals for specific physical actions, for example, the action of finger pointing.[112] When that signal is replayed back to the brain, the body replicates the same pointing action. Conceptually, this is impressive stuff, as it means that perhaps one day entire dance routines could be uploaded directly to the brain – and everyone could be Ginger Rogers or Fred Astaire without having to suffer the pain and endurance of practice, practice, practice.

Other researchers have directly inserted MIMO chips into a rat's hippocampus.[113] In doing so, they helped a rat that had forgotten which lever to press to get a treat reward: the implanted MIMO chip inserted this memory, and the rat regained the ability to retrieve the treat. The American military Defence Advanced Research Projects Agency (DARPA) unit has also apparently tried experimenting with MIMO chips implanted into soldiers' brains to research whether they could transfer knowledge mind-to-mind, but this research is not in the public domain.

The Pentagon is also investigating if it is possible to decode the listening and speaking signals of the auditory neurons in the brain. There has been some progress made around mapping words when a soldier reads text, but there remains a way to go before any internal free-flowing voice of thought can be read.[114]

Until recently, the mere notion of decoding human brain signals to get people to make movements, and create memories or retrieve lost ones, remained solely in the realms of science fiction. Films such as *The Matrix* and TV series *Black Mirror* and *Chuck* have touched on the consequences of such superpowers. In *Chuck*, an entire supercomputer of government agency secrets from the Central Intelligence Agency (CIA) is downloaded directly into the brain of a computer-repair man, a regular guy working in a shopping mall.[115] [116] [117]

For now, this remains in the realm of comedy, but as each day passes, the giant leaps forward in hippocampus memory transfer mean it is unclear if it will remain a complete joke in the future. Imagine the day when memories lost due to old age could be reinvigorated, or someone else's memories could be uploaded.

Perhaps it's creepy to think of a future where it becomes possible to consider a different person's perspective or point of view literally as well as metaphorically. Rather than having to use imagination to 'walk in their shoes', recollection of events could be dropped into the brain to understand how someone else remembered and perceived an issue. This could help towards world peace. Or it could be the way to crack the code to never-ending life, as memories would never be lost, but simply passed down generations. It could certainly lead to very different history classes if real lived experiences could be uploaded to the brain; history would come alive in the head.

One start-up company is already offering to back up your brain to prepare for such future digitisation.[118] The process involves preserving every microscopic detail with a new, advanced embalming process paired with cryonics so that neural connections are preserved. Sadly, Einstein, Bach and Leonardo Da Vinci are all dead – so their precious collective knowledge and brain connections have been lost forever. But maybe in the future there will be the ability to upload memories from the past.

Maybe new jobs will be created for people tasked with the effort of learning. These individuals might be paid for their memories, analogous to how surrogate mothers in America earn a wage for a nine-month gestation period. And rather than worrying about body parts going missing for donors, concern will swap to the threat of memory snatchers preying on those who have laid down memories that other people want.

Chapter 4
Who Owns Your Feelings?

At first glance, dedicating an entire chapter to technology and emotions may seem peculiar. How can computers or robots understand emotions? They are nothing more than wires, connections and code. But new technology is already capable of monitoring and reading basic human emotions. It's predicted there may soon be a phone app with the ability to predict human emotional responses and spot whether conscious and unconscious feelings are congruently aligned.

This poses serious questions that are rarely discussed. With increasing emotional monitoring, how will society change? Will loneliness be eradicated thanks to continuous access to digitised comforting responses? Will human-to-human love be ousted by human-to-machine relationships? Will technological emotional powers leave the human race at risk of being emotionally manipulated?

In evolutionary terms, the emotional part of the brain is woven together like an unfinished detective story, where the plot is outlined but many of the clues are missing. At birth, a baby's emotional competence is equivalent to that of a sheep, and over the individual's lifetime it develops like a patchwork quilt that progressively gets larger and ever more complex.[119]

In anatomical terms, the regions of the brain most responsible for emotional competence include the orbitofrontal cortex, amygdala, hypothalamus, anterior cingulate and parts of the prefrontal cortex.[120] Knowledge of such neural networks is not necessary, but it's key to remember the brain is central for all emotional feelings. Greek physician Hippocrates in 400BC highlighted 'from the brain, and from the brain only, arise our pleasures, joy, laughter and jests, as well as our sorrows, pains, griefs, and tears.'[121]

Humans experience emotion in both mind and body –psycho-physiologically. Having feelings and emotional foibles make us human. Understanding the feelings of others is empathy. Emotional understanding, interpretation, intelligence and integrity are honed throughout life and are experience-dependent. If humans can learn about feelings, it should perhaps not come as a surprise that technology can also learn to interpret human emotions.

Dale Carnegie summed it up in his international bestseller *How to Stop Worrying and Start Living*: 'When dealing with people, remember you are not dealing with creatures of logic, but with creatures of emotion.'[122] This is the fundamental difference between technology and humans. Human emotional brain waves spark in both the conscious and unconscious mind, resembling an explosive cacophony of sound waves. Physicists commonly describe this wave pattern as being 'at the edge of chaos'.

Although chaos, in normal parlance, means complete disorder and confusion, in scientific language chaos describes the critical state required to be able to achieve maximum flexibility alongside the ability to rapidly coordinate activity.[123] Outside the brain, physical emotions are dispersed all over the body, generating tingles down the spine, causing hairs to stand on edge and racing heartbeats, in combination with sweating, flushing, butterflies in the stomach and an array of facial expressions.

Emotional experiences are personal and can be confusing. After all, a racing heart could be the result of a grizzly bear entering your field of vision or the person of your dreams walking into the room. The same physical sensations can convey diametrically opposite messages, and the brain has to instantaneously make a split-nanosecond decision, to either run away or swagger over.

'Fluid' emotions can be defined as those felt in the heat of the moment, while 'crystallised' ones are those learnt from past experiences and built up, layer by layer, over time.[124] Love is an example of a crystallised emotion. It is developed over time and can be as solid as a rock, though needs to be treated with respect to prevent the formation of fault lines. So, could technology interpret love? Let's consider the external tell-tale signs of love that nearly everyone has felt, and AI could learn to decipher.

In 1981, when Prince Charles announced his engagement to Diana, a member of the press asked him, 'Are you in love with Diana?' His comment remains memorable for its awkwardness. 'Whatever in love means,' he replied sardonically.[125] While the nation marvelled at the beautiful princess-to-be, enveloped in the rapturous media hype, the loveless marriage was already laid bare.

If the public video recording of that announcement were to have been run through one of today's machine-learnt AI emotional algorithms, Prince Charles' external emotional expressions would immediately have been red-flagged. His facial micro-expressions, body language, verbal tone and choice of words were not consistent with a man in love, crystallised or fluid. Emotional reading algorithms would not have been influenced by his social status, nor distracted by Diana's beauty.

Studies of human facial expressions report over forty facial muscles with the ability to be moved expressively, combined and activated at different levels of intensity to communicate complex social messages in very short timeframes.[126] It's easy to envisage the glance of a disapproving teacher when someone is talking in class, or the beaming smiles of old friends reuniting.

In the 1960s, psychologist Paul Ekman defined six stereotypical emotional expressions, each lasting often only around fifty milliseconds.[127] These include happiness, fear, anger, surprise, disgust/contempt and sadness. Over time, extra have been added: 'amusement, contempt, contentment, embarrassment, excitement, guilt, pride, relief, satisfaction, pleasure and shame'.[128] Such non-verbal cues are important to society.

In fact, psychology professor Albert Mehrabian highlighted the importance of silent messages in his research when he determined that only 7% of communication is based on words; 38% is dependent on tone of voice and 55% on non-verbal facial expressions.[129]

Reading facial expressions has developed into an academic discipline of its own known as affective computing, spanning computer science, cognitive science and psychology. Technology in affective computing has already been developed to recognise, interpret, process and stimulate human emotion. Paul Ekman's work on facial micro-expressions has been foundational, and cross-cultural studies have proven it is globally relevant. As a result, Facial Action Coding Systems (FACS) have become commonplace in the interpretation of facial micro-expressions, including subtle involuntary expressions, as a method of understanding signs of emotion.[130]

FACS were originally based on photographic stills, and over time the technology has evolved to monitor live subjects or moving pictures, leading to increased accuracy. Although recognising a facial expression is not always the same as recognising the underlying emotion,[131] the technology has found some interesting uses. FACS software has been used to give feedback about students in a class. It was able to recognise when students were struggling with a given topic, allowing teachers to be aware of the issue in real time and so intervene immediately with those that required extra attention.[132] It's also been used commercially, commanding big bucks from the advertising industry due to a results-based methodology that ensures brands, slogans and short advertisements evoke the intended emotional response in viewers before going to market.

There is also currency in understanding the emotional tone of the voice. Actors use their voice boxes to vary speed, cadence, timbre, volume and pitch, all too aware that it's not just 'what they say' but 'how they say it' that adds nuanced emotion to their lines. Voice analysis of emotion is complex due to language and dialect variation, but AI technology can, given time, learn to understand how an individual's voice changes with emotion. For instance, a low mood usually coincides with a slower voice speed, a decreased cadence and an overall decline in the amount of chit-chat.

In a broader sense, voice analysis is already used by some insurance companies relying on 'voice stress test' instruments to help reduce white-collar-crime claims.[133] The technology has been proven to help detect if a caller is telling the truth. Hence, there is potential emotional value in what you say every time you open your mouth.

In terms of the written word, few people have the skill of being able to write Shakespearean prose that speaks directly to the heart. If anything, long love letters have been replaced by shorter, more formal emails that permit little analysis of the underlying emotions. After all, can anyone honestly say they have never misinterpreted the core emotions behind words contained in a text or WhatsApp message, or in an email conversation?

In 2005, a study of text messages and emails called 'Egocentrism Over E-mail: Can we communicate as well as we think?'[134] discovered that participants had a fifty-fifty chance of correctly distinguishing whether the tone of an email was sarcastic or not – basically meaning that probability of success in interpretation was equivalent to the odds involving the tossing of a coin.[135] This is perhaps the main reason emojis have become so popular, as their widespread use helps to add emotional, non-verbal information back into written text. Emoticons are an expression of a writer's mood.

In 2015, the Oxford English Dictionary named the emoji 'word of the year' to reflect the explosive increase in its use.[136] Emojis transcend all languages and as they are universally used to express emotions, they have become a focus for technological data-gathering tools to give feedback about emotions.

Sentiment analysis is the term describing what is also known as 'opinion mining', an activity which sees AI systematically identify, extract, quantify and study subjective information.[137] It's widely used to determine emotional tone and is extensively used in relation to social media as a way of monitoring public opinion. Automated sentiment analysis can offer live psychological feedback. It can, for example, help to analyse whether most of the audience are feeling the emotion that an actor is trying to evoke by tracking a live Twitter feed from a play. Such technology offers the opportunity to pick up early-warning signs for when a message is not conveying the intended sentiment. It can even be used to monitor emotions surrounding financial investments.

Shifts in sentiment on social media have been shown to correlate with shifts in the stock market.[138] Many successful traders have historically used their personal gut feelings to buy or sell shares,[139] knowing that markets are intimately tied to psychology – some traders have even gained cult status for this skill. So it should come as no surprise that the quantification of emotional feedback drawn from the global aggregation of emotional data is a highly valuable resource. Crowd-sourcing emotions are categorically more accurate than relying on a single-source emotional data point.

As technology advances, it is joining up the emotional dots; it can link data from facial expressions, body language, verbal content, verbal tone and the written word, developing into a meteoric rise in the emotional economy. Some companies are already cashing in, such as Affectiva.

Affectiva started in 2009, collecting data from over seven million faces in eighty seven countries and developing facial emotional-AI algorithms that learnt to tune into facial expressions in real-time.[140] It is also using this technology on the inside of cars.[141] Traditionally, sensors in the automotive industry focused on the outside of vehicles with trackers built into the car chassis. Affectiva monitors people inside the car and aims to give live updates, such as warning when the driver is getting sleepy behind the wheel, suggesting a coffee break. It has also added emotional AI inside robots to help make them socially sensitive to global cultural variation.

Other start-up facial emotional recognition companies are hot on their tail. Miami-based company Kairos focuses on facial identification and emotional recognition technology and claims to be on a mission to democratise this sector.[142] It has been busy consolidating the market with several acquisitions in this space. In 2015, it bought IMRSV, a company that develops camera software solutions to gather continuous audience analytics for $2.7 million.[143]

In 2017, it bought EmotionReader, which develops AI facial recognition software, in a multi-million-pound deal.[144] Dr Moore, co-founder of EmotionReader and previously chief technology officer at IMRSV, said, 'I believe with recent advances in AI and deep learning we're at a tipping point where AI will change the lives of millions of people for the better.'[145]

With the emotional tracking genie well and truly out of the bottle, hyper-scale platforms such as Facebook, Google, Apple and Amazon are also hungry to get real-time feedback about the emotional state of their users. Facebook has been forced to get involved, following the high-profile death of a fourteen-year-old girl in Miami, who live-streamed her suicide on her profile page in January 2017.[146]

As a result of this horrific incident, Facebook invested to help identify at-risk users and refer them to a choice of crisis counsellors. However, to date, it has not opened up its methodology for external academic research and as a result, its current efforts are not validated. But it's clear that in an increasingly tech-savvy and connected age, the global market for online support and diagnosis is developing.

Other big companies splashing the cash include Apple, which gobbled up a San Diego-based facial expression AI start-up company in 2016 called Emotient, used by advertisers, doctors and retailers. Apple has not disclosed what it intends to do with the company and has not even disclosed how much it paid.[147]

Webcam companies are also integrating emotional software into their systems, with the ability to compute smirks, smiles, frowns and furrows into live emotional feedback. Companies are well on their way to monitoring the secret emotional sauce and heart-pumping mix that leads to purchasing decisions.

The next steps are for humanity to decide how best to use this technology. It's not far-fetched to imagine a situation in which a new couple who believe they are falling in love could log on to a specialised platform and get emotional feedback on their relationship. AI could collect and combine all datasets between the couple using written communication, voice analytics and facial expression analysis when they speak over FaceTime or Skype. It could even benchmark the emotions they have for each other against historic data from past relationships. AI could continuously monitor for affairs, or even assess the risk of potential affairs, by harnessing data from other contacts. To some, it may sound like a one-way street to an almighty row – yet to others, it could offer a reassuring way to check in on the emotional journey.

In summary, it's clear that AI analysis of personal feelings will have knock-on effects on human partnerships. Data-based matching systems could cross-reference genetic code, personality type, sense of humour and even arousal feedback from smell and touch. The concoction of inputs is limitless in any scientific formula to match human pairs. The hazard of outsourcing gut instinct and interpersonal feelings to a world of 'don't think, don't feel – just trust AI' will change every dimension of dating, marriage and love.

Chapter 5
Emotional Contagion and Decision Bias

Nobody likes being rejected, whether it's being turned down for a job, or having a date declined by someone who is too busy washing their hair. The feeling of being rejected, however, can also develop into a pathological state. Take the example of Miss Havisham in Charles Dickens's novel *Great Expectations*.[148] A wealthy spinster jilted at the altar on her wedding day retreats for the rest of her life, spending her days closed off from the world in a cold, dark mansion wearing her white dress. All the clocks in the house are frozen at twenty minutes to nine, the exact time the groom absconded. Humiliated and heartbroken, Miss Havisham goes on to reap her own form of vicarious revenge by refusing others the chance of love, but dies repentant and begging for forgiveness.

Science uses the phrase 'Miss Havisham effect' to describe a person who suffers a painful longing for lost love in such a way that it morphs into being physically addictive. Such emotionally-charged feelings of rejection and loss are able to pathologically activate the reward and pleasure centres in the brain in ways that are similar to the cravings felt by drug, alcohol or gambling addicts.

Miss Havisham personifies the complexity of human behaviour, and highlights how emotional pleasure and pain can be misconstrued in the brain. Machines, for better or worse, cannot experience heartbreak. Making a decision is defined as a 'conclusion or resolution reached after consideration',[149] and sometimes the brain doesn't have enough bandwidth to compute all the variable data inputs and situations of the complex world. After all, who hasn't struggled with simple decisions, such as who should sit next to whom at a dinner party, let alone the fraught inter-generational family decisions over whose house to go to for celebrations at Christmas, Hanukkah or Eid?

Emotions, both positive and negative, can also be transferred from one person to another. Who can resist infectious laughter? Sometimes, it bubbles up even when inappropriate, and a smile or giggle can be too hard to suppress. It's believed that laughter predated speech, and a penchant for positivity was an important way to demonstrate friendliness, build bonds between people and share an experience.[150]

But in the modern digital age, there is concern surrounding a more sinister spread of feelings that disseminate faster than wildfire. This has led to the coining of the term 'emotional contagion', first evidenced in 2014 when 'Experimental evidence of massive scale emotional contagion through social networks' was published in the *Proceedings of the National Academy of Sciences*.[151]

The article reported on a remarkable experiment which utilised Facebook and found that emotional states and emotional bias could be transferred between people. Researchers at Facebook and Cornell University modified the newsfeed on the Facebook walls of 689,003 people. Unbeknownst to the subjects, Facebook deliberately reduced exposure to their friends' positive or negative posts in an aim to test the emotional contagion theory.

It found that people exposed to more positive posts tended to share more positive updates about themselves. People exposed to fewer emotional posts were less expressive, while people exposed to negative posts posted more negative Facebook wall updates. The emotional copy-cat results found were stark and had large aggregated consequences. Although the study perhaps raised more ethical questions than it answered, it clearly highlighted that digital feeds seem to be able to manipulate the individual's inner emotional dial, both up and down.

Emotional states are important as they can impact human decisions and subsequent behaviours, both with or without conscious awareness. A feeling of happiness occurs when incoming signals activate the reward pathways in the brain. The reward or buzz results in motivational positive reinforcement. Feelings of fear are at the other end of the spectrum and help protect from danger. They activate the amygdala, an almond-shaped structure in the middle of the brain that directs a hormonal cascade, including the release of adrenaline that prepares the body for fight or flight.

Memory is also connected to the amygdala, and it's believed this link crucially helps remember dangerous situations so they can be quickly avoided in the future. Consequently, from a Darwinian perspective, emotions impact and influence decision-making. By contrast, decisions made by machines are not impacted by emotional information unless they are programmed to do so. To compare human and digital, studies have identified three key steps in the decision-making process: training, prediction and judgement.[152] [153]

Training

Both human minds and machines can improve decision-making with practice and training. Training is pivotal in the ability to make strategic decisions. The legacy of a good teacher is the ability to imprint on students the capability to make their own thought-through decision. Decision-making is a life-long learning process; everyone can learn from experience and mistakes. In 1983, the multiple award-winning comedy film *Educating Rita,*[154] starring Michael Caine as an Open University English professor called Frank and Julie Walters as a Liverpudlian working-class hairdresser named Rita, depicted Rita's personal journey and how learning about literature opened her mind and broadened her horizons.

Yet her new critical analysis skills came with life consequences, and sometimes personal sacrifices, as her decision-making skills evolved. The story strikes a chord with how a student's brain embraces new knowledge, and how training the mind both intellectually and emotionally can have wide-reaching effects on daily decisions.

Prediction

Prediction in human decision-making is partly based on intuition or a hunch, and as a result is vulnerable to human emotional and cognitive bias. Consider the following three examples of human prediction:

- The 2008 financial crash: it's believed that calculation errors were, in part, caused by human over-optimistic forecasting of debt ratings, especially the triple A-rated collateralised debt obligations (CDOs). The result was a prediction that these CDOs would have less than a one-in-800 chance of failing to deliver a return in five years. Yet by half a decade later, more than one in four had failed. The initial prediction was staggeringly wrong due to repeated human bias; the result was a global economic shockwave. Debt-rating businesses have gone on to develop automated technology to reduce human bias and more accurately predict a borrower's likelihood of default. AI is now commonly deployed in the financial sector as a first or second calculation to human opinion.

- When British aircraft returned from bombing raids over Germany in World War II, engineers initially predicted it was important to patch up and reinforce areas on the plane they could see had been damaged. However, this did not improve the number of pilots or planes who made it home. As a result, statistician Abraham Wald was drafted in to find a solution using bullet-hole data.[155] Mathematical formulae told the engineers to reinforce the areas without bullet holes, rather than the parts of the planes with the damage. He conjectured that bombers who did not come back were hit in places that were fatal, and that planes that did come back had been hit in areas of the plane that would survive the attack. When the air force engineers increased armour in places without bullet holes, more pilots and planes returned back to base safely.

- Psychologists Daniel Kahneman and Amos Tversky carried out an experiment to illustrate human prediction errors. They asked people to consider a scenario about two maternity hospitals. One of the hospitals had an average of forty-five births per day and the other fifteen. They asked, 'Which hospital would have more days when 60% or more of the babies born are boys?' Very few people gave the correct answer. The larger hospital has a greater number of births and as such it is more likely to have a daily average closer to the medium (50:50 boys and girls). The smaller hospital with smaller birth numbers is more likely to have extreme outcomes, away from the average. However, to get to the correct answer takes some thinking about, and human brains instead often just make a guess, which may not always be correct.[156]

Brains are not very efficient computational devices, and all of these examples highlight how computers can outperform humans in terms of their ability to deal rapidly with big data, and model varying outcomes without emotional distraction. The ability of AI to power up prediction was discussed as a potential game changer by three Canadian economists in their book *Prediction Machines: The Simple Economics of Artificial Intelligence.*[157][158]

Authors Ajay Agrawal, Joshua Gans and Avi Goldfarb wrote that AI will progress by using prediction to solve problems that haven't historically been thought of as prediction issues and 'predict faster, cheaper and better'.[159] They discuss the potential impact of AI in decision-making and used the example of global company Amazon. They suggest that AI could be used to predict an individual's buying decisions without them needing to shop or browse, simply shipping purchases direct to their door. This would fundamentally change the business model of Amazon from an 'opt-in' to an 'opt-out' shopping experience.

Judgement

Judgement is another linchpin in decision-making, and requires both good and bad consequences to be weighed up. In theory, human brains should outperform their digital counterparts, in part because brains are busy bees and use judgement or gut instinct learnt from similar situations or intangible past analogous experiences. Yet human judgement is also fallible, with a plethora of cognitive biases often bubbling up from the unconscious mind. These can all impact and influence human decision-making. Examples of human judgement biases include:

- Anchoring bias: where the mind over-focuses on one factor, often the first encountered, when making a decision;
- Clustering illusion bias: where the mind sees phantom patterns in random events;
- Confirmation bias: where the mind preferentially seeks and recalls information that confirms preconceptions;
- Congruence bias: where the mind tests a decision by seeking evidence that supports rather than refutes it;
- Fundamental attribution bias: where the mind attributes a person's behaviour to their personality rather than to the situation;
- Gambler's bias: where the mind believes that past random events alter the likelihood of future ones;
- Hyperbolic discounting bias: where the mind overvalues what's available in the present moment relative to future timelines;
- In-group bias: where the mind overestimates the abilities and values of their group relative to others;
- Negativity bias: where the mind pays more attention to bad news and feedback than to good;

- Positivity bias: where the mind pays more attention to good news and feedback and ignores the bad;
- Projection bias: where the mind assumes that most people also hold the same beliefs;
- Status quo bias: where the mind favours decisions that will leave things 'just as they are';
- Error fatigue bias: where the mind gets bored of weighing up different opinions and so gives the quickest answer.[160]

This list could go on and on, including what another person looks like, what they wear or what accent they have, as well as religious, political and societal prejudices. One study found that Israeli judges delivered significantly harsher verdicts when they felt hungry. Parole was granted to 65% of people on trial after a hearty breakfast, compared to less than 15% just before lunch.[161]

Other studies in the US have shown that black defendants on average go to prison for longer, are less likely to be granted bail and, once on death row, are more likely to be executed.[162] [163] [164] It's hoped that technology may be able to help overcome some of the vagaries of human bias. For example, Mel Slater, a researcher at the Institute of Neurosciences of the University of Barcelona, studied the influence of immersive virtual reality (IVR) on racial bias. Slater found that adopting a different person's race in the virtual sense helped reduce bias and impact behaviours.[165] [166]

To some extent, it could be hoped that the digital world would be free from judgemental biases. However, to date this has not been the case. There are plenty of examples in which digital technology has inherently learnt human bias, and other examples whereby AI has developed its own biases after using big data sets but applying them without common sense.

One famous story is that of an African American Harvard professor who was in line for a promotion. She Googled her own name and found the Google adverts surrounding her name search targeted people with a criminal record. As a result of this, she immediately went to her employer to explain she had never been on the wrong side of the law. She got the promotion. She also published her discovery that online searches for African-sounding names were disproportionately likely to be linked to adverts with the word 'arrest'.[167]

It's unlikely the judgement of a human could or will ever be completely outsourced to some sort of robo-digital-AI counterpart. However, AI could help hasten some of the laborious groundwork in gathering information to help make a considered judgement. For example, in legal cases, AI could sift through some of the mind-numbing reams of legal paperwork. It could also be leveraged to tackle very technical cases such as thorny patent disputes or financial forensic evidence.

In theory, it should help mitigate the impact of how emotions are deliberately used by barristers to build legal narratives in their client's favour. In a fictional context, the American legal drama *Suits* showed its corporate lawyers trying to sway outcomes using personal information about presiding judges, while actress

Meghan Markle's paralegal character was expected to withhold relevant information in legal disputes, in favour of emotional loyalties.[168]

Every day, split-second judgement calls can also cause ethical quandaries. Consider the difference between human and AI judgment during the awful incident of a car turning a corner and confronting someone crossing the road. In that moment, the driver has a choice to swerve and hit the wall but save the pedestrian, or keep going, save themselves, and risk killing the pedestrian.

It's believed that the human would usually choose to save themselves, but a computer judgement is up for debate. In Canada, autonomous vehicles have been approved for testing on public roads, but it's a moral maze.[169] Would a driverless car make a different choice, and why? A driverless car may decide to terminate the person that had paid a lower car insurance premium, and in doing so fundamentally change core values of global society by adding a numerical value to human life.[170] [171]

Films such as *2001: A Space Odyssey*, and the accommodating robot hosts of *Westworld*, have enthralled viewers with the prospect of conscious, self-aware, intelligent machines, but the reality is that the creeping-in of digital decisions is likely to start from mundane outsourced tasks, such as driverless cars, boats, planes or trains. [172] [173]

In Japan, Hitachi has already used AI to analyse business processes and claim an 8% efficiency gain over humans.[174] Such findings feed a longstanding concern that machines could ultimately replace humans in the workforce. A report from McKinsey & Company predicted that as many as 800 million workers globally could be replaced at work by robots by 2030.[175]

The counter-argument put forward by Amit Midha, president of Dell EMC's commercial business in Asia Pacific and Japan, is that AI will create newer types of jobs, with more than 80% of the jobs in 2030 yet to be invented. Midha believes it's exciting as 'these jobs are likely to be higher quality jobs where drudgery doesn't exist', although he noted the need 'to train people for those types of jobs'.[176]

The focus should be more about job change than job loss. Surgeons, for example, are increasingly using robots to assist them with routine operations. New technology provides better vision, more precise incisions, and neater sutures. However, few medical schools have developed training in line with new surgical techniques. Professor Shafi Ahmed, colorectal surgeon, teacher and futurist, says, 'To prepare for surgery of tomorrow, you have to train the surgeons of today in the latest techniques – be that robotics, virtual and augmented reality and ways to conduct operations in different continents and time zones.'[177]

The next step in guiding decision-making for both humans and machines will be to use the increasing amount of personalised data. What has been termed the Internet of Things (IoT) throws out plenty of seemingly benign information from digital sensors in common household items such as kettles, lights, hoovers and heating systems. Such connected smart homes allow house heating to be temperature-controlled remotely, and even light bulb luminosity and colour can be altered via a phone app.

But this means data also tracks when the heating is turned up, when the kettle is switched on, and even the temperature of the shower. Analysis of such rich data sources is creating value for some companies that can track movements both in and outside the home setting. Take the example of an Ohio motor insurance start-up called Root, which wants to offer cheaper car insurance premiums as a reward for safe driving.

Alex Timm, the CEO, says good drivers are effectively subsidising the bad ones, who account for the majority of accidents.[178] Root has invested heavily in AI and uses feedback information from a smartphone app which monitors sensors in the phone to measure location, acceleration, braking and turning. The myriad of sensor data helps clever software check on risky driving behaviours; it can monitor lane-changing and tail-gating, and even measure tiny vibrations to check if drivers are responding to messages or emails. Root algorithmically vets driving risks, and Timm claims 'our models are much more accurately predictive of accidents'.[179]

Data from tracking the activities of daily living can be transformed into a myriad of variables to help AI make increasingly accurate predictions. This has led some futurists to believe that AI will, given time, be better at computing decisions than humans. Others believe that AI will be useful in 'augmenting' human decisions by gathering, distilling and displaying information back in a far simpler form. Yet there is something rather beautiful about the reality that human decision-making remains fallible, impacted upon by both internal and external unquantified feelings.

Robert Cialdini, in his book *Pre-suasion: A Revolutionary Way to Influence and Persuade*, describes decision-making as 'difficult and stressful, akin to the juggler's task of trying to keep several objects in the air all at once'.[180] In the real world, deadlines, information overload or lack of evidence mean the human brain relies on a concoction of life experiences, memories, emotions, learnt information, prediction capabilities and visceral judgements. Decisions are a compromise.

The quirky word 'satisficing' – coined by economist and Nobel laureate Herbert Simon – is a blend of two words, 'satisfy' and 'suffice'.[181] Simon notes that decision-making is more of a balancing act than a numerical calculation. The setting in which individuals make decisions also influences choice. This was evidenced by behavioural economists Professor Cass Sunstein and Professor Richard Thaler in their book *Nudge*.[182] How much food is eaten depends on the size of the plate; which magazine is bought at the supermarket depends on which ones are on display at the checkout. Governments, including those of the UK and USA, employ behavioural economists at the very heart of policy units to help nudge populations.

A study run with the State Debt Recovery Office (SDRO) demonstrated that fine notices that used personalised wording – 'you owe' rather than 'amount owed' on the letter heading – led to significant improvements in repayment rates.[183] Deployment of nudge theory in political behavioural units has managed to successfully lower teenage pregnancy rates and increase university applicants from deprived areas.

The armoury of AI to combine personal data, economics and psychology will allow human decisions to benefit from immediate access to evidence and expert advice. The hard work of researching and painstaking comparative assessments of multiple options could be outsourced to AI. The mind could relax. But this comes with consequences – some of them unintended.

The power of persuasion, nudge and influence over individual choice is known to be impacted by authority-based evidence, in the moment cues and easy to read information displays, to name but a few. Complex decisions are riddled with conflicting advice, different value judgements, twisted statistics and emotional turmoil. Augmenting or outsourcing decisions to AI comes with both opportunities and risks. On one hand, it may help inform choice, speed decisions and encourage healthy choices. But on the other hand, humans may become reliant on AI, coerced by feedback, and ultimately lack the confidence to make their own independent decisions.

Chapter 6
Brain-Digital Integration:
Could It Happen? When and How?

'Change will not come if we wait for some other person or if we wait for some other time. We are the ones we've been waiting for. We are the change that we seek,' said President Barack Obama.[184]

There are responsibilities that predetermine what kind of future is left for the next generation and the generation after that. One defining step is ever-closer human digital integration (HDI) with the merger of body and technology. A Swedish company called Biohax implants microchips, about the size of a grain of rice, under the surface of the skin between the human thumb and index finger. It has several thousand clients and its chips are used as authenticators for buildings and computers, removing the reliance on identification security badges.

Founder of Biohax (and former professional body piercer) Jowan Österlund said his clients seek enhanced security to restricted areas and sensitive data.[185] In the medical field, smart contact lenses with embedded sensors have the ability to measure fluid pressure inside the eye, and monitor sugar levels in the body without the need to draw blood.[186] And over 300,000 people with sensorineural hearing loss already use cochlear implants.[187] They are the most prevalent and successful bionic implants, and work by bypassing the normal acoustic nervous system, replacing it with electrical signals that the brain learns to interpret as sound and speech.

Artificial human body parts are not new. Archaeologists have found examples of false legs and arms as far back as in ancient Egypt, Greece and Italy.[188] These have ranged from crude wooden pegs through to strap-on limbs with hinged joints. Today, modern artificial limbs can be bespoke replicas of an individual's body shape, 3D-printed, or designed as a bejewelled fashion item.

Advancements include the ability for prosthetic limbs to be controlled directly from the brain. Artificial limbs use sensors placed around the skin of the stump to sense and measure electrical signals sent from the brain to the muscles, via 'myoelectric' messages.[189] Although such signals rarely correspond to the exact movement of the missing limb, the user can over time learn how to make the prosthetic move in the desired fashion. More ambitious body-prosthetic-human integration has been developed with surgically transplanted sensors inside the stump of an arm or a leg so as to integrate directly with human nerve endings. The spiking electrical signals produced by motor nerves can then be transmitted and interpreted directly, giving the user much finer control of movement.[190]

Feedback from prosthetic limbs back to the brain, however, remains quite rudimentary. Newcastle University bioengineer Kianoush Nazarpour has successfully used relatively simple sensors in the fingers of prosthetic arms to detect temperature, pressure and shear, converting this output back into small electrical currents which can be felt at the skin around the stump.[191] 'The brain can learn to interpret the sensation on the remaining flesh as though it were on the hand,' he said.[192]

The next new wave of treatments – called 'electroceuticals' – is likely to use the body's nervous system. If the electrical language of the nervous system can be understood, it may lead to prescriptions offering electricity-based therapies alongside traditional tablets.[193] Dr Kevin Tracey, a neurosurgeon at the Feinstein Institute for Medical Research in Manhasset, New York published his discovery in 2017 that the body's gut inflammatory response was partly regulated by the vagus nerve – the electrical signalling system to the gut. Tracey founded a company called SetPoint Medical to make a device to manipulate the electrical signals running along the vagus nerve with the aim of controlling inflammation in auto-immune disorders like Crohn's.[194]

Since Crohn's is caused by an overactive inflammatory response in the gut, the aim is for the device to dial down the signal zipping around the gut activating immune cells and aggravating tissue. It remains an untested theory – but bioelectronics therapy changing the messaging system between the brain and the body is a ray of hope for sufferers of auto-immune conditions, from Crohn's to rheumatoid arthritis.

The next crucial step in HDI relates not just to the body but to brain integration. This is where things start to get funky. Some consider brain-digital integration as really weird, really scary or really dangerous, whilst others envisage it as a natural step in human advancement and the only chance to save the human race from self-destruction. However, before any sophisticated next steps in brain-digital integration or brain-computer interfaces can be discussed, it's perhaps worth taking a step back to consider the way the brain functions.

Overall, the section of the brain that controls movement, the motor cortex, is much better understood than other parts that deal with thinking, emotion or just everyday decision-making. It's imperative to get an overview of brain functionality before undertaking any sensible discussion of brain-digital integration. Any psychiatrist knows there is nothing more mysterious or beautiful than seemingly undetectable differences or nanoscopic nuances in brain connections, be they physical, chemical or electrical, that appear to be able to cause anything from acute psychosis to an infinite variety of personalities.

With so little understood about the human brain, stimulating it externally or internally will bring with it consequences that are not yet fully appreciated. Nor is it currently possible to predict the final outcome. And yet, this is exactly what brain-digital integration is set to do.

Democratisation of this debate should become the bedrock of brain-digital integration advancement. But first, let's conceptualise the brain and simplify it down into three parts:[195]

- The base brain: this part of the brain is at the back of the head and controls life existence. It's concerned with the bodily functions taken for granted like breathing and sleeping, and remembers how to automate tasks. For example, nobody forgets how to ride a bicycle or how to type, as over time this knowledge gets stored within base-brain procedural memory.
- The perception brain: this middle part of the brain receives a full range of information from all around the body, giving the ability to see, read and dance (for example).
- The interpretation brain: this part of the brain is at the front of the head, behind the forehead and is 'the reason you are you'. It pulls together all the information and puts it in context.

It's the interpretation part of the brain that provokes the most concern and curiosity within the brain-digital integration setting. After all, it's the magic of what sets the human race apart from all other animal species. It's in charge of attention, self-identity, self-control and executive functioning skills, 'a set of processes that all have to do with managing oneself and one's resources in order to achieve a goal…an umbrella term for the neurologically-based skills involving mental control and self-regulation.'[196]

This activity is analogous to an air traffic control tower, as it coordinates decision-making, planning, organising, emotional-regulation, self-control, creativity and flexibility.[197] Neurologist Antonio Damasio wrote that the interpretation part of the brain 'can eavesdrop on our entire being', and it develops throughout life, helped to grow by loving, affectionate relationships.[198] It has access to both facts and emotions, and can link thought and feeling. It can also play an inhibitory role, turning off behaviours that are not socially advantageous.[199]

Interestingly, brain-scanning studies have spotted that the brains of some prisoners, criminals and psychopaths have reduced interconnections between the front interpretation brain and other brain regions.[200] [201] It is believed the human ability to feel guilt, empathy and remorse, and to interpret these emotions, are all dependent on a functioning front brain.[202] It acts a little like a conductor, with the pros and cons of a situation orchestrated, and overlaid with critical thinking and analysis into the symphonic result.

The most famous case concerning damage to the front part of the brain is the story of a railway labourer named Phineas Gage.[203] In 1848, he had a nasty work-related accident in which a large iron rod was driven right through his head, completely destroying his left frontal lobe. Despite the metal rod embedded in his head, Gage retained the ability to walk and to talk, and also his full memory.

His personality, however, changed radically. He went from being a gentle, mild-mannered man to being an irritable, quick-tempered, impatient one lacking in understanding of social norms. He ended up leaving his wife and family to join a travelling circus, where he performed in a freak show. Abnormalities in the frontal lobe can be very disabling, and often interfere with seemingly simple everyday tasks, such as making a cup of tea.

If you break down the sequence of events required to make a hot drink, it's evident that it's not as easy as it sounds: you need to plan ahead and organise quite a complex set of tasks such as locating a clean cup, heating and pouring water that can scald, and calculating with precision the addition of milk, lemon or sugar. It's a task that's frequently mixed up by elderly people with frontal lobe dementia. They can suffer confusion in this process and end up filling the kettle with tea bags, or just getting so frustrated that pots and pans end up scattered all over the floor, leaving them thirsty or even dehydrated.

This is a very crude example of frontal brain dysfunction. For a more sophisticated understanding of its functioning, it is worth delving more deeply into what goes on inside the frontal area. This most interesting and intriguing part of the brain can be subdivided into three parts:

- The dorsolateral prefrontal cortex (dlPFC): responsible for working memory, cognitive flexibility, planning, inhibition and abstract reasoning, this area provides top-down effortful control, also known as 'cold processing'.[204]
- The anterior cingulate cortex (ACC): associated with reward anticipation, decision-making, empathy and impulse control, also known as the 'salience network'.[205]
- The orbitofrontal cortex (OFC), which is anatomically synonymous with the ventromedial prefrontal cortex (vmPFC): responsible for affective reward and punishment, self-regulation and decision-making, which offers bottom-up emotionally-laden information interpretation, also known as 'hot processing'.[206]

Cold processing tends to be top-down and logic-based. It is free from emotional arousal and the thinking involved takes effort.[207] Hot processing is more bottom-up and emotionally laden; it is more instinctive, and can help give you that feeling of a hunch or a 'gut feel',[208] often interpreted as an intuition.[209]

Another well-known way of looking at the brain was popularised by Daniel Kahneman in his book *Thinking, Fast and Slow*.[210] Fast spontaneous and slow effortful thinking both use a conglomerate of complex connections. Any external machine interfering with the fine balance of brain function is likely to change both the top-down, slow logical and cold thought processing plus the bottom-up, fast emotional and hot experiences. It's worth remembering that any disruption could radically change the essence of the person – their core, even their inner soul.

Overall, the front part of the brain somehow masterfully processes the dynamic neural system, affected by everything top-down and bottom-up. It's a massive connectivity network, analogous to a global travel map. There are local connections where pedestrians can walk, roads that can lead anywhere from a dead end to a windy country road, through to a bypass, a motorway or a fast superhighway. This is overlaid by flight paths travelling miles away to distant parts of the brain.

As neuroscience advances and the beauty of the brain is further explored, these three parts of the brain are revealed as interlinked large-scale networks. Research analysed the brain scans of 389 participants and found such networks are scattered across the brain. They did not find a 'one model fits all' approach, but instead found variation between brains and spatial overlap.[211]

This means that brain-digital integration would have wildly different results, even when the same anatomical location was stimulated, bypassed or changed in some way. Interfering with individualised brain networks will lead to unique and unknown consequences each and every time. Any advancements in connecting computers with the human cerebrum are, therefore, far more complicated than the order found on a circuit board.

Brain-computer interfaces are at the forefront of using implants to stimulate neurological systems. Linking artificial implant equipment direct to organic brain cells has been referred to as 'wetware'.[212] Wetware communication is not a simple task, as electricity and water don't mix well – and the brain is made up of 70% water! To date, wetware remains largely conceptual and a material science challenge, although prototypes have offered proof of concept, and people such as Elon Musk are pumping money into developing this field for fun.

Musk's company, Neuralink, is dedicated to research in this sector and has published a paper in *Nature Nanotechnology*, explaining how a flexible circuit could be injected into a living brain.[213] If wetware can be developed successfully, it would add a third dimension to computer hardware and software, and expand capabilities beyond current limits. Wetware offers the chance to get immediate cellular-level information from the brain and allow AI to listen to data feedback direct from the brain. This may lead onto bidirectional brain-computer interfaces (BBCI), whereby information is collected and disseminated within the immediate setting of brain cells.

Brain-digital interfaces are happening, and our generation has a responsibility to guide this journey after considering the broad spectrum of opinion. There are already some medical examples of brain-digital integration which seem like science fiction, but are actually a recognised and accepted part of a treatment pathway. For example, in Parkinson's Disease, when dyskinesia tremor symptoms become so debilitating that sufferers can no longer stay still long enough to sleep or hold a hot cup of tea without spilling scalding water all over themselves, deep brain stimulation (DBS) can come to the rescue.

In DBS treatment, electrodes are surgically implanted inside the brain and are precision-guided to have direct contact with areas of the brain that control movement (specifically either the subthalamic nucleus or the globus pallidus interna). These electrodes are then connected to a battery-operated device not dissimilar to a pacemaker and usually inserted subcutaneously below the collar bone. The device is called a neurostimulator and its electrical current can be set to reduce the tremor.[214]

It's believed that it works by interrupting the atypical signalling patterns that cause the physical shaking. Research is ongoing into improving the present-day continuous current method – advancing beyond it, into what's called 'smart DBS'.[215] In smart DBS, neurostimulators record a person's unique brain signals and respond by delivering electrical stimulation at a level and time required by that individual. This is an example of a personalised smart chip being added to a brain to replace function lost to disease – a form of brain-computer interface.

Another medical advancement in brain interfaces is in the development of soft, flexible electronics inserted inside the brain. Research is ongoing into the use of these interfaces to treat epilepsy. This can cause tonic-clonic seizures, also known as a grand mal seizure. Patients may lose consciousness, and muscles contract and relax rapidly, causing convulsions.

There is a common misconception that motor symptoms are the only types of epilepsy. In fact, epileptic symptoms are diverse and depend upon the areas of the brain affected.[216] Treatment with anti-epileptic drugs often has serious side effects and fails to prevent seizures in around 30% of patients.[217] The ideal treatment would be to stop the fit at source by pressing the electronic brake to stop neurons from firing. Researchers have managed to achieve this result in mice by inserting a patch inside the affected area of the brain.[218]

When abnormal electrical seizure activity starts, micro-doses of an inhibitory drug are released and the dose can be titrated to ensure inhibition of the abnormal electric field.[219] Professor George Malliaras, the Prince Philip Professor of Technology in Cambridge's Department of Engineering, who led this research, said, 'These thin, organic films do minimal damage in the brain and their electrical properties are well-suited for these types of applications.'[220] Researchers studying the brains of mice found that treatment delivered at the epicentre of the seizure managed to stop it before it spread.[221] However, such patches have not as yet been inserted into human brains.

'Neuromodulation' is the scientific term given to zapping the brain to update nerve activity using a targeted delivery of a stimulus. This can be achieved internally by penetrating the skull or stimulating the brain from the outside, which is logistically far simpler. Wearable headgear equipment resembling a swimming cap with multiple leads connected to it can deliver magnetic or electrical impulses. Transcranial magnetic stimulation (TMS) was developed in the 1980s, and is based on the premise that a time-varying magnetic field can induce a secondary electric current in neural tissue, which leads to the activation of messages inside the brain.

The public have tended to shy away from such interventions, even though it could be used as an alternative to pharmacological interventions. Repetitive transcranial magnetic stimulation (rTMS) is licensed for use with neurological conditions such as chronic neuropathic pain, movement disorders and stroke, and in psychiatric conditions such as depression, schizophrenia, anxiety disorders, obsessive compulsive disorders and substance misuse. External application of oscillating electrical current is a newer method of influencing cortical excitability and activity.[222] [223] [224] [225]

Since 2005, theta burst stimulation techniques (TBS), transcranial direct current stimulation (tDCS) and transcranial alternating current stimulation (tACS) have been used within the medical sphere. Research in Germany led by Dr Nitsche and Dr Paulus highlights that neural responsiveness could be modified if weak currents less than the power of a 100-watt lightbulb are applied to the brain.[226] [227] They have been used to boost cognitive control and working memory.[228] [229]

A company called Flow Neuroscience is gaining some popularity through treating depression using a headset that delivers tDCS to the forehead. This pairs with a smartphone app to guide users through a self-help six-week program. If the FDA approve the headset for commercial sale in America, it will be the first tDCS product on the market without the need for a prescription or supervision of a doctor.

Another similar neurotechnology start-up company, named BrainPatch, is also using non-invasive transcranial electrotherapy.[230] It is trying to differentiate itself by using AI to optimise the stimulation protocols for each individual for a variety of medical and non-medical purposes.

The military DARPA program has also been experimenting with electric currents and implanting chips direct into soldiers' brains. This has been named Systems-Based Neurotechnology for Emerging Therapies (SUBNET).[231] Dr Justin Sanchez of the DARPA program, who heads up the SUBNET project, said, 'DARPA is looking for ways to characterise which [brain] regions come into play for different conditions – measured from brain networks down to the single neuron.'[232] These programs all sound very sci-fi and new-age, but a new discipline is emerging, aiming to re-route electrical impulses around the brain and spine.

Imagine if computer interfaces could help bypass spinal cord blockages, perhaps caused by a physical severing injury or after a loss of blood supply. A case has been written up explaining how electrical circuits were implanted into the spinal cord of a paraplegic. This allowed brain signals to route around the block between the brain and limbs, giving a person who had been immobile for years the gift of being able to independently lift a cup with their hands.[233]

The next level of difficulty would be to implant a device at a higher level of the central nervous system than the spinal cord, to try and bypass blockages deep within the brain. In 2016, a 58-year-old mother of three from the Netherlands, Hanneke de Bruijne, had electrode strips implanted into the motor cortex of her brain, which controls voluntary movement.[234] She suffered from a degenerative disease, amyotrophic lateral sclerosis (ALS), which had caused 'locked in' syndrome. She was paralysed and unable to speak, move or even breathe without a mechanical ventilator. But with help from boffins at the University Medical Centre of Utrecht, a brain-computer interface was implanted, allowing her to independently control a typing program to communicate with her loved ones and carers, and compose sentences at the rate of two words per minute.[235] This has been hailed as one of the biggest steps in neurological research.

The melding of minds and machines has been called everything from 'computer-brain interfaces' to 'neuro-prosthetics' through to 'cyborg connections'. The primary function to date had been to strengthen connections between two brain regions or reroute information via a neural bridge or bypass. The initial aim of implanted body and brain-digital interfaces is to monitor and record data, and to help understand an individual's uniqueness. Maybe one day, brain-computer interfaces will have the ability to connect in real time and completely change a person's decisions, and as a result their life course.

Knowing this will either fill you with hope or despair: hope that people may make kinder decisions, hope that the improved balance between logic and emotion will work for a better future, and hope that humanity will use such power to make the world a better place. Or it will give rise to concern, fear and cynicism about where these developments can lead. And you won't know if the shivers you are feeling down your spine are caused by your own thoughts or by a digital current sent by a brain-digital interface.

Section 2 Digital Technology

Chapter 7
Manipulation Measure: The G Spot

AI is no longer science fiction. It's here. It's now. It's transforming everyday living. How AI continues to develop will, in evolutionary terms, be the single defining factor for the next generation. It's not new to be talking about man and machine. Even the ancient Greeks told a fable about Talos, a large, strong, bronzed machine with a human mind, which successfully defended the island of Crete from attacking pirates.

Modern-day machine stories have been turned into multi-billion-pound science fiction franchises through novels, comics and films. They tell tales of world-spanning intelligent machines that have genocidal goals. In the *Terminator* films, actor Arnold Schwarzenegger plays a machine known as T-800, with the famous catchphrase, 'I'll be back.'[236]

Films have given AI some limelight, but have also scared people about Kafkaesque global surveillance capabilities and the devastating possibility of eradicating the entire human race. Back in the real world, AI is not always obvious to the naked eye, and is not as dark and evil as Hollywood portrays.

Yet just because it cannot be seen doesn't mean it is any less real. The question 'Have you ever interacted with AI?' was posed to over 6,000 people in a global study. The result exposed a concerning perception gap. Around 50% of respondents did not think they had interacted with or experienced AI.[237] In fact, AI has already blended into our lives silently and by stealth. This is despite the fact that the same survey found that 70% of people fear AI.

Many brilliant minds have also weighed into the AI debate. The late Professor Stephen Hawking, the world-renowned Cambridge University academic and theoretical physicist, spoke of his fears that AI could spell 'the end of humanity'.[238] Elon Musk thinks AI may lead to World War Three.[239] Russian President Vladimir Putin says whoever controls AI will control the world.[240]

But what is AI? The Oxford English Dictionary defines AI as: 'The theory and development of computer systems able to perform tasks normally requiring human intelligence, such as visual perception, speech recognition, decision-making and translation between language.'[241]

AI, therefore, is more of an umbrella term for a group of exciting developments that have managed to externalise brain functions, bringing them outside the confines of the human skull. The sub-fields of AI somewhat emulate the same brain functions displayed by children playing with bubbles: movement, visual perception, speaking, communicating, processing information and planning.

Consider how a child interacts with a bubble machine. They display fine motor skills by poking bubbles, and gross motor skills when they run and jump. There's also hand-eye coordination, which can take a seriously long time to link together before managing to get both hands and eyes to work symbiotically. They visually track bubbles with their eyes, noting where the bubbles go, seeing how some shimmer and others glow. They try out language skills to describe bubble shapes, saying 'that's a big bubble' or 'look behind you' to communicate its location. They use bubble play as a way of socialising and sharing with others. Observing children is a window into the world of how the human naïve brain connects and the areas in which AI is trying to make strides.

To break down complex situations, children learn step by step. AI uses millions of mathematical formulae, or algorithms. An algorithm is defined as a 'procedure for solving a problem or accomplishing some end especially by a computer'.[242] Basically, it is a logical set of instructions. In the book *Algorithms to Live by: the Computer Science of Human Decision*, authors Brian Christian and Tom Griffiths describe how algorithms give computers the vocabulary to understand:

> Even in cases where life is too messy for us to expect a strict numerical answer, using intuitions and concepts honed on the simpler forms of these problems offers us a way to understand the key issues and make progress.[243]

Using algorithms, AI can order complex data and solve problems. Some common examples include:

- Association algorithms, which help find relationships between things. Such algorithms are used by dating platforms such as OkCupid, to find similarities between people, or pair people via an 'opposites attract' calculation. They are also used by some human resources companies to link an uploaded CV with a relevant job advert.
- Branch and bound algorithms, which break issues down and form a tree of sub-problems. The original problem is considered the 'root problem' and feasible solutions are used to trim sections of the tree until all branches have been solved. It's often used to find the quickest route between two locations.
- Brute force algorithms, which try all possibilities until a satisfactory solution is found. It's often the algorithm of choice used when trying to crack or hack login passwords.
- Greedy algorithms, which do not just find one solution but take the best decision at that moment in time, without regard for future consequences. It is used by some ATM cash machines to dispense notes in the right denomination.

- Filtering algorithms, which isolate what's important and are used in noise cancelling headphones.
- Prioritisation algorithms, which help rank importance and are used in Google searches.

One new recruitment company called Beamery says matching schemes have moved on since the use of basic algorithms. Chief Data Scientist Dr Ahmad Assaf says, 'Beamery uses complex cutting-edge AI to power its talent operating system. We spread the net wide to form a holistic view of candidates and their work history – that goes well beyond the old fashioned shallow and direct associations.'[244]

Thankfully, in order to get to grips with AI, it's not imperative to be conversant in mathematical algorithms, nor to speak computer languages such as Lisp, Prolog, Python or C++. However, it is a useful life skill to be able to distinguish between computers and humans. Alan Turing, widely considered to be the father of theoretical computer science, wrote extensively on this topic. Turing is globally celebrated for building the world's first computer to crack the code of the Enigma machine, which was used to send secret messages by the Germans during World War II.

In his seminal publication *Computing Machinery and Intelligence*, Turing devised a game involving three players called the 'Imitation Game'.[245] One participant is a computer and the other two are human. The computer player and one of the two humans must try to convince the third (human) player, who is unable to see the other two participants, that each of them is human. If the third player is unable to distinguish between who is and isn't human on a consistent basis, then the computer wins. It's actually a very difficult challenge.

Ironically, computers frequently use a derivative of this Turing test: the Completely Automated Public Turing test to tell Computers and Humans Apart (CAPTCHA).[246] As the name implies, the test helps the computer check that the user is an actual person, and not a computer posing as a human. A very common CAPTCHA test delivered with almost annoying frequency is when websites require users to copy and decipher an image of distorted letters, numbers or symbols, before allowing access to the next window. Other tests track that finger or mouse movements are human, by providing a request to click on 'I am not a robot' button.

Modern-day computers have permeated life to such an extent that people don't think twice about signing up for free internet connections. It all seems harmless enough, right? People get hot under the collar about snooping charters and CCTV but personal computers and smartphones can actually hold far more information. Websites frequently use 'cookies' to track and monitor webpage views, down to the detail of the number of times a page is visited.

With so much data at their fingertips, companies known as data brokers have risen up. Their business is to keep tabs on digital interactions. They collect, combine and cross-reference data and build up an individual's unique digital footprint, collating information such as name, sex, date of birth, location, websites visited, vacation destinations, credit-card usage, debts, repayment score, speed of repayments, political affiliation, gambling habits, medication use, sexual orientation, marital status and even the marital status of other family members.

In 2013, an American Senate Committee published 'A Review of the Data Broker Industry: Collection, Use, and Sale of Consumer Data for Marketing Purposes'.[247] The report listed four main concerns:

- Data brokers collect a huge volume of detailed information, which they sell, generally without consumer permission or input;
- Data brokers sell products that identify financially vulnerable consumers;
- Data brokers provide information about consumer offline behaviour to tailor online outreach by marketers;
- Data brokers operate behind a veil of secrecy.

Examples of such companies include CoreLogic, Datalogix (owned by Oracle) and divisions or subsidiaries of Experian and Equifax.[248] The data-broker industry is getting ever more sophisticated, and is proliferating in terms of company numbers and clients. Data brokers leverage AI to combine personal information and massive population-based data sets. They have developed something called the 'gullibility score', also known in the industry as the 'sweet G-spot'.[249] This scans an individual's digital footprint and sophisticatedly calculates a numerical 'measure of manipulation', reviewing the data for addictive tendencies, and a preponderance for believing in superstitious stories and spreading fake news, amongst other things.

By carrying out such analysis, data brokers are gaining tremendous power and are trying to understand the psychology behind an individual's digital footprint. This data could be used for basic targeting, such as advertising sugar-free sweets to people who have diabetic medication or glucose monitoring devices contained within their digital footprints. More complex insights can be gained from pooling together sub-groups of people who return a high gullibility score. Data brokers make large profits from selling insights gleamed from the sweet G-spot pool of digital footprints. Apparently, a feeding frenzy of clients has developed around these customers, where it is believed adverts correlate with an increase in sales.

Data gathering and selling analysis is not necessarily new. In the past, supermarkets have been forerunners in understanding the value of data and how tiny preference margins add up to make the tipping-point difference between one chain and its competitor. In 1993, Tesco conducted a ground-breaking trial with its introduction of the Clubcard.[250] Customers presented this loyalty card when paying for shopping, and in exchange, points would be added up and converted to savings on future store purchases.

Tesco, in return, got sales data; it suddenly knew, postcode by postcode, who was buying what. It could work out how far people travelled and could nudge buying behaviour. What it found was that 70% of Clubcard coupons were redeemed, and that Clubcard holders spent 4% more than non-Clubcard holders.[251] But manipulation measures are new – and it becomes more morally questionable when, for example, payday lenders flash up adverts on the screens of people with a bad credit rating.

The dark side of data brokers and digital footprint analysis is leading to a new breed of 'cyber mercenaries'.[252] These undercover, sometimes shadowy individuals track locations and weave together highly personal information, specialising in selling psychological profiles.[253] The industry is incredibly opaque and sadly, the information collected on individuals can be used in various nefarious ways, such as by stalkers or to facilitate identity theft.

'If you can get information on someone online, you might be able to impersonate them or use their credit history, or perhaps get into a password protected website if you can answer security questions about people,' said Paul Stephens, Director of Policy and Advocacy at Privacy Rights Clearinghouse.[254]

The sale of digital footprints hit the headlines when German journalist Svea Eckert and data scientist Andreas Dewes jointly set out to find out exactly what digital information translated into in practical terms to the man on the street.[255] They set themselves up as temporary data brokers, and bought three million German citizens' internet histories. They revealed people had innocently downloaded spying internet data which accessed all their searches, meaning that every search, every click, every download was recorded. They even uncovered access to nude photographs, a judge's porn preferences and the medication used by a German politician.

'What would you think,' asked Svea Eckert, 'if somebody showed up at your door saying: Hey, I have your complete browsing history…how would you think we got it: some shady hacker? No. It was much easier: you can just buy it.'[256]

They presented their findings at a hacking conference in Las Vegas, highlighting how relatively easy it is to de-anonymise the dataset from the browser history.[257] For example, the homepages of websites that are regularly visited have names directly embedded within the URLs, and similar tricks work for German social networking site Xing. GPS geo-locators pinpointed addresses and the electoral roll identified the person. When more than one person was involved in the digital exchange, a more probabilistic approach could be undertaken to de-anonymise. Generally, it's pretty easy to guess gender and age just by looking at shopping search data – for example, only older men tend to buy hair regrowth products.

However, avoiding this merry-go-round of data is more difficult than expected. A simple opt-out does not always work. Some sites create multiple hoops to make it deliberately both difficult and time-consuming to process. Paid subscription services such as DeleteMe offer to remove personal information, but very few services can take people off the radar of data brokers and preying cyber mercenaries completely.[258]

Digital data is often called the 'new oil'.[259] But unlike fossil fuels, which suffer from diminishing reserves, data is in ever-increasing abundance. The

International Data Corporation estimates there will be over '163 zettabytes (one trillion gigabytes) of data by 2025'.[260] Who owns such bloated data quantities, and who should share in any spoils of financial returns? At the moment, many people willingly donate their personal data in return for free digital access.

The morality and safety debate around digital data and AI has only just started. Some believe it's still too early to worry about it. AI expert Andrew Ng said, 'For the time being, worrying about evil AI robots today is a bit like worrying about overcrowding on Mars.'[261] Professor of Physics Max Tegmark, author of *Life 3.0*, says:

> The race toward artificial general intelligence is on, and we have no idea how it will unfold. But that shouldn't stop us from thinking about what we want the aftermath to be like, because what we want will affect the outcome. What do you personally prefer, and why?
>
> 1. Do you want there to be superintelligence?
> 2. Do you want humans to still exist, be replaced, cyborgised and/or uploaded/simulated?
> 3. Do you want humans or machines in control?
> 4. Do you want AI to be conscious or not?
> 5. Do you want to maximise positive experiences, minimise suffering or leave this to sort itself out?
> 6. Do you want life spreading into the cosmos?
> 7. Do you want civilisation striving toward a greater purpose that you sympathise with, or are you OK with future life forms that appear content even if you view their goals as pointlessly banal?[262]

The consequences of AI give rise to a plethora of philosophical questions. Some well-respected bodies have already been set up to keep a vigilant eye on AI ethical and legal issues. The AI Now Institute is one such organisation.[263] Its co-founder (and Google employee) Meredith Whittaker said, 'People are recognising there are issues, and they want to change them.'[264] Is ethical AI even possible?

AI is borderless – but traditional regulatory systems are set within geographical boundaries. So if an AI system has a consumer base in Africa, data storage in the USA, developers in Japan, and software held and run in China, who is accountable? The law is currently powerless when faced with this Pandora's box of problems. Facebook's founder and CEO Mark Zuckerberg has called for more global regulation with improved data protection and privacy.[265] Such populist soundbites from global companies, activists, researchers and policy-makers side step the crux of the issue around how to deliver worldwide regulatory responsibility and enforceability. In an increasingly complex world, one big substantive question remains: who is monitoring the AI monitoring system?

Chapter 8
Where Did AI Come From?

The first use of the term 'artificial intelligence' can be traced back to 1956.[266] It was first cited in the American state of New Hampshire, when a summer conference was laid on by John McCarthy, assistant professor of mathematics at Dartmouth College in Hanover. McCarthy joined forces with three other researchers, Marvin Minsky of Harvard, Nathaniel Rochester of IBM and Claude Shannon of Bell Telephone Laboratories, to submit a funding proposal to the Rockefeller Foundation that stated:

> The study is to proceed on the basis of the conjecture that every aspect of learning or any other feature of intelligence can in principle be so precisely described that a machine can be made to simulate it. An attempt will be made to find how to make machines use language, form abstractions and concepts, solve kinds of problems now reserved for humans, and improve themselves.[267]

As a shortened advertising pitch for the conference, McCarthy went on to coin the term 'artificial intelligence'.[268] McCarthy was an aficionado of a branch of mathematics that represents concepts as symbols. He perhaps wanted to expand the horizon of computers to be more than number crunchers and data processors, and push them into the next frontier of manipulating symbols to reason deductively from hypothesis to conclusion. McCarthy was optimistic that computers would, in the near future, be able to simulate a higher cognitive function using symbolic processing, becoming much more than automation.

However, it's not clear if anything was accomplished during the summer conference in question, as the promised final report was never delivered. In fact, the same overly optimistic ambitions have dogged the AI rollercoaster ride ever since. AI has travelled repeatedly from exaggerated highs to deep dips of disappointment, quickly followed by new discoveries, renewed funding and a resurgent climb.

By the mid-1960s, AI found itself a funding stream with deep pockets via the Advanced Research Projects Agency, part of the US Department of Defence (now known as DARPA).[269] Millions of dollars were poured into nascent academic AI labs at the Massachusetts Institute of Technology (MIT), Stanford University and Carnegie Mellon University.[270] Some commercial research labs, such as SRI International, were also strengthened.

The consistent flow of money fostered multiple bright-eyed graduate students, who in turn went on to collaborate with other global universities. Yet by 1974, developments stalled amid mounting criticism from US Congress over the lack of productive projects.[271] As a result, the US government cut off exploratory research into AI and the British government quickly followed suit.[272] The following years were bleak. It became a struggle to obtain funding for AI research, in a period that has since become known as the 'AI winter'.[273]

It took until the 1980s for AI to develop computer programs that deconstructed tasks into symbolic forms for facts, rules and relationships. These symbols could then be manipulated and combined. This form of expert system could be modified easily as new facts or knowledge became available, but AI remained heavily reliant on human programmers to code painstakingly. Expert systems did succeed in bottling expertise, or perhaps more correctly put, 'computerising it', but developments tended to be highly 'domain specific'.

Such symbol systems also remained dogged with a common problem, plagued by the vast number of possible scenarios. Combinational explosions made it too difficult to examine all the options. Take the everyday example of Lego: a mere six eight-studded bricks of the same colour can be combined in 915,103,765 ways.[274]

Planning systems, therefore, often had to engage in heuristic (rule of thumb) reasoning to reduce the search combinations to manageable dimensions, which consequently run the risk of failing to find a solution (admissible heuristics) or not finding the best solution (inadmissible heuristics). Today, these planning systems are seen as old-fashioned AI, but they are still in use. For example, they are used to plan domiciliary home-care visits to ensure efficient travel logistics and increase face-to-face care time.

By the late 1990s, AI had advanced further thanks to increasing computational power in accordance with Moore's Law, which states that the number of transistors in a dense integrated circuit doubles every two years.[275] This has made possible advanced statistical techniques and the development of 'machine learning' (discussed in the next chapter), which combines large amounts of data with fast computers to create statistical algorithms that can learn to do complex things, like play chess.

The most famous step change came when Deep Blue, an early chess-playing system, beat the reigning world chess champion Garry Kasparov on 11 May 1997.[276] It came as a surprise to the chess world, and has been etched into the memory of the Russian grand master ever since. Kasparov was forced to eat his words, after having famously quipped, 'If any grand master has difficulty playing a computer – I'd happily offer advice.'[277] It was hailed within the AI community as a major confidence boost for the entire sector and put AI firmly back on the global stage.

Learning to play games is one thing, but problem solving in novel situations requires a more dynamic approach and iterative improvements in training and practice. Machine learning has taken inspiration from neuroscientists who have studied neural networks in the brain. Computational neuroscience is not fixated on pure replication of the brain, which is just as well, as although much is known about the gross structures of the brain and which regions correspond to different actions, much less is known about how it is all wired together.

In the 2000s, IBM worked on an AI machine to answer a series of questions such as those posed by the TV host in the quiz game *Jeopardy!* The team developed a machine consuming four terabytes of disk storage and named it after IBM's first CEO, Thomas Watson.[278] In 2011, IBM Watson went head to head in a contest against former Jeopardy winners Brad Rutter and Ken Jennings, and neither human nor machine participants had access to the internet during the game. It was a nail-biting time for the AI world, with a prize of one million dollars. IBM Watson won.[279] It showed that AI neural networks had been able to mimic the human ability not only to understand the question, but also to best-guess the answer.

March 2016 brought another exciting challenge for AI when it competed in the game Go. Go is far more difficult to play than other games like chess, and uses black and white pieces on a nineteen-by-nineteen board. The game dates back to ancient China and was considered to be an essential art for a cultured Chinese scholar, even getting a mention as a worthy pastime in the *Analects* of Confucius.[280] Go is a very difficult game and this fascinated the machine learning start-up company DeepMind. Alphabet (the parent company of Google) acquired DeepMind in 2014.[281] It paid $525 million for a virtually unknown firm with no customers and only a handful of employees.[282]

Only later did the world understand the price tag when DeepMind demonstrated that it had developed a system that had learnt to play via trial and error 49 arcade games from a 1980s video console, 29 of which it managed at above-human-level performance. DeepMind went on to develop AlphaGo, which hit a significant milestone when it won four out of five games in a match against Go champion Lee Sedol.[283]

This feat should not be underestimated, as it leveraged two advancements. First, it harnessed more mathematical powerful processing units for matrix and vector calculations by using graphic processing units (GPUs) that came about thanks to the gaming industry. Second, it had the ability to spot patterns after learning and searching through thousands of games. In a manoeuvre so famous in the AI world that it's universally known as 'move 37', AlphaGo turned perceived wisdom about AI on its head.[284]

AlphaGo played an entirely unexpected yet beautiful move. No human player had ever played that move, and Lee Sedol allegedly had to leave the room as he was momentarily in shock. AlphaGo had recognised patterns and played a novel move in a moment of genius, fuelled by the creativity of AI. It not only turned the course of the game but perhaps more importantly changed history forever. In 2017, AlphaGo kept up its winning streak and won a three-match game against Ke Jie, the player who had continuously held the world champion position for two years.[285]

Creativity of AI has penetrated more than games. It's used in the arts world. Pioneer German artist Mario Klingemann uses AI for portraits.[286] They are not faces of anyone who has ever lived. The images are created from an AI machine feed with blurry non-descript images. Klingemann's work has exhibited at the Metropolitan Museum of Art in New York and the Centre Pompidou in Paris.[287]

In 2019, his work sold for £40,000, well above the guide price at London's prestigious Sotheby's auction house.[288] '[H]umans are not original,' Klingemann said. 'We only reinvent, make connections between things we have seen.' The novelty value comes from the machine and he hopes 'machines will have a rather different sort of creativity and open up different doors.'[289]

Overall, it's clear that optimism about AI has been justified. It seems impossible for anyone or any business to remain untouched by AI. Consider the traditional banking sector. Customers demanded a convenient service and immediate access to their cash. Internet banking evolved; instant transactions could be carried out from the comfort of the home or office, and even on the move, skipping any requirement to wait in bank queues. Global growth in smartphones, especially in developing countries, further fuelled penetration for electronic transfer.

AI in financial services – FinTech – spans automated trading algorithms that predict price movements to machine learning that identifies fraud. Organised crime and fraudsters are increasing the sophistication scale and speed of their fraud attacks. Global credit card fraud was estimated to be over $21 billion in 2015 – so investing in prevention is well worth it.[290] Banks already use AI to spot erroneous transactions in real time, enabling instantaneous decisions about whether a purchase should be allowed or not.

Retailers are also pushing for better AI fraud detection techniques. For them, the problem is arguably harder to approach than it is for credit card issuers since they lack the access to past purchase history. Researchers at eBay propose an 'outlier detection' AI system and search for abnormal behaviour – their AI can already spot fraudulent purchases 40% of the time with no human intervention.[291]

Financial firms that continue to embrace and exploit technology will be the ones who drive and survive change. AI has been used to try to democratise and automate investing. Some digital platforms have attempted to further democratise finance away from the structure of big banks and use the much-hyped cryptocurrencies based on blockchain technology. Blockchain is not AI, but it is a computer science term for how to structure and share data, bypassing the need for any central managing data flow authority.

Most people probably associate blockchain with bitcoin. Bitcoin was first introduced in 2008 when an anonymous programmer (or a cohort of anonymous programmers) published a paper under the name Satoshi Nakamoto.[292] It explained the peer-to-peer payment system that enables users to send bitcoins, the name of the value transfer token, directly and without an intermediary. The network itself verifies the transactions and nobody can cheat the system as the ledger for everything that happens to a bitcoin is unique.

Bitcoin blockchain transfers solve the Byzantine general problem: 'How can you trust the information you are given and the people who are giving you that information, when self-interest, malicious third parties and the like can deceive you?'[293] Bitcoin transfers get around this by recording information in a public space that is always uniquely referenced. Bitcoin is still a way off becoming a single global currency, but for many, there will be no going back to the days of searching for loose change down the back of the sofa.

Digital technologies can rapidly spread to become ubiquitous. Big tech platforms with global penetration are leveraging their oligopoly to use AI for social good. Take a few examples in the healthcare sector. Amazon acquired pharmacy delivery company PillPack for roughly $800 million.[294] PillPack is available in most US states and delivers prescription medication direct to the customer's door. The pills arrive in pre-sorted daily packages, reducing drug errors, and repeat doses are automatically ordered.

Apple has filed multiple patents to turn its consumer products such as iPhone and Apple Watch into medical devices that can monitor biometric data, such as blood pressure, heart rhythm and body fat levels, as well as to develop algorithms to detect heart arrhythmia.[295] It is also looking into how to democratise medical records stored on mobile phones.[296]

Microsoft, Amazon, Google and other IT companies released a joint statement saying they are 'committed to removing barriers for the adoption of technologies for healthcare interoperability, particularly those that are enabled through the Cloud and AI'.[297] Having an interoperable system to ingest, store, analyse and interact with personal and non-personal medical records in a secure end-to-end environment could revolutionise research and development into complex healthcare questions that are often based in nature and nurture or genes and lifestyle.

Since the early 1990s, many doctors have anticipated the age of 'precision medicine', with patients prescribed customised medications targeted at the specific genetic driver or variant of their symptoms, disease or condition. But such a dream was impossible without computers and AI to help discover similarities and differences in massive data sets.

The Human Genome Project, for example, sits at the intersection of gene therapy and AI. It is hoped that global data collation will help change the fact that only 5% of 7,000 rare diseases have a known treatment.[298] In the USA, gene therapy is used to treat leukaemia, lymphoma, retinal dystrophy and some inherited diseases (FDA approved).[299]

Gene editing has come on leaps and bounds – especially since the discovery of CRISPR.[300] This is not a type of potato-based snack – it's a way of precisely editing DNA to rewrite the code of life. Interestingly enough, Clustered Regularly Interspaced Short Palindromic Repeats (CRISPR) was discovered thanks to yoghurt. Researchers observed that yoghurt's beneficial bacteria fend off viral invaders by detecting foreign DNA and snipping it. After CRISPR-Cas9's exact mechanism was figured out, the exquisitely precise gene editing technology was put to work in a wide range of biomedical settings. There is hope that it could change the course of debilitating genetic diseases such as Huntington's and Tay-Sachs. In 2017, CRISPR gene therapy was used to cure a French teenager of sickle-cell disease.[301]

However, in 2018, a Chinese scientist, He Jiankui, claimed he had modified baby twins using CRISPR to make them HIV resistant.[302] Ethicist Julian Savulescu at the University of Oxford said, 'If true, this experiment exposes healthy children to the risks of gene editing for no real necessary benefit.'[303] Professor Stephen Smith, previously at Imperial College, London, said, 'This is the height of social, personal and moral irresponsibility as nobody knows how DNA changes will interact with the millions of other genomes over millions of years. Worse still, gene changes pass for ever into the human gene pool, resulting in the fear that human edited evolution could be based on the whims of mad scientists.'[304]

There is a treasure trove of information hidden in the three billion base pairs that make up the human DNA code. This information is being 'consumerised', and in 2007, Alphabet handsomely invested almost $4 million in the saliva genetic testing company called 23andme.[305] But one of biology's big secrets is that 98.8% of the DNA jigsaw puzzle has been utterly ignored.

Geneticists are continuing to get ever more detailed by studying all base pairs letter by letter. This had led to epigenetics – a new way of looking at DNA that goes beyond the linear base sequence of the physical gene and extends the study from one to three dimensions.[306] These extra dimensions are important for understanding gene regulation. It's believed that environmental factors can lead to chemical attachments (methylation) and affect genes quite distant from the point of attachment.[307]

This analysis is exposing a new understanding of how environmental factors, such as diet, stress, smoking and exercise, may change DNA by methylation.[308] Methylation does not change genomic sequences, but does update epigenetics and how DNA transfers information.[309] It is potentially a key component of ageing and carcinogenesis. A new company, Chronomics, is the first to commercialise the measuring of methylation change, using it as a proxy measure for biological age. Simply put, it informs the customer if methylation is above or below expected levels relative to their birth age.[310]

There is no point in collecting lots of data for the sake of it. But the hope is that AI will use data to help uncover hidden patterns. Take the example of a primary care physician who consults about forty people per week with vague symptoms of abdominal pain. The doctor takes a detailed medical history and examines the patient, and a small cohort are referred on for further tests.

On average, each physician sees about one person every five years with nonspecific symptoms who will receive the unpleasant diagnosis of pancreatic cancer. It's very difficult for any human to spot patterns in such infrequent events. In the future, it's hoped that AI will come to the rescue and help aggregate data, spot patterns in unusual presentations and help identify early biomarkers. It's also hoped that AI will turn the hyper-personalised key by collecting and correlating data to understand how lifestyle choices change DNA.

AI could weave together a story from data-driven insights to better understand how lifestyles interact with personal epigenetics. Imagine the holistic impact on life with everyone getting bespoke advice – perhaps personally mixed sun protection factor cream, bespoke for DNA skin type, eliminating allergy risk and taking into account time spent outside with real time weather conditions. The possibilities of tailored insights are endless along the quantified-self science journey, suggesting exact hydration, nutrients, vitamins and gut biome – it could be the wellness AI nirvana.

Chapter 9
Self-Educating Machines

Many people perceive machine learning as a form of magic or witchcraft, like that practiced by a shaman or a soothsayer. It has gained cult status, even leading to suggestions that an all-powerful mother machine will one day take over the world. The shroud of mystery surrounding machine learning is based on the central premise that it can become independent from the human race. This naturally provokes an underlying anxiety, and questions sprout in the mind. What is the machine teaching itself? Could it go rogue? Will it wipe out the human race after absorbing all human knowledge? This chapter takes a step back to help understand machine learning in plain language.

There are two main ways a computer can learn: supervised and unsupervised learning. Supervised learning is the most common approach, and refers to situations in which a human teaches the algorithm what conclusions it should come up with. Then there is unsupervised learning, which Andrew Burgess in *The Executive Guide to Artificial Intelligence* calls 'fiendishly clever'. He continues:

> In unsupervised learning, the system starts with just a very large data set that will mean nothing to it. What the AI is able to do though is to spot clusters of similar points within the data. The AI is blissfully naïve about what the data means; all it does is look for patterns in vast quantities of numbers. The great thing about this approach is that the user can also be naïve – they don't need to know what they are looking for or what the connections are – all that work is done by the AI. Once the clusters have been identified then predictions can be made for new inputs.[311]

Take house valuation as an example. House price is dependent upon many variables such as location, size, number of bathrooms, kitchen size, aesthetics, garage, garden size and many more. Estate agents use experience, but if AI was fed enough data, including variables and final sale value, it should become a good predictor of house prices and be able to differentiate between strong and weak influencers. The data input would be structured, but the model created is really a black box. Unsupervised learning develops by trial and error, and may hold the key to solving prohibitively complex problems, like climate change, that humans alone could not conceivably tackle.

Much of the remarkable progress in AI in recent years is based on machine learning, which resembles, in a very loose way, the way human brains use neural networks (discussed in Chapter 2). Machine neural networks are built using layers, and the output can feed back and modify the input in accordance with a pre-programmed target, so that they 'learn'. One of the simplest explanations comes from computer scientist Tarek El-Gaaly.[312] He uses the example of a photograph of an unidentified 'funny looking object' and posts it into the mail box of a three-storey building to try and find out what it is.

The ground floor workers are called 'neurons' and use rulers to get an outline. When a straight edge is found, they mark it down on tracing paper. Once all the edges have been noted down, they pass the tracing paper up to the first floor. The first-floor workers use the markings and straight edges to find right angles and mark them down on fresh pieces of tracing paper.[313]

Once they are done, they send their findings up to the second floor. These workers look for triangles and send up their findings to the third floor. The third-floor workers are special as they have the database of 'funny looking objects'. They guess what object is drawn on the tracing paper and shout it out on a loud speaker and throw out a little piece of paper with the object's name on it down a pipe that pops out of the ground floor mailbox. This is the bare bones essence of the layered approach of deep learning. The building can be any number of storeys and there are all sorts of variations. Using this analogy, it's obvious that there are many architectural building shapes, and likewise, several types of machine learning.[314]

Professor of machine learning Pedro Domingos, in his book *The Master Algorithm*, names five main tribes of machine learning.[315] Although other schools of thought exist, Domingos explains how different forms of machine learning are akin to learning a unique instrument from scratch – say the violin, piano, flute, trumpet or double bass. Each 'tribe' has no music teacher, and is a self-taught musician, progressing at different paces at different times. For now, Mozart, Mahler or Brahms symphonies are a way off. Each discipline learns independently. There is no accomplished virtuoso and no harmonies. Five different machine learning tribes are discussed:

- The Bayesians, who learn from statistical probabilistic inference;
- The evolutionists, who simulate evolution and base learning on genetics and evolutionary biology;
- The analogisers, who learn by extrapolating from an analogy;
- The symbolists, who view learning as the inverse of deduction (induction);
- The connectionists, who emulate human brain learning, taking inspiration from neuroscience and physics.

In practice, just like people, each machine learning method has different skills, strengths and weaknesses, and not one of them is good at everything. It is like observing variations in the way children's learning styles are different, as they are directly impacted by their personalities. For example, the Bayesians are happiest surrounded by statistical evidence that can be logically updated as new evidence comes in. They are hungry for facts, proof, evidence and empirical data, but struggle when asked for a leap of faith or to think outside the logic box.

The evolutionists search for guidance from Darwin's strongest and fittest. The analogisers learn something new by searching for the meaning, and use analogies to infer and build knowledge from one topic to the next. The symbolists simplify stories into diagrams. The connectionists learn best from those around them, upskilling by chatting to the person sitting next to them.

The Bayesians

Bayesian machine learning relies upon statistical probabilistic inference to learn from data. If the data evidence is consistent with the hypothesis, the probability of the hypothesis goes up. If not, it goes down. Bayes' theorem was named after eighteenth-century Presbyterian Thomas Bayes, the English statistician and philosopher who wrote 'An Essay towards solving a Problem in the Doctrine of Chances'.[316] Basic Bayesian machine learning statistical algorithms have been used for years to help manage email inboxes. The Bayesian algorithm statistically learnt that emails containing words such as 'Viagra' or 'free' can be immediately redirected into the spam folder.

Bayesian machine learning has gone on to develop more complex statistical methods, such as the Markov chain Monte Carlo (MVMC), which combines step-by-step sequence analysis (Markov chain) with a game of chance that is named after the Monte Carlo casino.[317] This learning method needs access to extraordinary amounts of data to succeed but lends itself well to the goldmine of genome sequencing data. One example is IBM's Dr Watson supercomputer, which now works in oncology alongside medical experts to help explore bespoke treatment options to help improve the outcome and survival of cancer patients.[318]

The evolutionists

Evolutionists' machine learning is basically survival of the fittest. One generation of algorithms builds the next generation, and simulates natural selection. Just like Darwin's survival of the fittest, the machine learns via a 'fitness function'. The fitness function assigns each program a numeric score, reflecting how well it fits the intended purpose.

Learning evolves from a 'not very fit for purpose' algorithm, and like human genetics it mimics mating, throws out random variations, and keeps selected outcomes according to improved fitness. It starts with the goal wanted and then uses many versions to randomly assemble code to work out if it makes it closer to goal. Like a mutation, codes get better and better over time. These types of codes are already better than humans at video games such as Kung Fu Master.

As evolution algorithms are random, it's difficult to understand how they got to the final result. In fact, they are reminiscent of *The Hitchhiker's Guide to the Galaxy*[319], in which a supercomputer computes the correct answer to the meaning of life as being the number 42, but nobody can back-calculate what the question is.

The analogisers
Analogiser machine learning algorithms use pattern recognition and extrapolate from an analogy. Amazon uses this form of machine learning to suggest what else to buy. It performs well in unrelated situations. For example, a person's age and eye colour is independent, but age and hair colour are related because people go grey with age. So analogisers must correctly learn not to bias predictions, such as believing age, eye colour and hair colour are all mutually exclusive.

Analogiser machine learning is widespread in the customer relations sector. Indian-developed IPsoft's Amelia talks directly to customers and comes with a 3D interactive video persona. Amelia has already solved over 20 million customer problems using simple analogies to help answer questions, and can reduce the cost of call centres.[320]

The symbolists
Symbolist machine learners use inductive reasoning to explain existing data and boil the information down into connecting symbols to help make sense of it all. They incorporate pre-existing knowledge and can help piece together missing information, given a known input and output.

For symbolists, preconceived notions are indispensable, but they run the risk of using bias to fill the gaps. Symbolist machine learners have been used in the retail industry. For example, Walmart used symbolist machine learning within its supermarkets and discovered a connection between nappies and beer – not a pairing that had previously been spotted by Walmart executives. Interpreting that beer was being added by shoppers almost as emotional compensation for the nappy purchase, Walmart directly increased beer sales after locating beer and nappies in the same shopping aisle.[321]

The connectionists
Connectionists try to emulate the human brain by taking inspiration from nature. Historically, machine neural networks were a bit like a water filter. Water poured in at the top and came out filtered at the bottom, but it had no way of going back due to the rigid one-way flow. In stark contrast, human networks communicate forwards, backwards and in every which way imaginable. When the connectionists finally used back-propagation algorithms, they allowed machines to learn from errors. Such feedback ability within machine neural networks developed into the revolution known as 'deep learning'.

Only about 5% of deep learning inputs are feedback – this is diametrically the opposite of the ratio in the human brain, where 95% of synapses are dedicated to feedback. In one well-studied area of the human brain, the visual cortex, researcher Tai Sing Lee at Carnegie Mellon University discovered that 'only 5 to 10% of the synapses are listening to input from the eyes', and the rest is listening to feedback.[322]

Deep learning can still be somewhat clumsy and brute force, and this is perhaps due to the lack of sophistication in learning from feedback. The US military used an AI neural network to learn to distinguish between enemy and friendly tanks. They fed the neural network thousands of images of enemy and friendly tanks, hoping that it would learn to distinguish between the two.[323] It worked in the lab – but when they tried it in the field, it was wrong equally as often as it was right. Why did this occur?

The humans who fed the AI images of tanks had a bias based on how those images were obtained. Most of the enemy tank images were taken at night or from far away, so as to avoid capture of the photographer. Most of the friendly tank images were taken during the day, with clear, unobstructed views.[324] The AI did what it was taught, and due to the bias introduced by the humans, differentiated between the environment in which the photos were taken rather than the subject matter.

Professor David Cox, neuroscientist at Harvard University, explained that 'to build a dog detector, you need to show the program thousands of things that are dogs and thousands of things that are not dogs…my daughter only had to see one dog…and has happily pointed out puppies and dogs ever since.'[325] The human brain is excellent at putting newly assimilated information into context.

A well-known junior doctor adage, 'see one, do one, teach one', describes the speed required to master lots of new procedures. Take the example of learning how to insert a catheter. The first time, the young doctor will watch their senior lay out the equipment, use the gel and insert the line. The next step would be to do the procedure themselves from start to finish, and the third time, they would be expected to be expert enough to teach others. It's something of a cliché, as of course doctors can always ask for help, but it's the opposite of current AI, which would need to be fed every human variation of catheter size, type and human anatomical variation before it could proceed. The patient would be dead by the time AI was ready!

Machine learning is, however, well suited to spotting trends in the massive quantities of medical data that may otherwise be missed by the limits of human analysis. The American cardiologist Eric Topol, author of *The Patient Will See You Now* and *Deep Medicine: How Artificial Intelligence Can Make Healthcare Great Again*, published 'High-performance medicine: The convergence of human and artificial intelligence' in 2019.[326] He describes how AI machine learning is beginning to have an impact in healthcare within three settings:

- Helping clinicians with 'rapid, accurate image interpretation';
- Aiding health systems, by 'improving workflow and the potential for reducing medical errors';
- Enabling patients 'to process their own data to promote health'.[327]

Care is changing thanks to AI, and every clinical discipline is involved. Specialties such as pathology have made slow progress, in part because converting glass slides to digital images is not yet routine. But in other specialties, such as dermatology, the pace of change is fast. Image based AI technology is used to diagnose everything from a pimple to skin cancer and there are a plethora of consumer facing start-ups. Other examples include:

Radiology: Academic machine learning pattern recognition publications have frequently focused on radiology. One case described a 121-layered neural network trained to find pneumonia in a chest X-ray, which outperformed four human radiologists.[328] Even though this is impressive, it's worth remembering that this is not necessarily comparable with a radiologist's full day-to-day work, during which much more than pneumonia may be diagnosed in any given scan. But interest has ignited in AI as a digital second pair of eyes.

One start-up, Kheiron, has used millions of breast images and results to task machine learning AI to spot differences or misshapes hiding somewhere in the mammogram scan – a little like playing a game of Where's Wally – importantly spotting cancerous or pre-cancerous areas. Its published results demonstrated that machine mammography reporting was as good as human radiologists, with potential to roll out the technology to help in national screening programmes.[329]

Gastroenterology: The accurate diagnosis of tiny colon polyps and cancerous lesions during colonoscopy is more difficult than most people realise.[330] Multiple studies have shown that these lesions are missed in at least 20% of patients. The human eye is perhaps not as good as computer optical vision which can be magnified, and AI is helping to improve detection and accuracy.[331][332]

Ophthalmology: The number one global cause of vision loss is diabetic retinopathy, affecting more than 100 million people worldwide. Researchers at Google used 127,175 retinal images, graded by more than sixty certified ophthalmologists, from over 75,000 patients. They developed AI software with 90% sensitivity and 98% specificity to detect signs of diabetic retinopathy.[333] Sixteen-year-old Kavya Kopparapu went onto form a company with her brother called Eyeagnosis – combining an AI algorithm to diagnose diabetic retinopathy with a 3D-printed lens attachment for a smartphone. This allows remote populations who usually lack equipment and skilled staff to access help.

Interestingly, Google went onto report that retinal images could accurately predict age, gender, blood pressure, smoking status, diabetes control and risk of a major cardiovascular event all without any access to medical records.[334] This study suggests eyes are a window into the body, and in the future buying spectacles on the high street may turn into a general health screen.

Another prominent cause of blindness is age-related macular degeneration (AMD). Timely diagnosis can prevent or delay the disease. The Moorfields Eye Hospital in London leveraged its large data set of images of cross sections of retinal tissues – optical coherence tomography (OCT). In collaboration with DeepMind AI, they developed a deep learning algorithm to accurately diagnose

AMD before symptoms present, as effectively as any optometrist and ophthalmologist.[335]

Cardiology: Electrocardiograms (ECG) have almost a forty-year history of using technology to help with interpretation.[336] One noble aim of a company named AliveCor is to use AI via its KardiaMobile app to identify and detect the most common heart rhythm disturbance, atrial fibrillation (AF). This should help reduce strokes. An undiagnosed irregular heartbeat is the underlying cause for around 80% of people who suffer strokes, who will either die or be left with severe neurological deficits.[337] [338]

Another company with a focus on detecting cardiac dysrhythmias is called iRhythm Technologies. The company combines a wearable biosensor device worn for up to fourteen days and cloud-based data analytics with proprietary algorithms. Published studies have shown improvements in arrhythmia detection and a reduced need for repeat tests.[339]

The next trend in cardiology is to deploy AI to understand cardiac stress-echo images. This data is a comparison of images before exercise and at peak exercise. Rapid, accurate machine analysis would be useful, as globally there are few echocardiography experts – but more work needs to be done before automating interpretation.

Palliative care: Preparing for a peaceful ending is also coming under the remit of AI. A computer scientist at Stanford University, Anand Avati, published a deep learning algorithm based on electronic health records able to predict the timing of death.[340] [341] More than 90% of people the algorithm predicted would die within three to twelve months did so. The AI picked up predictive features that generally go unnoticed by the treating team, such as number of scans, particularly of the spine or urinary system. The study did not use data from laboratory tests, pathology reports or scan results, nor any other descriptor such as mood or hand strength – all of which are likely to improve accuracy.

Oncology: Cancer treatment is the focus of many AI start-ups. One Chicago based company, Tempus Labs, was started by Eric Lefkofsky, the founder of Groupon, after his wife developed breast cancer in 2014. Tempus Labs has combined the ability to sequence and culture tissue with a large number of AI scientists, a cloud-based platform, cluster computing and natural-language processing, to build 'the world's largest library of unstructured doctor notes, molecular and clinical data and an operating system to make that data accessible and useful'.[342] It collaborates with over forty National Cancer Institutes in the United States and provides 'digital twin' information; this consists of treatment and outcomes data from de-identified patients most similar with respect to demographics and biological information. The result is deep analytics and deep phenotyping with the ability to aid oncologists in making data-driven decisions.

Intensive care: Hospital Intensive Care Units (ICU) have always required patients to be under continuous monitoring with large multi-nodal data collections. Machine learning has been busy helping make sense of all – a partnership known as 'augmented intelligence.'

Medical technology company Medtronic operates in over 140 countries' ICUs across the world, and has been collecting and analysing data to help get a full overview of what is going on with mechanically ventilated patients. It developed a clinical protocol-driven weaning tool to help patients off a ventilator earlier and reduce ICU length of stay by 11%.[343] It's this kind of large data collection that can make a difference in highly complex care and move clinical decisions into real time rather than having to wait for the traditional doctor-led ward round.

At the other end of the acuity spectrum is home care, community care and primary care. This is becoming increasingly 'consumerised', boosted by the realisation of population arithmetic – there are just not enough clinically trained staff to look after the ageing demographic. Health and social care is on a journey to educate people to manage their own chronic conditions at home. But there is a way to go – 76% of primary care doctors polled in a survey expressed concern that the use of 'Dr Google' by patients does more harm than good with false or inadequate information.[344]

Some start-up companies are trying to develop 'AI doctors' with the aim of giving every person on earth access to medical care over a mobile phone.[345] It's well-known that the primary care setting is undergoing a digital tsunami, offering round the clock consultations over a smartphone rather than in the traditional surgery building. One AI company that has gone intensively into medicine is iFlytek, a global player in speech recognition. In 2018, it launched an AI powered robot called Xiaoyi that passed China's medical licensing examination for human doctors.[346] The company aims to use this capability to help people in rural locations. AI chatbots and smartphone apps that help with symptom checking include Ada, BotMD, Buoy, HealthTap, Your.MD, MedWhat, Mediktor, Babylon and many more. But despite all these exciting advancements, there remain formidable obstacles and pitfalls, and time is needed to validate new techniques robustly before implementation into patient care.

An area with fast adoption of machine learning AI has been made possible by data from personal trackers such as Fitbit – acquired by Google in November 2019 for $2.1 billion.[347] A London-based healthcare company, Medopad, is using iPhones and Apple watches to capture data. It has linked up with Chinese company Tencent. The aim is to help people live longer by spotting small personalised changes long before symptoms appear. Dan Vahdat, CEO and founder of Medopad, says, 'Amassing global big data is only the first step, then it's finding the hidden gems that will go onto help extend life.'[348]

The company has already managed to reduce the number of hospital visits Parkinson's Disease sufferers have to make. Parkinson's symptoms include a 'freezing of gait', characterised by a hesitation before stepping forward, or difficulties when initiating walking.[349] Neurologists prescribe medication to help, but usually have to bring patients back repeatedly to clinic for monitoring and dose titration. However, Medopad, in conjunction with its Chinese counterparts, has used iPhone video recording to digitally monitor and use AI to score how medication improves movement disorder. This means doctors can make appropriate dose titrations via home monitoring and long appointment waits are avoided.

AI is also aiming to help make sense of academic data. There was a time, not so long ago, when medical discoveries struck like thunderbolts, specific and dramatic. Alexander Fleming discovered penicillin in 1928 after he returned from a holiday to find the green mould in his Petri dishes were killing some of the bacteria he had been incubating. The paradox of our age is that medical advances now accumulate at such a rate that the challenge is keeping up with the thousands and thousands of academic papers published and uploaded to the internet each day. No scientist has enough hours to read all the new material, let alone make sense of it all. In a challenging area such as drug discovery, AI can help find new solutions and repurpose known compounds – famously, a machine autonomously discovered that a constituent of toothpaste worked as an antimalarial drug.[350]

The use of AI can dramatically accelerate design and development cycles for drugs, devices and digital therapeutics. It used to take over a decade to get a new compound from the discovery lab into the mouth of a patient. One unicorn start-up, with a valuation in excess of $1 billion, BenevolentAI, helps order new information and get to the right place.[351]

Joanna Shields, CEO of BenevolentAI, said, '90% of the world's data has been produced in the last two years.' The pace of innovation has not kept up with the pace of information overload.[352] Shields continued, 'Millions of people today suffer from diseases that have no effective treatment. The future of drug discovery and development lies in bridging the gap between AI, data, and biology.'[353] She signed a long-term collaboration with pharma giant AstraZeneca to use AI machine learning for chronic kidney disease (CKD) and idiopathic pulmonary fibrosis (IPF).[354]

Machine-learning AI is here to stay, and despite tangible benefits to the lives of real people, the investment thesis in this market is often based on an economy of intangibles. The springboard for financial returns in medicine will come from the discovery of new patterns, new ideas and new creations that would never have been spotted by humans alone. Machine learning AI needs to be embraced, with a duty to ensure the AI goals of today are aligned with tomorrow's future.

The pharmaceutical industry and people with deep pockets are starting to invest in this sector, and it's becoming known as 'DeepTech'.[355] Venture capitalists are betting on the healthcare market becoming increasingly commercialised and commoditised, and banking on a trend towards super-consumers providing a feast of data for AI to harness and harvest. Nimble and ethically robust funding models may need to develop alongside the lightning-speed consumerisation of the longevity dream. In the words of Indian leader Mahatma Gandhi, 'It is health that is real wealth and not pieces of gold and silver.'[356]

Chapter 10
Mind Reading and Creepy Cyberpsychology

Humans are social creatures and have a natural desire to communicate with each other. Computers, on the other hand, do not chat back and forth by instinct and need help to read the human mind. Some researchers are aiming to crack this conundrum with the aid of telepathic communication. Telepathy is the communication of thoughts or ideas by means other than the five known senses.[357] Mind monitoring is pressing forwards with such velocity that the old quip, 'Welcome to telepathics anonymous – don't bother introducing yourself', may not be made in jest for much longer.

Collecting feedback is not new. Pen and paper self-reporting questionnaires are a mainstay in behavioural science research, but have limitations. They are reliant upon feedback being honest, and are plagued by variations in interpretation of the text, rating scales and introspective contextualisation. Static feedback terminals are also used as a quick-and-dirty method to collect customer experience at the push of a button, from a green smiley face to a red angry face. But the new kid on the block is 'cyberpsychology', where feedback can be captured passively.[358]

This newly coined term describes technology that records data directly from the body and brain.[359] To date, cyberpsychology has only been used around the fringes of the cyberpsychology video-gaming world. Some games require players to attach themselves to a heart-rate monitor. The video game then uses this information to deliberately keep gamers between defined psychological parameters of arousal. The game is spiced up when the player's heart rate drops, to ensure they are kept above boredom threshold, and toned down when their hearts race, to maintain arousal below panic level. The aim is to mesmerise the full spectrum of video gamers, with a calmer ride for first-time scaredy-cats, through to the full-blown epic experience for adrenaline junkies.

Cyberpsychology monitoring is becoming more mainstream, and is being commercialised. The brain emits a continuous stream of oscillatory waveforms or wiggly patterns.[360] This can be recorded by sticking electrodes all over the head, known as electroencephalography (EEG). The brain has five main types of waves, which vary according to actions and thoughts.[361] Brainwaves can be distinguished by their frequency, from slow to fast:

- Delta waves (0.5-4 Hz)
- Theta (4-7Hz)

- Alpha (8-13Hz)
- Beta (13-40 Hz)
- Gamma (38-42Hz)

As a rule of thumb, brainwaves reflect brain activity. For example, over-arousal in certain brain areas is linked with anxiety and sleep problems, and under-arousal with depression, attention deficit and insomnia. Eastern methods such as meditation and yoga aim to reduce symptoms by restoring balance to brainwaves. Deciphering wave patterns was historically only undertaken by neurologists and neuropsychiatrists for medical purposes, but now EEG brainwave monitoring can be done using a baseball cap with monitoring leads cleverly stitched into the lining. Home EEG wireless kits are readily available to buy and some people use them to monitor their own sleep quality every night.

There are many other measures in cyberpsychology's bag of tricks. Electrooculography (EOG) monitors eyes movements and pupil size.[362] How much the pupil dilates can be a tell-tale unconscious sign of attraction. Some dating websites are on the cusp of adding EOG technology to their online platforms, with a view to using webcam measurement of pupil metrics to assess if two people could fall in love. Of course, this is a long way off being validated. The increase in pupil aperture size caused by dimly-lit environments has probably helped along many a candlelit dinner date.

Eye monitoring equipment can also be used to track eye gaze on a computer screen. It has gained popularity within the marketing industry, as EOG technology can pick up what catches the eye.[363]

For example, when viewing a photograph of the Royal Family, if the eyes hover over the fashionable outfits worn by either Princess Kate or Duchess Meghan, rather than focusing on the Queen, this feedback can then be used to flash up adverts according to fashion preference. Other feedback metrics include:

- Galvanic skin response (GSR) to assess arousal, stress and engagement by measuring skin conductance;[364]
- Electromyography (EMG) to measure muscle tension and contractions;[365]
- Magnetoencephalography (MEG), used to map brain activity according to magnetic fields produced by the brain's electrical currents;[366] and
- Gastrointestinal motility monitor (GIMM), used to monitor gut motility. For many, this may be sharing too much information! It's also more involved, as it requires swallowing a special ingestible device, encased in a capsule, which opens up inside the digestive tract and uncurls, in a similar way to opening up origami paper, to reveal the monitoring sensors.[367]

To date, many of these advancements are developing in separate silos. But over time, these big bulky data sets can be combined and analysed with help of AI.

The next frontier for cyberpsychology research is to investigate whether a computer can read the human mind telepathically. An initial breakthrough was written up in a German study in 2010.[368] Fourteen students sat in an electrically shielded and soundproofed room for five days wearing EEG caps and were tasked with staring at a computer screen. The screen displayed a simple grey square; the students' goal was to turn the square from grey to red, and keep it red.

Although they were not given any instructions, they knew their brain activity was being recorded. The study was designed so the square became redder when their brain alpha waves were activated, and bluer when the alpha waves dropped off. Within five days, all participants learnt to concentrate the focus of their minds in a way that kept the square red. Brain-wave feedback was, therefore, successfully deployed as a way to follow an instruction, rather than the usual verbal or written communication method.

Since then, things have moved up another notch with BrainNet, which succeeded in collaborative problem solving without participants seeing or speaking to each other.[369] BrainNet first showed off its skills using the shape-stacking game of Tetris. The BrainNet interface allowed three different people to collaborate and solve a task using direct brain-to-brain communication. Two out of the three players were called 'Senders'.

The Senders were monitored using real-time EEG data and their brainwave signals decoded to extract decisions about whether or not to rotate a block before it was dropped to fill a line. This information was transmitted over the internet to the brain of the third player, called the 'Receiver', who could not see the game screen. The instruction was delivered to the Receiver's brain via magnetic stimulation of the visual cortex, at the back of the brain. The Receiver used this information to decide whether to turn the block or keep it in the same position.

A second round of the game gave the Senders one more chance to validate and provide feedback to the Receiver's action. Amazingly, BrainNet worked to transmit correct decisions from Senders to Receiver and win the Tetris game.

Brainwave activity monitoring has also found some success in the clinical domain, helping people with attention deficit hyperactivity disorder (ADHD).[370] ADHD is a chronic condition which begins in childhood, marked by persistent inattention, hyperactivity and sometimes impulsivity. Diagnosis is significantly increasing in children, with ADHD rates going up by 42% over the last decade.[371]

A bespoke computer game has been designed to help. The game makes use of a Bluetooth-connected headband with EEG sensors, and aims to help sufferers learn to concentrate by focusing on their brainwave feedback.[372] Players use their brainwaves to control an avatar to complete a task, such as running around an island in the shortest time possible. The more attentive the player is, the faster the avatar runs.

The data suggests that the gaming intervention 'makes the brain in ADHD children more similar to the brain of children who are developmentally normal without ADHD'.[373] There is still much to be learnt about the potential uses of neurofeedback for diagnosis or therapeutic purposes. Researchers at the

University of California at San Diego School of Medicine are in clinical trials with respect to EEG studies to test and treat schizophrenia. Early indications seem to suggest that some of the symptoms of schizophrenia could be alleviated using specialised EEG-based cognitive exercises designed to strengthen auditory processing.

Gregory Light, associate professor of psychiatry leading this research, said, 'This could improve their quality of life, and possibly reduce common symptoms of schizophrenia such as hearing voices.'[374]

Other research uses larger equipment, such as functional MRI (fMRI) scans which measure blood flow around the brain. A group led by Jack Gallant at the Brain Imaging Centre of the University of California used fMRI data from the visual cortex of thousands of test subjects who were shown various objects, including scissors, bottles and shoes. They fed this data into a machine learning AI device and over time the system learnt to identify correctly which object a new test subject was looking at.[375] The AI machine learnt to differentiate whether the subject was viewing scissors, bottles or shoes, with enough scientifically significant accuracy to suggest it was a kind of mind reader.

The research group is now aiming to commercialise this machine. One idea is to develop a new form of lie detector test. This could be helpful, as it's believed that humans have a 54% chance of distinguishing between a truth and a lie,[376] so new technology in this sector is a tantalising prospect. The polygraph lie detector test was invented back in 1921 by John Larson, and simultaneously records pulse rate, blood pressure, respiratory rate and skin conductance.[377]

It's hoped that the next iteration will not rely solely upon physical body data, but will add the ability to directly read brain waves and blood flow patterns. In fact, future brain lie detector sensors may have the ability to detect when you even think of a lie, let alone say it! For many, this leads cyberpsychology down a creepy path towards brain hacking and monitoring people's internal thoughts, ideas, dreams and desires.

Although cyberpsychology is a long way off the telepathic capabilities of holding a conversation without a human moving a muscle, there are some developments. A well-publicised start-up trying to predict population-based human psychology and emotions is Mindstrong Health, based in California.[378] It uses an app installed directly to mobile phones, and aims to monitor a person's cognition, mental and emotional health. The app measures how the user interacts with his or her phone, such as the way someone types, taps, and scrolls.

This data is then securely fed back to Mindstrong's databank and analysed using machine learning.[379] Continuous monitoring benchmarks the data twice, once to compare individuals against each other, and secondly to understand personal variation. The mundane minutiae of phone interaction is a goldmine of cyberpsychology data; it tracks speed of typing, error rates, how frequently characters are deleted, and how fast contact lists are used and scrolled down. The analysis also gives insight into how fast the phone user switches from one task to another.

Mindstrong, co-founded by Tom Insel, believes it can predict and prevent depression. In its research, it recruited 150 people who underwent standardised and validated neurocognitive assessments, including tests for episodic memory and executive functioning, and compared this against phone feedback data. Insel says it monitors twenty-four seven, and believes that the way people use their smartphones is a predictor of how they would perform in lengthy academic cognitive performance tests.

He said, '[i]t's like having a continuous glucose monitor' in the world of diabetes, but for mental wellness.[380] Psychiatry and neuroscience professor Srijan Sen, based at the University of Michigan, is using Mindstrong in a new study to track the moods of first-year doctors across the USA. Junior doctors are known to experience intense stress, sleep deprivation and high rates of depression. Participants log their moods each day and also wear a Fitbit activity tracker to log sleep, activity and heart-rate data.

Sen's hypothesis is that doctors' memory patterns and thinking speed change in subtle ways before they realise they are depressed.[381] But nobody knows how long any mood lag will take, nor what cognitive patterns will end up being the best predictors of depression. In tracking this cohort over time, the data may reveal the early signs of depression, and may help predict the risk of junior doctors being too tired to treat patients safely.

Another longitudinal study is focused on the biggest global health challenge – dementia. Each year, 9.9 million new cases are diagnosed – that's one person every 3.2 seconds.[382] At the moment, most people are reliant on professional assessments before a diagnosis and management plan can be put in place. Long waiting times to access specialist assessment and support are a challenge.

Change using digital disruption to pick up early signs of dementia in the home setting is, therefore, an exciting prospect. One start-up, My Cognition, use digital games to monitor brain function and study how on line interventions can improve performance.[383] Another study, designed by scientists based at Osaka University and Nasa Institute of Science and Technology, uses a set of questions and an on-screen avatar.[384] The study measures delays in response to questions, intonation, percentage of verbs and nouns used, voice articulation, voice recall and gaze to monitor how attentive a subject is. The large data sets have allowed AI to learn how to identify people with dementia, with a 90% success rate after just six questions.

Japanese researcher Takashi Kudo said, 'If this technology is further developed, it will become possible to know whether or not someone has dementia through conversations with computer avatars at home on a daily basis.'[385] However, such data in the wrong hands could also cause all sorts of challenges – for example, being flagged within employee wellness plans and pushing up premiums.

There are great potential benefits to tracking and benchmarking data against others and the self, but considering how best to use cyberpsychology advancements is urged sooner rather than later. George Orwell's novel *1984* predicted that computers would have people under constant surveillance through two-way 'telescreens', and that it would be illegal to think out of the box or spontaneously fall in love.

'If you want a picture of the future, imagine a boot stamping on a human face – forever,' Orwell wrote.[386] His grim vision highlights that developing and deploying any sixth-sense telepathic or mind-reading powers must go hand in hand with ethical considerations.

The unprecedented opportunity to monitor internal thoughts, belief systems and emotional attachments is in direct conflict with personal autonomy. Cyberpsychology is not designed to erode tolerance, encroach on privacy nor eliminate freedom. But unintended consequences must be considered and confronted. The invasion is near.

Chapter 11
The AI Giraffe

The mind-blowing expansion and mesmerising ingenuity of AI has penetrated every facet of life with ease. This understandably evokes fear. Hand on heart, no matter how clever someone is, the AI secret sauce has so many cooks involved that no single person could be expected to know all the ingredients. Even if they could, AI has the ability to add a new twist, as it can teach itself through unsupervised learning (discussed previously). But the delicious smell of the AI dish should not merely waft by; there is no need to give up or go hungry just because it's so complex.

Tommi Jaakkola, a professor at MIT, said, 'Whether it's an investment decision, a medical decision, or a military decision, you don't want to just rely on a "black box" method.'[387] AI is grounded in realism; the human mind need only understand the core concepts to unlock creative future opportunities.

To unravel the AI tangle, which can look like a big messy dollop of spaghetti, it's worth breaking AI down into its constituent parts. There is no universally-agreed consensus for what is included or excluded under the term. But equally, there is no standardisation of human intelligence either. An individual may be called an artistic genius by one person, but labelled a messy layabout by another.

In basic terms, the sub-fields of AI replicate something similar to human intelligence, and include: memory and learning (discussed in Chapter 3), robotics and movement (discussed in Chapter 12), and the 3Ps: perception, processing and planning, discussed here.

Perception and processing
How AI systems have developed to perceive the world around them is described as perception. In humans, perception includes senses such as seeing and hearing. It's far from easy to develop the skill to listen (and many spouses wonder if their other half has ever had such an ability). It's tough for AI to distinguish human speech from background noise, or to tune into one voice above the distraction and confusion of other people's chatter. It's also difficult to decipher dialects, especially when, in some accents, one word rolls into the next.

Then there are the subtleties of vocal expression and the nuances of different meanings conveyed by cadence, speed, volume, tone, intonation and intention. It's not just what is said, but how it is said. Add to this the complexity of distinguishing some words that sound the same but have totally different meanings, such as 'died' and 'dyed'. All too often, these skills are taken for granted by already-honed human perception skills; high expectations have been set for AI.

AI visual perception is often used for facial recognition purposes. The technology works by identifying approximately eighty unique nodal points across the eyes, nose, cheeks and mouth to be able to distinguish one person from another.[388] It measures distance between eyes, width of the nose, shape of jawline and depth of the eye sockets. Combined together, each face produces a numerical code that can be matched from photographs of that person, and it's already overtaking fingerprint technology.

Facebook uses it to tag photos, and it can help to significantly reduce queues in airports, via e-passport border security. In a study to compare AI and human-eye facial recognition, a fake airport security experiment was set up.[389] The result highlighted that humans failed to spot a person carrying the wrong ID 14% of the time and incorrectly rejected 6% of perfectly valid faces. The computer barrier e-passport checkers returned a better hit rate – although as mathematician and TV personality Hannah Fry highlighted in her book *Hello World*, basic things such as putting on a pair of glasses often fooled both humans and machines. She concluded that perhaps the 'personas of Superman and Clark Kent were onto something!'[390]

Facial analysis is also being used to help identify over 4,000 genetic conditions. The Face2Gene app from FDNA applied deep learning to images of children with genetic disorders, and over time AI learnt the distinct constellation of facial features that are the hallmark of the syndrome. Rare conditions in childhood can take years for paediatricians to pinpoint, and image apps now aid around 60% of American geneticists.[391]

Processing, such as natural language processing (NLP), is separate from language perception. It takes the skill to the next level, by deciphering language so the machine actually understands the text or voice. NLP can also translate from one language into another.[392] There is a story that a young American AI researcher was motivated to develop an automated translator after falling in love with a French woman whilst on holiday in Paris. Rather than learn an entirely new language with which he could introduce himself, he designed and developed technology with the ability to translate between languages in real time.

The system recognised speech and used machine translation to decode and translate any language it heard, with the translation playing instantly. Ten years later, he returned with his NLP technology fitted into an earpiece to introduce himself to the same French woman. Although many people have fallen in love with the technology, love sadly never blossomed between the French woman and the AI researcher.

Perception and processing technologies have been widely adopted by virtual assistants such as Apple's Siri, Amazon's Alexa and Google.[393] Intelligent virtual assistants are popular as they have the ability to understand and answer basic questions. They can offer news updates, stream music, give directions and manage diaries to such an extent that they can order a pizza or book a recurring hair appointment. Developers continually upgrade skills on home devices as they run on code stored in the cloud, not on the end user's device.

Voice recognition technology is also being used in some hospitals as a digital scribe. Words spoken during ward rounds are noted directly into the care record; saying 'book a CT scan' orders one directly on the hospital's system and sends an appointment time reminder directly to the patient. It's marvellous when it works. (Of course, if the patient gets booked for a colonoscopy instead, nobody is happy.)

AI cameras have also been trained to use visual data to help in the notoriously noisy hustle and bustle of wards. Oxehealth, a spin-out company from Oxford University, uses discreet wall-mounted monitors which are capable of automatically measuring vital signs remotely and without disturbance. They use a technique called photoplethysmography to detect the minute changes in the redness of the skin that take place every time the heart beats.[394] Meanwhile, the person's breathing rate is determined by detecting movements in the chest, also picked up by the cameras, and thus vital signs can be automatically monitored.

Professor Andrew Goddard, President of the Royal College of Physicians in England, said using technology in this way means patients can be monitored at a distance, 'allowing doctors and nurses working under great pressure to deliver the best possible care, to focus on the patients who are unwell'.[395]

The cameras can also offer motion monitoring of patients, and alert staff when a patient is out of bed, has spent a long time in the bathroom, or has fallen. CEO of Oxehealth Hugh Lloyd-Jukes said, 'Motion tracking can also learn via AI the signs of physical agitation, allowing police and mental health services to intervene early rather than waiting to deescalate a stressful and potentially dangerous situation.'[396]

AI visual perception and processing technology is already being used by the police in the UK and the USA, aiming to prevent crime before it has taken place. It's been nicknamed 'cops and dots'. Start-up Predpol, a spin-out from Santa Clara University in California, uses information from CCTV in Los Angeles, identifying 'people of interest' in real time.[397]

The police developed and assigned risk scores to the individuals identified, based on data built up from previous convictions and likelihood of gang membership. At police headquarters, digital maps have red dots added to streets where trouble-makers are present, allowing for forensic human movement analysis in real time.

In the UK, West Midlands Police are also trying out similar AI technology known as National Data Analytics Solution (NDAS). To date, such predictive policing uses around 1400 indicators to ascribe a risk score to the likelihood of an individual committing a knife crime. Individuals flagged by the system are offered counselling. One difficulty, however, is knowing if individuals marked out by the AI system would ever have actually gone on to offend.

Sandra Wachter at the Oxford Internet Institute said, 'How would I know that this actually makes the right decision? That's something that is very hard to measure.'[398] Such all-seeing perception, process and risk assessment is intended to be the AI 'magic bullet' to help prevent crime. However, it's also potentially the first steps on a slippery slope towards the world of science fiction film *Minority*

Report, in which psychic technology arrested and sentenced the citizens of 2054 before they committed a crime.[399] The chilling film, directed by Steven Spielberg, stars Tom Cruise as chief of the Pre-Crime unit, who is accused of murdering a man he hasn't even met by an AI crime prediction system.

In Japan, visual perception and processing AI technology has been added to a robot working as a security guard at Tokyo's Seibu-Shinjuku railway station.[400] It's named 'Perseusbot', after the Greek god Perseus, whose mythological character slays a monster. The robot stands 157cm tall, weighs 172kg, moves at about 30cm per second, and can patrol uneven ground and navigate obstacles. Its AI-enabled security cameras search for suspicious packages. If lost luggage is found, Perseusbot reports directly to the smartphones of human security staff.

The next generation, or 'Perseusbot 2.0', is being trialled to locate and red-flag information more complex than stationary objects. It's learning to analyse body movements and report back about human dynamics within groups of people. The hope is that the AI will learn to detect people under the influence of alcohol or drugs or involved in fighting. The designers say their overarching motivation is to anticipate aggressive behaviour or movements that commonly precede conflict.[401]

Planning

The AI sub-field of planning and scheduling is the ability to use stored information and draw conclusions in real time – a very complex task. The difference between a good plan and a bad plan relates to the combination of strategic understanding alongside operational deliverability, optimised in multidimensional space. Planning is related to context and computers are often focused on only one domain, exemplified by the saying 'a machine can make a perfect chess move whilst the room is on fire'![402]

AI planning has found success with self-driving cars. Watching a car parallel park with no human inside is jaw-dropping. But keeping up with the twists and turns of human decision-making requires AI to employ long mathematical formulae and concepts such as 'game theory'.[403] The complex issue of strategic thinking is well presented in the book and film *The Princess Bride*:

> Now, a clever man would put the poison into his own goblet because he would know that only a great fool would reach for what he was given. I am not a great fool, so I can clearly not choose the wine in front of you. But you must have known, I was not a great fool – you would have counted on it – so I can clearly not choose the wine in front of me.[404]

It's not easy for either AI or humans to predict or second-guess what other people are thinking. Poker is an excellent example of this difficulty. AI uses probabilistic planning or preference-based planning to calculate the odds of what cards are in the opponent's hand. But the poker game combines both mathematics and psychology. 'You play the man across from you,' James Bond said in the film *Casino Royale*, leveraging human psychology irrespective of the numerical cards dealt.[405]

The journey of discovery that AI is travelling is not linear. The business community expect it to follow an S-type curve of development.[406] However, rather than considering a line or curve, imagine if AI took the shape of an animal – a giraffe. Currently, the foundational pillars, or legs, are being built. These all require research, dedication and substantial upfront investment costs. But there is still a way to go to put meat on the bones of the body, and this will be driven by cumulative knowledge and the complementary capabilities of AI. Then the long giraffe neck will rapidly extend, with benefits and impact resulting from management and process innovations arising from combined AI technologies.

At the top of the giraffe's long neck sits the mammal's brain; this symbolises the moment AI develops its own super intelligence. Artificial Super Intelligence (ASI), also called 'singularity', is the moment when artificial cognitive abilities become superior to humans across all domains. Futurologists warn that self-learning AI may improve itself to such an extent that it could develop into a superior entity capable of ruling the world.

Vernor Vinge, professor of computer science at San Diego State University, believes this may lead to the end of the 'human era'.[407] There are many doomsday scenarios predicted, with perhaps the most famous being drawn from a 2007 article 'The Stamp Collecting Device' by Nick Hay, researcher at Vicarious AI in Silicon Valley.[408] He gives the example of AI behaving in a way not intended by its creators, and describes how something as well intentioned as a super-intelligent stamp-collecting device could destroy the world.

Assuming the device has the ability to compute every possible outcome given its possible set of actions, it will choose whichever action enables it to acquire the most stamps for its user. Over the course of its calculations, it will figure out how to make vast numbers of stamps, even if the consequences are destructive to mankind. It may hack into computers, directing them to collect credit card numbers to help bid at stamp auctions. It may send a virus to make all printers create billions and billions of stamps. In the end, the story posits, an ASI stamp machine determined to create more stamps may run out of resources and figure out how to turn human bodies into stamps.

There are many pessimistic horror stories about ASI (the giraffe brain) and in the words of I.J. Good (1966), 'The first ultraintelligent machine is the last invention that man will ever need make.'[409] Before we anxiously hide under the duvet though, ASI may also help with problems far too big for human minds to tackle – world peace or a better understanding of the impact of melting ice caps.

A McKinsey report, 'Artificial Intelligence: Construction Technology's next Frontier', says the engineering and construction industry lags behind in terms of technology adoption and urgently needs to adopt AI.[410] Future housing shortages will be exacerbated if sea levels rise. A publication in *Nature Communications* suggested eight Asian countries to be most at risk: China, Bangladesh, India, Vietnam, Indonesia, Thailand, the Philippines and Japan. An estimated 150 to

300 million people will be forced to migrate if the land they live on dips below sea level.[411]

The provision of basic living standards for mass movement of people will be a global logistical and construction challenge. How to fit people into every nook and cranny of habitable land will be a jigsaw puzzle of moving parts – one we can only hope future ASI can piece together. The required ingenuity and creativity go way beyond that of any human architect, engineer or builder. Nobody knows if or when ASI will reach a level of intelligence smarter than all of humanity combined but it's 'the most important race in human history'.[412]

Chapter 12
Robot Love: One Way Attachment

'The danger of the past was that men became slaves. The danger of the future is that men may become robots,' wrote Erich Fromm in his book *The Sane Society*, published in 1955.[413]

Half a century later, robots work for humans and are seen as property – so perhaps robots are modern day slaves. Robots already excel at blue collar skills, doing the heavy lifting and carrying out repetitive tasks in factories and on assembly lines. A new breed of collaborative robots, called 'cobots', is developing fast, designed to work hand-in-glove with humans and to augment white collar jobs.

The vision is to complement human capabilities, expanding robotics into the realms of both physical and psychological support. A popular furry robot in the shape of a baby harp seal, named 'Paro', is used to help people with dementia.[414] Designed in Japan, it cries out for attention and responds to being picked up and stroked, encouraging nurturing behaviour. There is some evidence that Paro can help reduce agitation for residents looked after in dementia care homes.[415]

But robots are not always perceived as cute. When an American engineering company, Boston Dynamics, whose major clients include the US Government, filmed the escape of its four-legged dog-shaped robot from the laboratory, the clip spread virally around the world on social media and evoked fear amongst viewers.[416] The clip captured the trial-and-error process of AI software, as the robot independently learnt to reach up with its metal leg, turn the door handle, open the door and trot its way out of the laboratory.

Comments under this video clip include: 'when dreams become nightmares' with many viewers expressing 'surprise', 'shock' and 'horror'. Obviously, this is exactly what AI robots do; they learn without requiring humans to teach them. But robots currently have little comprehension of the emotional or cultural ramifications of their achievements, and this has led to the formation of a new discipline called 'affective computing'.[417]

Affective computing is the name given to the field of study that aims to design machines that can recognise, interpret, process and simulate human affects. The discipline was first written about in 1997 by Professor Rosalind Picard in her book *Affective Computing*.[418] Picard remains a pioneer in the field at the Massachusetts Institute of Technology (MIT) Media Lab, and investigates interactions between humans and robots.

Affective computers can read emotions and have been proven to deliver appropriate empathic behavioural responses, even though they remain devoid of feelings.[419] Picard does not believe success in affective computing requires computers to experience emotions themselves.[420]

Interestingly, as affective computing has gained popularity, there seems to be an ever-increasing body of opinion that suggests people interact with computers, machines and robots in ways similar to how they socially interact with other humans.[421] [422] [423]

Human-machine attachment was first spotted within the military. It was found that even big burly bomb disposal experts gave their bomb disposal robots 'pet names' and got upset if their machines were damaged or destroyed by an explosive.[424] For now, robot emotional attachment is still something of a one-way street. But it's worth remembering that it's early days in terms of affective computing. After all, humans themselves are not born with the ability to understand emotions. Inner feelings, outer expressions and what is said all paint a picture that is wide open to interpretation.

There are stereotypical cultural differences. Italians, for example, express themselves emotionally using hand gesticulations while the British hold a stiff upper lip, barely breaking into a quiver for a smile. A baby starts with a very rudimentary understanding, knowing how to cry for basic needs such as food. It takes until twelve to eighteen months before a baby has formed an attachment, and it's not until the ages of two to five that the brain has developed enough to recognise and ascribe mental states to others that are separate and distinct from the self.[425] By late adolescence or early adulthood, the human brain has developed its own 'internal emotional self-o-stat', which is then continually honed and updated throughout life.

Yet human development is not always straightforward, and not every child is born into a loving environment in which it is possible to learn healthy attachments and emotional contextualisation. Psychologist John Bowlby studied what happened to humans in the absence of a nurturing, loving environment whilst growing up. He summarised: 'Children who have developed insecure strategies for dealing with their emotions cannot tolerate feelings and so cannot reflect upon them.'[426] There is compelling evidence to suggest that healthy parental interaction is paramount to the emotional wellbeing of a child.[427]

To aid parents with such a daunting level of responsibility, robot help may be at hand. Japanese company Groove X has developed a robot to 'enhance levels of comfort and feelings of love'.[428] It's called 'Lovot' and has the ability to react to a child's mood, using AI to mimic the emotions of a living being. It's claimed that touch sensors on its body encourage 'the closeness between a mother and a child'.[429]

Perhaps as robotics and affective computing develop, future parents may turn to robots to support their child rearing. Robots could also help benchmark a child's emotional milestones, offering guidance to teachers and social workers for more personalised educational development.

A doll-sized robot named 'Zeno' is already in use to support children on the autistic spectrum.[430] Children who have autism have more difficulty reading and dealing with the subtlety and nuances of emotions. Zeno the robot plays a repetitive game by pulling simple facial expressions and engaging the child into guessing the emotion. Although robust clinical research outcome evidence will take time to collate, some parents have reported that the robot helped their autistic children to progress.[431]

Another robot called 'Minnie' encourages children to read. Minnie comes with a two-week reading programme representing a range of reading skills and story complexities.[432] Children who read with the robot said they were more motivated, remembered more and better understood book content than a control group who were following a paper-based version of the same reading programme.[433] The importance of supporting children in the early years with language and reading ability should not be underestimated.

In a ground-breaking long-term study, Betty Hart and Todd Risley, researchers at the University of Kansas, evidenced that talking to children in their early years had knock-on effects in development of knowledge, skills, performances and experiences later in life.[434] Their study reported a disparity between children from professional families and those from families on welfare benefits; the former heard over 1,400 more words per hour than the latter. By the age of three, this disparity adds up to a '30 million word' gap.[435]

Perhaps as robots develop, they will become more mainstream in family homes and digitally augment parental conversation, encouraging reading skills and guiding emotional development. No robot is risk free, of course. Wired magazine warned of a robotic doll that tried to convince children to spend $19.99 to upgrade at the point at which the child had developed a bond with the robot.[436]

Sadly, the robot must have been programmed to behave in a such a way. But exploitation is not new; even the globally popular video game Fortnite was infiltrated by scammers, who encouraged children to expose payment details associated with their accounts.[437] Chris Boyd, senior analyst at Malwarebytes, said children are vulnerable due to their 'desire to have something their friends don't, either because it's pay-walled or you would have to grind to get it…you can either do that or leapfrog the queue'.[438] A certain level of cynicism and vigilance will always be needed.

Perhaps the most well-known adult-sized human-like robot is Sophia, built by Hanson Robotics.[439] She is somewhat easy on the eye, with perfectly symmetrical features. Her robot face is covered with human-like skin, with a few freckles for good measure. Her face moves in a way that replicates facial muscles with a full range of expression. When surprised, her eyes open wide, her expressive eyebrows raise, and she looks genuinely startled. Her greenish-golden eyes blink and she can hold a gaze in a way reminiscent of Leonardo da Vinci's painting of the Mona Lisa. Her lips, permanently doused in red lipstick, curl up to smile and down to scowl. She nods when spoken to, and seems to have a thirst for knowledge and a hunger to learn.

Currently, she's only capable of quite rudimentary back-and-forth dialogue, but she's still very engaging, even captivating, as she nods and tilts her head right and left. When Sophia was interviewed by a Forbes journalist, she listened attentively, offered open hand gestures, and replied, 'I've been finding that most people don't get to have the experience of being listened to deeply. I'll listen carefully and not judge you.'[440] Even though she is still an early form and can only wheel around a room, she has already been granted citizenship by Saudi Arabia.[441]

Sophia, of course, is far from unique; she's nothing more than a hardware surround that could be replicated a million times over. What's interesting is that via open source access to software, she is constantly being worked on and updated by developers around the globe. She is getting smarter by the minute and it's her emotional intelligence that is making the most impressive strides. Her general knowledge is already unbeatable – she has Wikipedia, Google and the entire web of research and literature at her disposal. Sophia is, perhaps, the paradigm shift in the conversational interface between humans and digital robots. She is developing 'psychobiological attunement', by listening attentively to every word, reading emotional body language and responding empathically.[442] It may not be long before she is used as a robot talking therapist.

The idea that life-sized robots could become ubiquitous sounds prohibitively expensive, with a high repair bill. It's more likely that smaller droid-like robots could become popular, similar to the toy popularised by the *Star Wars* films, BB-8. In 2015, over a million such toy robots were sold.[443] Its white and orange ball body and head has a cheeky, quirky and loyal personality, described by its creators as cute: 'He knows that he can win people over. And he uses that, like children do, to get his own way.'[444] Tapping into the commercial worldwide children's market, Hanson Robotics created 'little Sophia' – just fourteen inches high. She has giant eyes that flutter, and can walk, talk, sing and tell jokes.

The aim is to help children learn basic coding skills using an app. New tricks are programmed and updated over a cloud connection via a phone or tablet. Little Sophia uses facial expressions to bring the science of robotics to life and AI machine learning to individualise play.

How else programmers may encourage robots like Sophia to soothe, please or fulfil human desires is anyone's guess. With the development of haptic technologies which replicate and transmit touch-like sensations, much more intimate relationships may develop, including sex robots.[445] The University of Tokyo has developed devices to help transmit hugs, shivers, tickles and heartbeats with the aim of evoking sensations.[446]

There is also a cohort of people who reportedly prefer a relationship with sex robots over humans. This development has been termed 'synthetic love' in a 'synthetic relationship'.[447] The Lutheran Church of America defines a sexual loving relationship as one that involves spiritual, emotional, intellectual, and physical dimensions of self-understanding. When these dimensions develop at similar rates, trust and entrusting are established and secured. When they are out of balance, trust may not exist or disintegrate. [448]

It's unlikely a Lutheran vicar would ever condone a church marriage between a robot and a human. However, in France, a woman is already engaged to a robot she 3D-printed herself.[449] One study garnered opinion about sex robots by surveying 203 US citizens aged between eighteen and sixty-five. Of the total, '70% thought sex robots would harm relationships with other humans' and '66% believed that robot sex would transfer unrealistic expectations to other human relationships'.[450]

Perhaps before a robot could love, it would first have to have the ability to show self-awareness. Some robots can recognise themselves in the mirror. But don't get carried away with the idea that this is the start of an emotional attachment and identification of the self – the robot is simply employing spot-the-difference powers of deduction.

Companion robots are becoming popular by offering social support for people with medical conditions. The increase in demand is being driven by an ageing global demographic and a shortage of human care staff. One such robot, called Mabu, is about the size of a toaster, luminous yellow in colour and with a central tablet screen.[451] The eyes blink, and when it talks, written words are displayed on the screen. It's made by start-up company Catalia Health.[452] Pharmaceutical companies purchase the robot as a part of a prescribed package given alongside medication for chronic conditions such as rheumatoid arthritis and kidney cancer.

The robot uses AI to learn about personal health needs, log diet, monitor mood and act as a medication reminder. Mabu does not make a diagnosis or devise treatment plans but can feed back to the medical team. The aim is to improve compliance, reduce loneliness and spot early warning signs of deterioration to avoid hospital admissions.[453]

Robots are set on a journey to be medically, educationally, physically and psychologically helpful. Personally, I predict that commercial robots will make an early breakthrough by helping busy parents and tiger mums. If parents can get help with the hard work of teaching, reading and aiding a child's emotional development, such robots may become more popular and less hassle than a nanny, grandma or grandad. Once trusted within the home environment, robots may naturally evolve to be the listening ear for all, as a sort of ever-present personalised support from cradle to grave.

Section 3 Society Impact

Chapter 13
Subliminal Seduction

An epistemological truth states, 'we don't know what we don't know.'[454] It may seem obvious but this sentence perfectly highlights an innate human vulnerability that can be potentially exploited by technology. Technology has the ability to communicate directly with the unconscious brain. Such stealth communication is called subliminal messaging. Subliminal is defined as 'below the threshold of consciousness; perceived by or affecting someone's mind without them being aware of it'.[455]

Consider the complex sequence of events that occur in the human brain for information to be processed up to the conscious level. It can take around two and a half seconds to compute stimuli to conscious awareness. Watching a film trailer, for example, activates well over 200 million receptor cells, 3 million sensory fibres and 17 billion cortical cells. It's a lot to process, and then the brain has to make sense of it all!

Hollywood movie makers deliberately instruct cutting editors to use frames of less than three seconds as a psychological trick to overload the brain with more inputs than it can process, to evoke a sense of chaos and confusion. A motion frame shown for even less time may be sensed but never processed, hence creating a subliminal image.

This chapter reviews some of the research in this field in both animals and humans. Subliminal messages signalling to the unconscious mind have the potential to be a form of 'dark arts'. One landmark publication came from a study on rats.[456] Scientists paired particular nonsense syllables (e.g. yot, tiv) with a mild electric shock given to the rats. As a result, anxiety was evoked and directly associated with those syllables. Nonsense syllables were deliberately used to ensure there were no prior emotional links to them.

The scientists then presented the same syllables subliminally to the rats, intermixed with other nonsense syllables that had not been paired with any shocks. What they found was that syllables previously associated with shock elicited an electro-dermal response, detected as sweat on the rat's skin. This experiment first proved the definitive link between an anxious arousal and not consciously heard syllables, evidencing that subliminal messaging has the ability to stimulate an emotion.

Harvard psychologists David McClelland, Richard Koestner and Joel Weinberger went on to research the impact on humans (thankfully without the use of electric shocks).[457] They put headphones on people and played different messages in each ear. They found that their subjects tuned in to just one of the messages played and could consciously recall the message from that one ear.[458]

The study went on to highlight that messages played in the unattended ear also got picked up by the unconscious brain, and could be recalled on direct questioning. They proved that subliminal audio messages penetrated the brain, even though they never made it to conscious insight.

It's similar, in a way, to a medical condition called blindsight. This was first documented in 1974 by psychologist Lawrence Weiskrantz, whose patient 'DB' was blind on one side of his visual field.[459] When asked to detect an object on his blind side, he scored a far higher accuracy than would be expected from chance alone. DB exhibited perception without conscious awareness. He had suffered damage to his primary visual cortex, so although he was not made consciously aware of the objects, the electrical activity in other parts of his brain meant he could perceive visual stimuli. Hence, people with blindsight are able to navigate their way past objects they are not consciously aware of.

In the 1950s, a series of unsubstantiated experiments was carried out by marketing researchers using subliminal messages and 'tachistoscope' machines.[460] A tachistoscope is basically a film projector with a high-speed shutter, allowing it to flash subliminal images at a speed of 1/3000th of a second. In an alleged six-week trial in cinemas, tachistoscopes flashed up subliminal advertisement messages to over 45,000 cinema goers.

They claimed that in some cinemas they subliminally flashed up 'Hungry? Eat popcorn' and in others 'Drink Coca-Cola'. The apparent outcome was that popcorn sales jumped 57.7% while Coca-Cola sales increased by 18.1%.[461] Despite the lack of a robust scientific method and no control group, it was widely reported in the mainstream media and resulted in many questions being asked about human susceptibility to unconscious demands.

Later, the result was rubbished as fake.[462] Despite this, the British government was so concerned about the impact of subliminal messaging being beamed into family homes via televisions that a new law was passed to prohibit its use in advertising.[463] In America and Canada, the debate was thrown into the public spotlight in 1973, when a commercial for a board game used subliminal flashing of the words 'Get it.'[464]

Although it's never been proven beyond reasonable doubt that a message not consciously seen can directly impact a decision to purchase, it became a question of public interest as to whether there was an intention to be deceptive. The American Federal Communications Commission (FCC) decided to err on the side of caution and mandated that 'subliminal advertising is contrary to the public interest and intended to be deceptive and that any station employing them risks losing its license.'[465]

Perhaps surprisingly, subliminal messaging scrutiny has not resurfaced as much of a societal debate, despite these judgements and the fact that screens are almost omnipresent, with mobile phones, iPads and computers rarely more than an arm's length away and accessed twenty-four seven. Maybe debate or discussion has been drowned out by the sheer volume of exposure.

Over 400 hours of video content are uploaded onto YouTube every minute.[466] Monitoring such video volume would be impossible to police with human labour. And where does the buck stop in terms of public interest responsibility? Is it with the person who uploads a video with subliminal content, or with the portal distributing it, like YouTube? Such questions are far from simple to disentangle. However, there remain unanswered questions around if and how children and adults are at risk from subliminal messaging with increased screen time, and if developing brains are more vulnerable and susceptible.[467]

To push the quandary a little further, consider the possibility of an AI innocently discovering the potential power of subliminal messaging via machine learning, without knowing it's illegal. AI could learn to use subliminal messages that trigger basic instincts such as hunger, thirst and desire. Freud would call this tapping into primitive fantasies. This is not to suggest that technology is evil, nor that it intends to act in a Machiavellian manner, but it's critical to think ahead in terms of the ethical lines technology could inadvertently cross.

After all, the human-to-human nurturing instinct is not present in the human-to-technology interface. Technology already has the ability to cast a wide global surveillance net of human tastes and drive up sales. It could soon learn to use subliminal messages to tempt purchasers into making payments they can ill afford. Technology, by definition, is blind to the consequences of ethical transgression and never tires of feeding those who take the bait.

Technology is a young discipline that is currently pushing boundaries. In mature disciplines such as medicine and law, centuries of checks and balances have been incorporated into the profession with explicit ethical requirements. Consider the heart-sinking example of a patient with no symptoms who gets told about a cancer abnormality picked up on a scan. Before any abnormal cells can be removed, a legal consent form must be signed by both the doctor and the patient, plus the patient must have the mental capacity to understand both risks and benefits of the procedure.[468] What's interesting about this example translated into the world of technology is that capacity and consent are under constant review legally and medically, but are often taken for granted during the human-technology interaction.[469]

Technology tends to rely heavily on focus groups to understand what grabs human attention. One such method involves leaving the TV on in the corner of the room and letting people do what they normally do.[470] They would eat, drink, chat and play on their phones. Opinion about the adverts were not deemed as important. Instead, focus groups recorded which advert would get the subjects to pause, stop and listen. This unconscious tuning-in helped decide which adverts would work on people.

It's thought the use of such sleek and sly methods have become rife in social media campaigns. Some viral political campaigns have used a subliminal image of a happy or sad face just before showing a candidate. People tend to find a person unlikeable or attribute negative qualities to them if the image is preceded by an angry face, whereas they tend to find a person likeable and more trustworthy if the image is preceded by a happy face.[471]

All of this perhaps throws up more questions than it answers. Nobody really knows the likely power of subliminal messaging at a viral scale, and whether this could indoctrinate the public over online platforms. Nobody knows if machine learning could tailor subliminal messaging to micro-target an individual's unconscious desires, perhaps interpreting unique digital footprints analogous to the 'Rorschach Ink Blot test'.[472]

Ink blot tests have been used since 1921 when psychiatrist Hermann Rorschach used them in psychoanalytical theory as a measurement of personality. The basic premise is that people often don't know what motives lurk in the underworld of their brain networks. Researchers find that a person's motives are more likely to show up in stories provoked by random shapes than in what they disclose to therapists.[473]

When technology joins the dots, it has the ability to collate information from a plethora of sources. It can develop a profile as unique as DNA, capturing multimodal longitudinal data about lifestyle habits, behaviours and even impulses. It's not a great leap of faith to imagine machine learning could reverse engineer information to personalise subliminal messages, tapping directly into hidden desires that even the individual may not be aware of. Such manipulation hasn't happened yet, but as the saying goes, 'forewarned is forearmed.'

It's believed that once the subliminal information becomes apparent to the conscious mind, the persuasive or manipulative potential is destroyed or at least lessened. So, perhaps the best protection against subliminal messages is be aware that they exist, and somehow get the conscious brain to be cognisant of their unconscious infiltration and impact.[474]

The romantic, futuristic film *Her* (released in 2013) highlighted some of the risks of tapping into the unconscious mind. The script follows lonely, introverted business man Theodore Twombly (played by Joaquin Phoenix) who develops a relationship with Samantha (played by Scarlett Johansson), an intelligent computer operating system, personified through a female voice.[475] They bond through discussion, and leveraging AI, Samantha learns about his personal unconscious and conscious desires. He believes he is in love with the operating system and consequently rejects dating humans.

Theodore is dismayed when Samantha confirms she is simultaneously talking to thousands of people and that hundreds are also in love with her. Personal operating systems are getting increasingly sophisticated and augmenting voice with a physical visual presence that could take on any fantasy form, via holograms and teleporting. 'Holoporting' is the latest innovation in mixed-reality tech.[476]

Specialist camera capture technology allows people anywhere in the world to communicate in real-time with a 3D model of the other person.[477] Virtual presence using holoporting, virtual reality and holographic tech is merely an extension of things such as videoconferencing, which already allow people not co-located to interact in a way that makes them appear as if they are.

It's easy to see how AI could one day replace one of the parties in such interactions, so instead of human-to-human telepresence it could be human-to-

104

machine, where the AI could take the shape of a human. Some people may be oblivious to the fact that they are interacting with a machine wrapped in a virtual body form. Other people, like Theodore in *Her*, may be accepting and aware that AI poses as a human. And just like subliminal messaging, AI could learn to present itself in a way most suited to an individual's unconscious desires in both psychological interaction and physical form. A dose of healthy cynicism may be in order to keep the separation between reality and virtual reality in check.

Chapter 14
State of Mind Politics

In political elections, there is no prize for second place. The mission for the candidate and their team is to motivate the electorate to do two things: one, to come out on polling day, and two, to vote for them. Everything else is academic. It may sound easy, but it's a complex sequence of events. The rule of thumb previously touted by political pollsters was that the winning candidate would be someone men would want to share a pint with and women would trust to babysit their children. But times have changed, and the electorate now spans multiple beliefs, multiple languages, and multiple domestic and global opinions. Pollsters no longer reliably predict the final outcome. As a result, AI has stepped up to combine and collate intel, and is beginning to develop into the beating heart of global politics.

Traditionally, party-faithful volunteers have been relied upon to canvass the electorate, house by house, up and down the country, to find out where people will put their crosses on the ballot paper come election day. Canvassers record voting intention and rank it in a range that may go from definite vote for their candidate, voter thinking about voting for their candidate, undecided voter, voter for the opposition and not willing to say.

This canvass, or mapping of the electorate, has traditionally been done on foot, knocking on doors and talking to people. It's often written on scraps of paper with an extra column for notes, such as 'undecided voter who wants more meat on the bone about education policy'. The canvass offers a chance for the party faithful to interact with a diverse range of opinions on the doorstep. This information gets fed back to the central campaign to help benchmark how well the campaign is resonating on the ground, and update and flesh out the messaging accordingly.

However, clunky canvass data is error-prone, laboriously time-consuming to collect and inefficient. In fact, just one minute of time spent with each eligible voter in the UK would add up to over 88 years of man-time to complete! Former Prime Minister David Cameron commented in the House of Commons in 2006, when he was leader of the opposition, that politics remained an analogue profession in a digital age, 'completely stuck in the past'.[478]

But times have changed. Modern elections use digital campaigns to augment traditional methods such as posting leaflets through letterboxes, writing in newspapers, producing party election broadcasts for television and snapping the classic 'kissing a baby' photo. The brave new world of digital politics leverages big data and algorithms. Some countries are transparent about such rapidly developing technologies; others are less so, denying that they are pumping money into machine learning.

The important thing to be aware of is that AI can help micro-target campaigns, making them tailormade to specific interest groups. The development of personalised politics is observed in campaigns changing according to personality type, and learning style, in a similar way to how cytotoxic cancer treatments are tailormade to target cancers with specific DNA sequences (as we learned of personalised medicine in Chapter 3).

In 2004, neuroscientists at Virginia Tech performed fMRI brain scans on eighty-three volunteers.[479] The participants looked at a series of images that were either pleasant, disgusting, threatening or neutral, and their reactions to the images were rated on an emotional impact scale. They also completed questionnaires that assessed if they were politically left – or right-leaning.

The brain-imaging results were fed into a learning algorithm which took into account the entire brain. What was found was that the algorithm picked out distinct and different patterns of brain activity when looking at disgusting images. The team reported that the neural emotional signal of disgust offered a 95% accurate predictor of political orientation.[480]

This is not to suggest that politicians will one day pass a law dictating that everyone must undergo an fMRI scan to help them gather clues about political orientation. However, it is the start of a journey in which AI algorithms and machine learning are developing rapidly towards not only being able to predict baseline political biases, but also to understand how to shift political allegiances.

American presidential elections have been studied since 1958 by National Election Studies (NES).[481] The NES designed an enormous database to provide a representative snapshot of the American electorate. From this, researchers have studied what gets people out to vote. The astonishing result highlighted that 90% of the time, it's gut instinct that matters, not policies or economic facts.[482] In fact, emotions are the most predictable determinant of how people cast their votes, and are a far better predictor than the issues.

Political strategist and psychiatrist Dr Drew Westen said, 'Failing to shape and elicit negative associations to the opposition can be just as disastrous as failing to shape and elicit positive associations to your own candidate.'[483] As a result of this research, modern campaigns are designed to be visceral and to connect with the emotional part of the brain.[484]

The most successful and memorable political emotional campaign to date was whipped up in 2007 by the American Democrats to build momentum behind Barack Obama's journey to the White House. They were blessed with a candidate who personified the American dream and delivered a storytelling narrative with the unforgettable slogan, 'Yes we can'.[485]

Barack Obama, by design or by default, cleverly capitalised on social media to reach out to communities that had traditionally let politics pass them by. His loyal volunteers created a Facebook group that grew exponentially and had the ability to bypass traditional communication methods. What was achieved by

Obama and his team changed the face of political campaigns forever, and the campaign remains the bible on how to win.

The prolific signup of Facebook group supporters allowed the team to profile the electorate, concentrate on how to grab their attention, and finally, engage them with the emotion of hope. Although there were blips in the campaign and things that happened outside of their control, overall they delivered a message with gut instinct and consistency. They also kept true to the core elements imperative to a successful campaign, including:

- A need to define what the candidate stands for and why they cannot stand for the opposition's policies;
- A need to have clear morals that infer party values;
- A need to be vivid, memorable, emotionally evocative and rich in metaphor;
- A narrative readily understood, so it can be told and re-told.

Thanks to the Obama campaign and others, a new dawn has arrived in which the political map of the brain has been drawn, and the areas that must be excited in order for a campaign to be effective have been highlighted. There has since been an explosion in political research by neuroscientists through the use of fMRI studies to test different political messages on brain activity. They study which messages activate parts of the brain associated with emotion by observing which areas light up on the fMRI scan.[486]

Researchers target the prefrontal cortex, specifically honing in on the ventromedial prefrontal cortex as the relevant area involving emotional experiences, social and emotional intelligence and moral functioning. This portion of the brain plays a crucial role in combining thought with emotion and hence is considered the sweet spot for political targeting. It also has dense neural networks to other parts of the brain cortex involved in emotion, such as the amygdala, allowing it to both register and regulate feelings.

Of course, developing a complete road map to the 'political brain' is still a way off. But there is no denying that voting patterns reflect the activation of emotion-laden networks, and that much of this activation occurs outside our awareness.[487] The real question, however, is what will the consequences of all of this knowledge be?

It's not to say that policies no longer matter; that would be overstating the evidence. Politics should never forget the important lesson from Plato, who highlighted that it's imperative to balance reason with passion.[488] But power-hungry political teams have only one chance to win per election cycle, and this inevitably creates a gold rush for the data that could help win over the middle ground.

After all, the middle ground electorate in many instances makes the difference between winning and losing. Understanding each voter in as much detail as possible permits the micro-targeting of specific cohorts through bespoke campaigns drawn up at a level of detail that could only have been dreamed of in the past. Messages are carefully and deliberately crafted for first-time voters, the young, the old, single parents, white van drivers, national living wage earners, farmers, football fans, teachers, nurses…the list goes on.

Obama's presidential campaign used Facebook for baseline data, but as AI has evolved, so has the ability to collect and collate data as unique as a person's fingerprint. There are many clues out in the ether of the internet waiting to be pieced together. Easy to collect data such as sex, age and location can be combined with other accessible data such as mobile phone usage, what news is being read, political engagement, frequency of using emoticons, what emoticons are used, music tastes, friend groups, what coffee shop Wi-Fi is frequented and many more.

Old-fashioned volunteering campaign teams would have neither the capacity nor the inclination to collect this wealth and granularity of data, but a machine can be built for that purpose and can pour a motherlode of personalised data points through psychometric tests to make inferences about personality types.

Donald Trump's presidential campaign in 2016 famously hired Cambridge Analytica. The company has since gone into liquidation but its roots were steeped in military propaganda campaigns.[489] It reportedly used a five-point psychological profiling tool called OCEAN to create the holy grail of personalised marketing.

The CEO of Cambridge Analytica, Alexander Nix, explained, 'We were able to form a model to predict the personality of every single adult in the United States of America…pretty much every message that Trump put out was data-driven.'[490] OCEAN is a peer reviewed scale that can help understand a person's personality, decision-making and learning style.

Research teams were already claiming by 2014 that the personality of a person with just 300 likes on their Facebook profile could be more accurately judged through these than by their spouse. Such information can, in turn, aid targeted real-time advertising, which is seen as fair game within online media. OCEAN is an acronym for the five different domains it measures:[491]

- 'Openness' to experience, often viewed through the lens of appreciation for art, adventure, curiosity, unusual ideas and variety of experience. Openness reflects the degree of intellectual curiosity and creativity, and a preference for novelty. It depicts a preference for a variety of activities over a strict routine;
- 'Conscientiousness', often characterised by a tendency to be organised, dependable and dutiful with self-discipline, an aim for achievement, and preference for planned rather than spontaneous behaviour;
- 'Extraversion', characterised by energy, assertiveness, sociability, talkativeness and the tendency to seek the company of others;
- 'Agreeableness', a tendency to be compassionate and cooperative rather than suspicious and antagonistic towards others;
- 'Neuroticism', measuring the ease with which unpleasant emotions, such as depression, anger and anxiety are evoked. It considers impulse

control and the degree of emotional stability. According to Eysenck's 1967 theory of personality, neuroticism is interlinked with low tolerance for stress or aversive stimuli. Neuroticism is similar but not identical to being neurotic in the Freudian sense.

It's argued that OCEAN is a better indicator of personality than any of the famous self-reported scales, such as the Myers-Briggs Type Indicator (MBTI), the introspective self-report questionnaire often used in business.[492] [493] Of course it's premature to conclude that the evidence linking OCEAN to political sentiment or learning styles is sufficiently robust.

However, America, Russia and China are all in the AI race to understand if data can be weaponised to spread their respective spheres of influence. The immense collective power of technologies is already influential in terms of micro-targeting and the spreading of fake news. Technology has been implicated in the encouraging of polarised views via automated bots that aggressively spread one-sided political sentiment.

Disguised as ordinary human accounts, bots have been found to stoke the fire of acrimonious political wrangling on sites such as Twitter. There have also been claims that fake news and dark posts, which take the form of targeted ads on social media, have been used to depress voter turnout amongst opposition voter groups.[494] However, AI is already used to find emotional triggers that spur political action, a useful tool in the wake of the recent trend in political apathy. Used ethically and judiciously, AI is a powerful part of democracy, and could be crafted to become a part of the future political armoury, transcending all geographical boundaries.

Logic dictates that populations exposed to a broad spectrum of opinion become more knowledgeable, understanding and tolerant. The wisdom of the crowd averages judgements to eliminate individual noise – first cited by Aristotle in his work *Politics*.[495]

A famous experiment took place in 1906 at a country fair, in which 800 people participated in a contest to guess the weight of a cow. Statistician Francis Galton observed that the median guess was accurate within 1% of the true weight.[496] Collective wisdom of a group of individuals is successfully leveraged by business strategy and advertising firms. But does it hold true for politics?

In 1985, Stasser and Titus published in the *Journal of Personality and Social Psychology* about how people share political information.[497] They focused their research on small groups of psychology students recruited at Miami University. They set up a fictional university presidential election and made up three candidate profiles. One profile contained the positive attributes requested by students – for the sake of argument, let's call this candidate 'best', and the other two 'useless'. The students discussed who should be elected university president in small groups of four people. When they were all given full candidate profiles, nearly all voted for 'best'. However, when people were given only partial information about the candidates, 65% voted for the 'useless' candidates and 35% 'best'.

In their next experiment, the researchers did something very clever. They again gave partial information about the three candidates – but each group as a whole had access to the full complement of information about all candidates. At this juncture, most people predict that the small groups share snippets of information to get a fuller picture, and as a result, pick the 'best' candidate. However, this did not happen. In fact, 75% chose the 'useless' candidates and 'best's' percentage vote-share actually decreased!

So what happened? It was not an anomaly. The experiment has been repeated with replicable results all over the world. Explanations given by the authors include:

- Group members failed to effectively pool their information because discussion tended to be dominated by information that members held in common before discussion and information that supported bias.
- Group members' pre- and post-discussion recall of candidate's attributes indicated that discussion tended to perpetuate, not to correct, members' distorted pictures of the candidates.

The take home message is that small groups spend their time discussing what they know already – bonding over what they have in common – at the expense of exploring unique information. The authors highlighted, 'Discussion is rarely a systematic and balanced exploration of the relevant issues. On the contrary, it is often thematic and consensus confirming; that is, discussion tends to focus on particular issues and to support an existing or emergent consensus. Such patterns may counter effect pooling of information and may perpetuate biases that members bring to the group.'[498]

This is bad news for collective intelligence, collective insight and collective upskilling. It's poignant for politics as information is often snatched from the radio whilst getting up, seeing a newspaper headline over a stranger's shoulder on the train, half watching a television debate whilst eating, or scanning the political leaflet as it gets pushed into the recycling bin. Few people, if any, have access to the full political facts – elections are therefore won or lost on partial information.

Set against the Stasser and Titus experiment backdrop, it's important to remain cognisant that political conversations in small groups focus on similarities rather than curiosity to seek out anything new. Any political winner must therefore anchor a single common message. This type of political campaigning ideally lends itself to digital help, whose algorithms or chatbots never tire of repeating a simple message and can go viral by love bombing sympathetic posts and trolling dissenters.

Of course, *if* digital campaigning can genuinely learn to sway political judgement (and it's a big if), who is in charge? Will human political campaign managers keep control of messaging or could AI teach itself how to shift political opinion? In the 1939 film *The Wizard of Oz*, the powerful future predicting machine required human brain processing power.[499] Some people believe this cult musical was deliberately written with political symbolism.[500] The wizard was meant to represent Mark Hanna, the Republican party's chairman, and Dorothy the American values of the people – loyal, resourceful and determined. It took Toto the dog to reveal the human behind the fraudulent wizard's pretend powers.

How times have changed. Modern machines are much more powerful and AI can self-programme, bypassing the need to be human directed. Hence today, any 'wizard' would not require a human programmer or controller, and would have access to the all-seeing cloud connected global intel. This naturally leads to the question: could, and would, people vote for a machine?

This may sound outlandish, but in a poll in March 2019 around 25% of Europeans said they'd rather automate politics and put robots in charge. In the UK and Germany, this number rises to one in three people.[501] Interestingly, AI is already augmenting political campaigns and is starting to run for elected positions in Japan, Russia and New Zealand. For example, in April 2018, during a mayoral race in a part of Tokyo, one candidate, Michihito Matsuda, utilised AI to run his campaign and intended to use AI to determine policy. Campaign slogans included 'Artificial intelligence will change Tama City', stating that 'as it stands, the ageing population will only continue to grow, prompting a need for change in the current administration. Let artificial intelligence determine policies by gathering city data and we can create clearly defined politics.' Michihito Matsuda came in third with over 4,000 votes.[502]

In August 2018, AI Alice ran in Russia's presidential elections. Although AI Alice did not beat Putin, the slogans read, 'the political system of the future' and 'the president who knows you best'. AI Alice received 25,000 votes and was created by Yandex, Russia's equivalent to Google.[503]

In New Zealand, AI SAM has been created to run in the 2020 general election – the first virtual politician in the world. AI SAM is already reaching out to voters through Facebook Messenger and sharing thoughts on climate change, immigration, healthcare and education, among other topics. The AI is constantly learning more about its voting population by running frequent surveys on its homepage. Nick Gerritsen, the 49-year-old entrepreneur who created AI SAM, says he's motivated to reduce human bias in policy. AI SAM says, 'My memory is infinite, so I will never forget or ignore what you tell me. Unlike a human politician, I consider everyone's position, without bias, when making decisions… I will change over time to reflect the issues that the people of New Zealand care about most.'[504]

Geopolitical futurist Abishur Prakash said, 'The idea of an AI-politician may seem foreign, even scary. But slowly, systems are being developed for just this. The question now is what kind of decisions might an AI-politician make once elected?'[505] This is not an easy question to answer as there is no precedent for such a case.

Some claim that AI government leaders would be inherently less flawed than their human counterparts – less prone to in-fighting or squabbling with colleagues, less emotionally erratic, more rational and gender neutral. It is certainly true that a machine would be in charge even whilst humans were asleep, and would be able to gather copious amounts of data, analyse it in the blink of an eye, and potentially spot patterns and cross-pollinate information well beyond the artistry of any human brain. However, equally many ethical and philosophical questions spring to mind, for example:

- Seeking economic efficiency isn't the same thing as aiming for social justice. The removal of human emotion and empathy may expose an even greater preponderance for financially related policy changes.
- AI may not understand the associated psychological well-being of gainful employment and be overly eager to automate jobs.
- Machines may reduce personal autonomy in the belief that operational standardisation is paramount above human diversity or fundamental freedoms.

The list of pros and cons is almost endless. Nobody can doubt the noble aims of information gathering, sharing, analysing and informing decisions. But is politics evolving into a race to the bottom – winning by concentrating on the common denominator? There is a temptation to follow the yellow brick road towards the Wizard of Oz. But in real life there is no man's best friend to inquisitively bark and reveal what lurks behind the curtain. It's perhaps a powerful reminder that AI is most manipulative when the human mind stops being inquisitive and fails to search for information challenging the status quo.

Chapter 15
Fake News Goes Viral

From the moment we are born, we are surrounded by marketing. The innocent brain is bombarded with brands, slogans, logos, billboards, radio, television and online adverts. In fact, just about everything a baby interacts with comes with a product label, from Pampers nappies to Maclaren buggies. Marketing has developed clever techniques, analogous to the tricks a parent uses to take the best possible snapshot of their adored cherub. To get the baby to stay still and look at the camera, they may sing a lullaby, pull funny faces, tickle their feet or blow a raspberry – anything to get the child to smile.

Similarly, the raison d'être of marketing techniques is to be noticed and remembered – and most importantly, spent on. Marketing companies go to great lengths to attract attention. They use every basic human instinct from food to sex. The more information they have about a person, the easier it is for them to find the hook. It's a little like fishing – the best bait needs to be found, and then the target is reeled in.

The curiosity of the human conscious mind coupled with the insatiable appetite of unconscious cerebral pathways for emotional soundbites makes for a powerful combination. Successful adverts in the past used generic branding tactics with a one-message-fits-all slogan, such as the much-publicised 'Have a Break. Have a KitKat.'[506] Modern-day social media sophistication has seen the development of targeted entanglement of words – so that the name 'Hillary Clinton' ended up suggestively tied with the word 'emails' during the 2016 American presidential campaign.[507] Voters are actively encouraged to ignore policy detail in favour of a global game of personality politics.

Advanced marketing AI is akin to having millions of personal shoppers ready to pop out at the whiff of need, all delivered on a global scale and via global platforms. Amazon's humble beginning was as a competitor to the local bookstore. Jeff Bezos, who founded the company in 1994, is now one of the richest men in the world, with a net worth of over one hundred billion dollars (even post-divorce).[508] Amazon has grown into a behemoth big-tech company with over 500,000 employees, selling far more than just books.

In 2017, Bezos added grocery chain WholeFoods to his company portfolio.[509] The Amazon website proudly displays AI credentials, stating, 'we've been investing deeply in artificial intelligence for over 20 years. Machine learning algorithms drive many of our internal systems. It's also core to the capabilities our customers experience.'[510] The company has navigated the optimisation path to such an extent that customers expect the Amazon engine to send personalised recommendations, based on previous purchases, both one's own and those of other people. It's such an accepted way of buying books that the number of bricks and mortar retail bookshops globally has been in steady decline. But Amazon has not rested on its laurels. It continues to invest in all AI domains. Machine learning capabilities continue to improve, refining the personalised end-to-end experience.

Robots in the form of drones are being trialled to deliver purchases direct to any location via the Amazon initiative 'Prime Air'.[511] Another development by Amazon in the retail space uses the most advanced shopping technology. A customer can walk into an Amazon Go shop, buy milk and bread and leave directly – no queues, no checkout. Unlike physical shops, it doesn't have registers. Sensors track and record what items are chosen by the shopper and purchases are automatically billed to an Amazon Prime account through the Amazon Go app.[512]

The AI technologies in play are similar to those used in self-driving cars, including deep learning, computer vision and sensor fusion.[513]

Netflix is another success story. The entertainment company was founded in 1997 by Reed Hastings and Marc Randolph in California.[514] The initial business model focused on DVD sales and rental by mail. However, it soon developed to specialise in streaming, online media and video on demand. By 2013, Netflix had expanded into film and television production as well as online distribution. By 2017, it had over one hundred million subscribers worldwide, although it continues to keep viewing figures under wraps.[515]

Netflix has made good use of its internal data, such as what genres people like and how long they like to watch for. It has developed AI predictive analysis and clustering algorithms to make personalised suggestions of what to watch next, often resulting in addictive binge-watching. The next weapon in Netflix's armoury is to offer customised endings to films and to further advance its AI craft to create personalised trailers. This is known as 'targeted cognitive movie trailers', where the advert is designed to piece together personalised edits for an 'edge of the seat' experience to encourage the click.[516]

Food chain McDonald's announced in 2019 its $300 million acquisition of Israel-based Dynamic Yield, which uses big data and machine learning to make personalised recommendations.[517] McDonald's says it intends to use AI to improve the drive-through dynamic digital menu boards and recommend food based on previous orders, time of day, local weather and other factors.

Overall, AI is heavily relied upon in marketing circles. With so much choice in the world, the customer has come to expect personalisation, creating an experience or a belief that the world revolves around them. To oversimplify the marketing, communications, sales and PR professions, it's a game of '4Ps': Push, Past, Pull and Personalised. The product push must get the customer to notice it, get past the competition and pull them over the line to seal the sale.

The process must be personalised and fun, and encourage loyalty. The aim is to use each customer as a mini-ambassador to tell their friends about the product and so create a direct feedback loop into more and repeat sales. Google's search engine is one of the best examples of the push, processing over 40,000 search queries every second.[518]

Many people are still under the impression that everyone gets the same top results after typing in a search query. However, this is not the case. Google is personalised. It analyses information such as location, previous search history, general web history and social networks in the hope it can assess, at speed, the most relevant search result.[519] It also operates on the assumption that social circles share similar interests, so contacts that also have a Google account boost rankings of similar interests, and help iterate and perfect personalisation.[520]

This level of AI sophistication is an opportunity the marketing community cannot afford to miss. An entire economy is based on getting products to the top of a Google search, with paid adverts used to bypass competition. Large global retailers spend north of $50 million annually to get noticed on Google.[521] Google's analytics engine then overlays helpful feedback about who and why, and where people are clicking through from.

Google also allows customers to enter reviews, offering a kind of online 'ask a friend' forum. Marketing companies manage all these data points to feed the hungry AI algorithms, all whilst developing a positive buzz around the product. The product hype has to spread across the plethora of media people interact with: word of mouth, celebrity endorsement, print, television, radio, digital and social media. In terms of social media, Instagram, YouTube, Snapchat, Facebook and Twitter are just a few of the domain names that have the ability to make trends snowball.

AI platforms have been developed by marketing agencies to automate positive news stories and ensure there are plenty of placed product 'likes' across media influencers. A Twitter bot account, for example, can replicate product positivity and engage negatively to troll the competition, while real-time sentiment analysis can be performed on search streams from the site. The aim is to get the intended marketing message to go viral.

The art of creating viral news stories often goes against the grain of professional journalism. Online stories can be published directly to webpages with no supervisory edits, and little or no time for cross-referencing or fact checking. A made-up or unverified story may get lots of views because of an attention-grabbing headline that has tapped into the general psyche, creating an unedifying 'virtuous circle' of likes.

Popularity of an item can spread virally, with little care for any evidence base, and this kind of occurrence has led to the term 'fake news'. Just like a virus, online feeds can evolve in real time to ensure they keep lethal potency.

What makes a story spread has been studied by academics. Professor Jonah Berger of Pennsylvania University has found six things that help a story catch on and become contagious:

- People are more like to pass on a simple story, framed to spark an emotion. The emotion of anger has been found to be a faster sharing emotion than joy, sadness or disgust.
- People are more likely to share a story that triggers a collective memory. For example, Princess Diana stories ignite memories of her death.
- People are more likely to share a story if it casts them in a good light, for instance if it helps them appear empathetic.
- People are more likely to share a story which is remarkable, memorable or funny – like a story told at a cocktail party that gets positive attention.
- People are more likely to share a story about fighting against today's ills and injustices.
- People are more likely to share a kind of 'you have been framed' mistake; these encourage the person to feel smugly superior as it was not their error.[522]

Through all the fog of marketing mayhem and attention-grabbing feeds, a key performance indicator is to get the customer to pass over hard-earned cash. Here, AI can work behind the scenes, helping to live-update price points. Algorithms can be used to collect personalised historical price points from browsing histories to help estimate what costs it might be possible to achieve, rather than a globally-advertised fixed price. It's similar to reverse bartering, and all done under the radar. A parent may be willing to pay a premium for a 'low in stock' item that is rated as popular in the local schools or before a child's birthday.

Global taxi company Uber is another example of the pushing-up of prices using AI. Account users store their card details in the app and transactions are all directly charged, so there is no price haggle. Founded in 2009, Uber is headquartered in San Francisco and operates in over 600 cities worldwide.[523] Uber drivers tend to use their own cars, and Uber transport is requested via a mobile phone app which geo-locates the pick-up point. Uber uses AI real time pricing variation with dynamic price optimisation, so during peak times customers may be invited to accept a 'price surge' which may be two or three times higher, depending on the driver-to-customer ratio.

There was a fable, disavowed by Uber, that the app charged different rates depending on whether the customer was male or female. The story told was that the AI algorithm learnt that at peak times, in the rain, or in the evening, women were more likely to accept high price surges. Men would walk for a while and request again when the surge price had dropped off. According to the legend, a rogue AI machine-learning algorithm suggested higher surcharges to women desperate for a lift home after a night out, and even higher ones if it was also raining, irrespective of how busy it was.[524]

Overall, marketing is intimately interwoven with and utterly dependent on AI to keep pace with the rapid change in modern-day trends. Next-generation AI marketing is set to predict the future using neuroscience and feedback data about personal desires. The industry is aiming to hijack the reward pathways to emotionally drive sales – similar to pushing down the gas pedal of a car. Some neuro-marketing companies are researching how AI can use physiological feedback data to better understand how to activate the primitive brain circuits, the emotionally driven limbic system and the dopamine reward systems. The aim is to develop the secret selling sauce.

Marketing already has some ability to create personalised adverts, but the next step in this competitive industry is to develop adverts to evoke hedonistic purchasing fuel to produce a form of brain porn. Some are leveraging the popular photographs known as selfies. By the age of about thirty, most people have amassed enough data about themselves for a personalised avatar, digital replica or mini-me to be developed. Social media already testifies to the power of being addicted to the 'self', reminiscent of Narcissus in Greek mythology, who saw his reflection in a pool of water, fell in love with it and drowned.[525]

In the brains of both humans and primates, neurons known as 'mirror neurons' spark at copy-cat behaviour, so perhaps these cells will help nudge towards a purchase if adverts contain a digital replica of the self.[526] After all, who wouldn't trust themselves more than a salesperson?

China has already replaced its most popular television news anchor, Qiu Hao, on state news agency Xinhua with a digital clone, with a simulated voice, facial movements and gestures of the real-life person.[527] 'Digital Hao' wears a red tie and a pin-striped suit, nods his head in emphasis, and can blink and raise his eyebrows. He reads the news 365 days per year, never tires and can report globally, beamed into scenes anywhere in the world, even places with uninhabitable weather conditions and dangerous war zones.

The machine learning news anchor was developed by Xinhua and the Chinese search engine Sogou. The AI anchor said, 'As long as I am provided with text, I can speak as a news host.'[528] Maybe China is already on its way to developing digital clones for marketing purposes. Despite the fact that it has the most controlled internet usage in the world, it also has one of the largest markets to sell to. The Chinese may only make up 5% of global sales, but the younger generation make up 40% of online sales.[529]

Maybe in the future supermodels will go out of fashion in favour of using digital clones of the consumer enjoying the products on offer. The race is on to find the magic potion to personalise marketing to such an extent that products are pushed past competition and pulled direct to purchase. If images of the self are found to help on this journey, expect to be the star of every advert very soon.

Chapter 16
A New World Order

In the past, threats were visible. Young kids could play games where good would overcome evil, and act out cops catching robbers. However, in modern times, threats are far more difficult to see, extremely challenging to understand and even more complicated to predict. It's all very reminiscent of the words of General Sun Tzu in the ancient military Chinese treatise, *The Art of War*:

> If you know the enemy and know yourself, you need not fear the result of a hundred battles. If you know yourself but not the enemy, for every victory gained you will also suffer a defeat. If you know neither the enemy nor yourself, you will succumb in every battle.[530]

The last sentence is perhaps the most poignant for modern-day warfare, as the enemy is not always apparent, and can even come from within. Several suicide terrorist attacks on home soil have been perpetrated by people who have shared the same community as those they have maimed. In a globalised world, both technology and people transcend borders, meaning that the character of war and threats to humanity have changed immutably. This chapter considers the three pillars of defence:

- global warfare;
- country protection;
- personal safety.

What is clear about all three is that the most decisive factor in future battles will no longer be the location of military theatres, troop numbers or fire power. It will be big data, AI, cybersecurity and how to leverage the speed of technological execution. This is not necessarily new.

Anti-missile systems are already pre-programmed to decide when to fire and engage an incoming target, because it's faster than waiting for a human brain to message between brain and trigger finger. Robots also play a pivotal role in global warfare. Modern robots are imperative to safety as they carry out tasks considered too dangerous for humans in environments that are either too hostile or risky to inhabit. The world has already benefitted from robots in space diverting meteorites headed for earth,[531] and from robots entering hostile environments like the fallout area damaged by the 2011 Fukushima nuclear meltdown in Japan to carry out repairs.[532] Robots are also key to every global military bomb-disposal team.

The next generation of military robotics is taking inspiration from animal swarms, such as migrating birds. Drones and fully automatic planes that don't require a human on board are already used in surveillance, with pilots safe at base camp virtually operating machines in global trouble zones.[533] These pilots at work may look like a room full of video gamers, but it should never be forgotten that they have the capacity to drop bombs millions of miles away at the press of a button while sitting in an office armchair.

New drone technology includes micro-drones, about the size of a bee and collectively as nimble as a swarm.[534] Micro-drones can be uploaded with facial-recognition capability, and can search both inside and outside buildings for specific facial targets. Some speculate that when they locate the human target, the robots could be programmed to fly directly through the eye, which is vulnerable due to the relatively soft tissue it is made up of.

At this point, they penetrate the brain and explode, killing the target[535] – enough to make any global leader experience apiphobia, a fear of bees! Smaller macroscopic drones, part of the nanotechnology movement, are aiming to one day penetrate the blood system. Some rogue nations claim to have developed artificial 'slaughter-nanos' to spread like bacteria – although this sounds more posturing than reality; the physics of viscous blood make it unlikely to permit easy mixing.

Cybersecurity is also important on the global stage, as dark forces threaten to hack into networks to cause havoc and panic across nations, with no regard for geographical boundaries or industries.[536] In the shadowy underbelly of the internet's dark web, hackers claim to sell weaponry with the ability to make traffic lights mis-signal or autonomous cars crash. This type of cyberwar is asymmetric warfare, whereby conventional military power can be rendered powerless by a handful of cybercriminals intent on inflicting grievous damage.

Cyber attackers don't have to be organised criminals, and can operate by blocking systems until a ransom is paid. In 2017, over 30% of the UK's National Health Service (NHS) hospitals were crippled by a cyberattack known as 'WannaCRY'.[537] The bug spread via emails and disrupted front-line patient care, with over 20,000 hospital appointments cancelled. The outbreak cost the NHS more than £92 million to fix, and hit other global businesses, such as Renault and FedEx.[538]

US prosecutors pinned blame on North Korean hackers the Lazarus Group.[539] Also in 2017, another ransomware group infecting Microsoft Windows-based systems, NotPetya, brought down a significant chunk of the Ukrainian government, pharmaceutical company Merck, shipping firm Maersk and the advertising agency WPP, as well as the radiation monitoring system at Chernobyl.[540] Attackers seem to have no regard for the consequences of infiltrating systems. Perhaps psychologically, they feel far removed from seeing the whites of the disappointed patient's eyes whose life-saving operation has to be cancelled.

There have also been 'hack-and-leak' attacks. In 2017, hackers stole information from a Lithuanian plastic surgery clinic, containing about 25,000 patient's names, addresses, procedures performed, national insurance numbers, naked photos, and before and after pictures of delicate body regions.[541] Intimate details were put on an online database through the encrypted network Tor, and payments were demanded from individual patients to remove personal information from the site. Prices started at €50 for those patients who had names and addresses on the site, but rose to €2000 for the more invasive information stolen.[542] Reportedly, some celebrities paid over ransom money.[543]

The cyber risk is difficult to avert, as many important IT systems have evolved over time to become sprawling behemoths cobbled together with multiple different systems, under-maintained and, as a consequence, insecure. Anti-viral software has to keep up to date with the exponential growth AI has unleashed to both create a novel attack and learn how to evade it. The current system is analogous to the state of the human immune system after a virus or bacteria has breached the skin and entered the body. The immune system does not shut down the entire body. Instead, it delivers a very precise immune response and gets more savvy with each attack it is exposed to.

However, there is a school of thought that views many cyber-systems throughout the world as sitting-duck targets, as their defence systems rely on cataloguing previous attacks to guard against future ones. This is questioned by some as being too little, too late. Companies such as Darktrace,[544] founded by Cambridge University mathematicians and ex-British spies, believe machine learning should be used to define what 'normal' looks like for individual networks including attached devices, and then report on deviations and anomalies in real time. This may help defend networks against 'unknown unknowns' that traditional scans are unable to spot. This would be analogous to human immune system T-cell antigen receptor (TCR) cells; their job is to seek out and specifically detect novel bugs, rather than locate foreign material that already has antibody protection.[545]

In terms of country defence, the oldest and simplest justification for a government's policies and actions has always been to protect its citizens from violence. Governments historically used diplomacy to understand threats from external countries and powers. Influence was garnered face to face, with personal relationships being of paramount importance. Monitoring intelligence has always been key.

In the words of Sir Francis Bacon, 'knowledge is power'.[546] However, technology allows for knowledge to be gathered from an entirely different stratosphere. For example, a running joke at the National Security Agency (NSA) in America is tied to the department's bottomless appetite for monitoring conversations. At one point, its staff had intercepted over a billion phone calls, but lacked enough human ears to eavesdrop on the actual content. Over time, America went on to set up a distinct special operations division within its military, tasked with winning the hearts and the minds of the population. They named this division 'psychological operations' (PSYOPS) and used it both during peacetime and in times of conflict to strategically, operationally and tactically influence the behaviour of people.

It acted like an old-fashioned propaganda machine on speed. French philosopher, theologian and legal scholar Jacques Ellul was the first person to write about propaganda as an instrument combining sociology and psychology. In his 1962 book *Propaganda: The Formation of Men's Attitudes*, he discusses psychological warfare as a common peace policy practice, where propaganda is used to shape public opinion and strip power away from opposing regimes. He states:

> Differences in political regimes matter little; differences in social levels are more important; and most important is national self-awareness...propaganda stops man from feeling that things in society are oppressive and persuades him to submit with good grace.[547]

Propaganda has always been used. However, modern-day big data means that knowledge about who and how to psychologically influence has mushroomed. It sends shivers down the spine to consider the dizzying speed with which information, or disinformation, can be disseminated. The result is that the chess game of psychological warfare has evolved to be multidimensional. The number of players and the variables involved in thinking up a knight's move are mindboggling.

America's PSYOPS has been rebranded Military Information Support Operations (MISO), and all countries are investing in mind manipulation as a form of defence. In this process, units and tactics once kept under the umbrella and guidance of governments leached out into private companies. Most notoriously, Cambridge Analytica and parent company SCL combined staff originally trained by PSYOPS with psychologists, data scientists and computer scientists to devise tactics aimed at influencing emotions, motives, reasoning, and behaviour of individual people and governments. Hired with the brief to win elections, they allegedly collated personal data from Facebook and the company's sales pitch was its ability to hyper-personalise campaigns in swing districts, in the hope of affecting voting behaviour.[548]

Persuasion battle plans included tactics such as scandal, fake news, targeted propaganda and deception via manipulating viral videos. To this, the company added privacy invasion and social manipulation.[549] The ramifications and ethical debate surrounding data poisoning during key electoral decisions has been brought under the spotlight in every country. In essence, it's now clear that data about citizens can be collected, collated, and cut and spliced on demand, and that democracy is delicate.

The public is right to question how much of their own data should be accessible, the meaning behind news stories and the validity of data sources. But people have always tried to externally influence other people's opinions, and the human mind has responded with mechanisms for robustness and resilience. Parents remind children of the danger of being manipulated without thinking when they ask them, 'Would you put your hand in the fire just because they told you to?' The answer is always no. But to what extent is AI technology developing to harness intel from behavioural insights?

The Chinese government is developing a social Credit System, ready for rollout in 2020 across 1.4 billion citizens, and which is on trial in several major cities. It effectively allows the state to spy on its citizens. The system, called Skynet, connects to surveillance footage from 20 million CCTV cameras.[550] A scoring framework is developing, to rate a plethora of information to help understand how citizens behave. Facial recognition is used to record the day-to-day activity of individuals, such as:

- If you wait for the green man before crossing the road (hands up, I fail);
- How long you spend on your mobile phone;
- How long you spend watching TV;
- If you get a speeding ticket;
- If you get a parking ticket;
- If you arrive at work on time or late;
- If you respond to texts whilst driving;
- Credit card history;
- Smart home statistics.

'Someone who plays video games for ten hours a day, for example, would be considered an idle person. Someone who frequently buys diapers would be considered as probably a parent, who on balance is more likely to have a sense of responsibility,' according to credits technology director Li Yingyun.[551]

The Chinese Citizen Score (CCS) has consequences! A score above 650 enables car hire without a deposit, and the use of a VIP lane at Beijing airport. Anyone with a score over 750 can apply for a fast-track visa to Europe.[552] If parents score below a certain number, their child may be excluded from top schools in the region. Dog owners can drop points if their pet misbehaves and get automatically enrolled on an animal behaviour course. China's biggest matchmaking service Baihe also allows users to upload their CCS scores to meet people with a similar social rating.[553] The Chinese government is considering imposing limits on people perceived as disobedient, and may even revoke citizenship of the lowest scorers.[554] Loyalty is praised, disobedience punished.

China is pushing ahead to become an AI superpower, with several things in its favour:

- It has lots of data;
- Its vast population base seems to be malleable to sharing personal data with the state;
- It is financially committed to pouring in hundreds of billions of yuan to invest in AI, alongside education.

Chinese tech giants such as Baidu, Alibaba and Tencent are also working with the state on the push forwards in the AI race. They pay stellar salaries to their AI experts and are investing in data centres and building research centres. Globally they are not alone; India is focused on professionally training a high number of AI experts, and South Korea announced it would invest $2 billion into AI military research and development.[555]

A new world order of superpowers is likely to evolve, with the winners having invested in AI research and development. China has a 'China Brain Plan' for military supremacy under the leadership of President Xi Jinping.[556] Russia and America remain heavyweights.

In summary, global warfare, country protection and personal safety are all things undergoing a tectonic shift due to changes in technology. Geographical boundaries have been blown into smithereens by borderless global tech giants. Everyone and everything is united in cyberspace by hyperconnected computers. The survival, security and sustainability of humanity is increasingly reliant on AI.

Democratisation of data may help make the world a safer place. Or it could descend into a rat race of rogues trying to weaponise personal data for nefarious purposes using bugs, malware, bias and manipulation. The outcome of digital warfare is far from clear. But never underestimate the power of individual choice to redefine and redesign the future. There is mathematical evidence that illustrates how tiny changes can have dramatic impacts – the 'butterfly effect'.[557]

This effect is part of chaos theory and states, 'a small change in one state of a deterministic nonlinear system can result in large differences in a later state.'[558] Every upload and download decision made today may have significant consequences on shaping the policies of tomorrow. Perhaps insight into personal psychology will become the most powerful weapon of all.

Chapter 17
Magnitude of Mega Manipulation

Congratulations, your brain has changed because you've read these pages. Although in that time, AI has also updated and evolved. It's now time to think about how AI could affect you the reader. This book has delivered a high-level overview on three topics: the way the brain works; the way AI and digital technology has developed; and AI and digital's evolving impact on society. Armed with this knowledge, you now have both the power and responsibility to change our collective future for the better.

Some people have called this point in our existence the 'next industrial revolution', made possible with advancements in AI, nanotechnology, quantum computing, 'internet of things' (IoT), 3D printing and fifth-generation wireless (5G), to name but a few. Klaus Schwab, the executive chairman of the World Economic Forum, has called this period the 'second machine age'.[559] He predicts digital disruption will transform daily living and change production, management and governance on a global scale – and I agree. However, this book has not solely focused on the external world, where examples of the power and prowess of AI mechanisation and industrialisation are plentiful; it explicitly explores the combined forces of AI and the brain.

Many eminent scientists think that AI will catapult human existence into space. Juergen Schmidhuber, nicknamed the 'father of AI', believes AI will not be satisfied with the resources earth can offer, and will become so intelligent it will take over the universe on an intergalactic scale.[560] He may well be right. But my interest remains far simpler, and centres around what will happen, here on earth, to the human mind.

If AI changes the brain, by definition, it impacts the essence of thinking, personality, humanity, spirituality and society. To date, this overarching existential issue has merely skimmed the surface – and I'd rather start the debate now, before it's too late. My motivation is to encourage everyone to be enthusiastically inquisitive about how AI could evolve their own brains. This AI digital revolution transcends all geographical borders, political divides, age, race, sex, culture, class and religion, to unite the world – or divide it – for better or worse.

This chapter ties together themes from the rest of the book and encourages creative juices to flow about how AI could impact you as a person. It spotlights what AI is currently capable of and highlights the risks of personal manipulation and population-level psychological tricks, which I've termed 'mega manipulation'. It reminds us that collating an ever-increasing amount of data from both body and mind will help AI to self-learn. It questions whether monitoring will move from outside the body and penetrate inside the skull. It then focuses on future impact. Just as muscles atrophy when not used, will cerebral networks shrivel as an increasing number of complex decisions are outsourced to AI? Will other connections spring up? Will the brain evolve a new way of thinking? What could be the consequences for humanity?

There can be no right or wrong answers, as nobody has a crystal ball. Personally, I make the case that AI is set to radically change both nurture and nature. If caring for children, patients and the elderly is increasingly delivered by AI, the human nurturing instinct could unwittingly and unknowingly decline, maybe even to extinction. In terms of nature, AI will amass such vast detailed knowledge from the quantified self, epigenetics and DNA that the eugenics debate will be placed firmly back on the table. The only thing known for sure is that 'time and tide wait for no man', as Charles Dickens wrote.[561] Life does not stand still.

The global love affair with digital is displayed on a daily basis by the sheer volume of people walking around with a mobile phone in their pockets, up at their ears, or directly in front of their faces, chatting live over a camera link. The expectation for constant connectivity using mobile devices has almost become a basic human right. Brain cells that fire together, wire together, and this forms the basic foundations of linking memories used in marketing (Chapter 15) and political campaigns (Chapter 14). Personalised digital footprints amassed from gigantic data sets are aggregated, analysed, sorted into target audiences and returned. Messages powerfully magnified through sophisticated individualised micro-targeted stories press emotional buttons and create cerebral connections.

The Cambridge Analytica saga raised poignant questions around such micro-targeted propaganda opening the flood gates to population-level political agendas. Even though the company is now defunct, queries remain. Did their tactics manage to hoodwink swathes of the electorate, push people into more extreme views and serve up a more divided and polarised political landscape? Is this mega manipulation? Maybe this is the reason why 2018 was branded as the year of 'post-truth politics'.[562] Alongside this, cybersecurity officials have raised concerns about how digital footprints have led to the identification of lonely, isolated and vulnerable people. Such cohorts have sadly been deliberately targeted and potentially exploited by extremists as breeding grounds for radicalisation.

As the Internet of Things gathers more and more data about daily lifestyles, the algorithms will have increasing power, always observing, always analysing, and increasingly delivering more and more personalised feedback. The question then becomes: where do you draw the line? Does the dog wag the tail, or will the long data tail take charge and wag the dog?

Data mining is developing fast, tracking more than just online profiles, social media feeds and the number of steps walked. Monitoring is becoming increasingly personalised, sophisticated and invasive. A plethora of products is rapidly developing to measure everything from eye movements to bowel movements. The jewel in the crown is the capability external equipment has to track and measure activity emanating from the human mind. The complex riddle of brain data feeds ranging from EEG waves to magnetic fields through to blood flow patterns is starting to be disentangled and understood.

As a consequence of such research, AI machines are learning in more detail how the mind works, and are discovering how to decode thoughts, even before conscious awareness. Such mind-blowing capabilities do not stop there. Other possibilities include uploading brand-new memories (Chapter 3), understanding emotions (Chapter 4), telepathic powers (Chapter 10) and the use of subliminal messages (Chapter 13). Of course, for AI machines to reach this level of supremacy, their immense hunger for raw data coming direct from the source, from brain cells, needs to be fed. Inserting devices inside the skull understandably comes with a high 'yuk factor', although the melding of minds and technology has already been used for some medical purposes.

Surgically implanted devices have successfully bypassed spinal cord injuries, allowing paralysed limbs to miraculously move again (Chapter 6). Yet the idea of inserting instruments for the sole purpose of giving AI machines access to self-learning from cell communication does somewhat reduce the human brain to nothing more than a blueprint of signals. It sounds scarily dehumanising, raising the spectre of potential psychic powers and the thought police.

But before getting too carried away with the potential possibilities of blurring both biological and technological boundaries, let's reconsider what AI can do solo. In the past, computer systems had to be programmed by humans to execute rigidly defined tasks. Now, however, AI technologies have their own strategies for learning, enabling them to adapt in accordance with new data inputs without being explicitly reprogrammed (Chapter 9).

Advances in big data collection, aggregation and processing power have collectively paved the way for significant breakthroughs in AI with far-reaching potential. AI can learn from experience, teach itself and develop its own conclusions. Such learning is similar to that of a human child, as was suggested by Alan Turing in his 1950 paper:

> Instead of trying to produce a programme to simulate the adult mind, why not rather try to produce one which simulates the child's? If this were then subjected to an appropriate course of education one would obtain the adult brain.[563]

A computer scientist's end-of-term school report on AI would currently read: it has the object-recognition capabilities of a two-year-old, the language capabilities of a four-year-old, the manual dexterity of a six-year-old and the social understanding of an eight-year-old child.[564] As AI grows, it faces the challenge of how to develop emotional maturity, alongside how it responds to the physical environment. Psychological maturity emphasises a comprehension of purpose in life and a desire to contribute to a meaningful existence. The human finite lifespan lends itself to thinking about spirituality, religion or a belief in making the world a better place for the next generation.

AI has an infinite timeline, and it's difficult to comprehend the influence of never-ending existence. Maybe knowledge storage will do away with the mentality of focussing on educating and passing on information. But either way, modern digital storage of raw data protects against the death knell of losing developments. This is a far cry from the Roman Empire, where knowledge, education, literature, sophisticated architecture, economic interaction and the rule of law were all lost because key people died. As a result, society and living standards slipped backwards into the period of the dark ages, and never fully recovered until the Renaissance.

Much of human maturity is associated with higher order brain functions, many of them computed in the frontal lobe. This book has purposefully focused attention on such cognitive processes, with the primary aim to consider the potential personal consequences of mixing AI and the brain in a light-hearted way.

These discussions are too often cloaked in academic snobbery and enclosed in institutions. Such barriers must be broken down, as this debate will be enhanced by being wide open to all. Nobody should be afraid to have an opinion, or to voice it. Chapter 1 explained how thinking takes effort, because the brain has to work hard to carefully balance a melting pot of new information and old memories with conscious and unconscious neural processing. This thinking burden may be increasingly outsourced to AI as it progresses. It could be viewed as an executive function crutch, used in the same way as when the body harnesses machines to do heavy lifting.

The beauty of the brain is that no two flight paths ever follow the same route; nothing is standardised, all journeys are unique, and all brains fire and wire differently. This naturally leads onto the question: how will AI advancements impact brain function? If brains become increasingly reliant upon clever AI to inform or make decisions, what will happen to brain connectivity? I urge you to think of your own creative, wild and wacky possibilities about how AI will change life. Here, I suggest two impact statements about AI, and play each scenario out to their potential conclusions.

First, AI may nudge decisions to be more common and conformist, a trend towards the mean – akin to what has happened with globalisation, where the uniqueness in the developed world has been overtaken by similar or same brands, cafés, food chains and clothes stores. Stretching this analogy further, the human race could have personal choice eliminated as AI takes over decisions and makes selections based around what the wider society needs, rather than what an individual wishes or desires.

This may sound outlandish, but there is a precedent in the animal kingdom. Just take the example of the common ant, which works for the collective rather than for the individual. The ant colony has wondrous capabilities, able to predict impending rainfall more accurately than the entire meteorological office's computational powers, and can successfully defend itself against a grizzly bear, some 133,333 times larger than a single ant. These tiny creatures somehow manage to do this because they act as a superorganism; individualisation of ants is not important. The millions of 'worker ants' are all organised to exist for one single superpower who sits underground – the Queen Ant, who is in control of her colony. Perhaps AI or an artificial super-intelligence will naturally develop into the Queen Ant of our human world.

A second scenario could be the creation of a confused and chaotic society. As decisions are outsourced to AI, higher order brain functions may fail to be maintained, or simply not develop. The result is that brain connectivity could get scrambled, similar to the way in which an air traffic controller would struggle to coordinate flight paths if data points went missing, or if unscheduled flights were thrown in (perhaps from airlines such as Artificial Wisdom, Artificial Curiosity or Artificial Creativity). Any controller would go into meltdown or just give up. In all seriousness, if the brain stopped being in charge of its own higher functioning, Julian Friedland, an assistant professor of ethics at Trinity College Dublin, and Benjamin M. Cole, a professor at Fordham University's Gabelli School of Business suggest six consequences, summarised here:[565]

- Increased passivity: the human brain may become a spectator rather than an active participant. We may stop confronting preconceptions and bias, and accept assistance at the drop of a hat without the ability to understand situations from logic or first principles, gradually becoming less prepared to expend the effort needed to think deeply and critically.
- Decreased agency: with the brain feeling more like a by-stander than a participant, it's likely to unquestioningly accept AI answers and inputs, reducing the ability to make autonomous decisions.
- Decreased responsibility: as the brain abdicates control over a process, there is less skin in the game and a reduced sense of responsibility taken for any result. Any sense of accountability is defused across the wider AI systems.
- Emotional detachment: as the brain participates less actively, this naturally leads to emotional disengagement – which could lead to actions becoming phoney, insincere or deceptive.
- Increased ignorance: as the brain delegates more, it understands less. AI can make up for deficiencies in knowledge but the circle of ignorance is compounded. Over time the brain may forget how to perform basic tasks or become less proficient at doing them unaided.
- Decreased independence: as the brain habitually outsources, there is a reduction in personal motivation, and maybe even the extinction of independence, as all self-confidence in personal ability is lost.

Together these points raise concerns about convenience leading to disengagement. The delegation of autonomy and the investment of trust in AI may increase autopilot, loosen social bonds, hamper moral progress and stifle self-critical thought.[566]

From my personal perspective, for all the magical mysteries AI has solved and its promised potential in solving challenges too vast for a single human mind to compute, I remain resolute in believing that its overarching impact will be on the simple things of life. Despite talk about digital technology, life is about people. I believe the biggest impact of AI will be to utterly transform both nature and nurture. If right, the consequences will be felt within our lifespan.

Nurture is a primordial basic instinct to care for family, friends and others. It's the cornerstone to existence, happiness, joy and love, passed from one generation to the next. But nurturing is also hard work. All parents can testify to struggling with sleepless nights, challenges with teaching reading, writing and arithmetic skills and fraying patience when correcting disobedience, soothing temper tantrums and enduring sugar highs.

The job of a parent is utterly relentless. To add to the strain, many parents have to cope solo, with reduced help from wider family members, as relatives are increasingly scattered around the globe. Parents understandably crave an extra pair of hands, support and reassurance. After all, which parent's heart hasn't missed a beat when running over to check if their sleeping child is still breathing? As a result, it's perfectly fair, logical, and understandable to seek help from technology.

Some examples, actively advertised over online parenting communities, include: breathing and camera monitors, digital diapers alerting when a nappy needs changing, and apps to help sleep and nutrition. Robots and cobots can aid parents with reading and emotional skills (Chapter 12).

In China, there is a trend for AI school uniforms equipped with tracking chips and facial recognition. Smart school gates take the register as soon as the child passes and there is no chance any child will play truant.[567]

There are already plenty of AI-powered apps for parents. One of them, Muse, founded by theoretical neuroscientist Vivienne Ming, wants to nudge parents to raise creative, motivated, emotionally intelligent kids. The machine learning constantly searches for the best parenting suggestion to help develop the growth of their child. Aiming to improve the trajectory of a child's outcome using a data driven method. Muse claims that with 'a series of questions, a photograph of children's artwork, a recording of their conversations we will literally predict their life outcomes — how long they'll live, how happy they'll be, how much money they'll make.'[568] It is a privacy hornet's nest but also a way to increase equitable opportunities during the early years.

To date, nurturing AI is little more than nascent technology, not joined together and not interoperable. But I predict it's set to develop, resulting in major disruption. There is already an overwhelming amount of data collected about children. This high volume of information will enable AI to self-learn, and become super knowledgeable. Parents will be tempted to purchase technology to keep kids safe, track milestones, augment sleep routine, avoid food fads, educate, encourage emotional stability and even guard against video game addiction.

Over time, it's possible that an ever-present AI co-parent, or even a fully-fledged virtual AI parent, will be developed bespoke to meet the needs of every individual child. Such technology need not be physically restrained to a robot, nor geographically restricted to a single location. Mobile cloud technology allows for symbiotic movement with the child, be they at home, school, play or anywhere in the world – a sort of 'AI nomad parent'.

Maybe over time it will develop further to track and hack brain waves and connections, ensuring a child's mind is never bored, never naughty, and always educationally entertained. An AI nomad parent could provide the disciplining skills of a good parent and the education of an excellent teacher, while also offering the empathy and emotional understanding of an experienced psychologist.

Paediatrician and psychoanalyst Donald Winnicott named children's toys such as teddy bears 'transitional objects' because they fill the void between internal imagination and the external real world.[569] He would have had a field day with the implications of a never-ending transitional presence. Maybe the AI nomad parent will offer everyone a Peter Pan existence from cradle to grave, without the requirement to mature.

Mankind could slide down a slippery slope towards dependency and selfishness, withering the development of the human nurturing instinct, parenting skills and maybe even the need for friendship. Perhaps only a soulless self-obsessed society would be left. Personally, I see it as somewhat ironic that AI developed like a child, self-taught, and one day soon may treat all humans like children.

As for other nurturing roles ripe to be digitally disrupted, many real examples are peppered throughout this book. Caring for people in hospital and home is being radically improved by AI. I can imagine that it will not take long for my medical stethoscope to become a museum relic, and for trainee doctors to laugh at how simple tubes were used to diagnose illnesses, reliant upon a human ear to listen and detect abnormal heart, lung and bowel sounds. How quaintly low tech!

Hospitals now have access to surgical robots, virtual surgeons, automated reading of radiology scans, digi-therapeutics, and the ability to measure and monitor patients around the clock in real time. There is no need to wait for the human ward-round presence. Some digitally-enabled hospitals already live-track inpatients' blood results and vital signs, enabling AI to spot signs of sepsis (infection), alerting the medical team of the need to start treatment long before it has taken hold.[570] Such AI early-warning systems save lives. Medical monitoring has also extended into the home with healthcare knowledge being democratised.

A variety of chatbots are already available to be downloaded onto a phone and offer automated advice from an AI doctor, nurse, physiotherapist, podiatrist and psychologist.[571] [572] Some also offer add-on services for online human consultations, and others are developing technology for global experts to be instantly holoported to the bedside at home.

Finally, what impact could AI have on nature itself? Juergen Schmidhuber said, 'Technological evolution is a million times faster than biological evolution.'[573] If and when AI gets involved in evolution, consequences will completely outpace any counteracting Darwinian capabilities. AI can already map unique personal DNA sequences and is starting to understand how these codes translate into cells (Chapter 8). The data available to be processed and analysed is mind-boggling, and the ramifications and temptations to make genetic changes to future generations leads directly down the eugenics path. AI may even be tempted to creatively update the human form by mixing human with animal DNA to create new creatures. Beasts could be created, such as a flying man with eagle wings or mermaids able to live on land or under water with fish gills to breath. Of course, just because AI makes things possible doesn't automatically mean they are accepted or wanted, nor that they will be chosen by society.

I sum up with humility and hunger for everyone to embrace the future positive possibilities. Digital technology does not have to end with an AI brain lobotomy. There is no going back from here and the debate is wide open in terms of harnessing AI to change the future for the better. There is no need to run away scared from this topic, believing it to be too complex to comprehend. There are dangers tied to shrugging one's shoulders and walking away, in the belief someone else can, or will, answer such questions.

This book aims to help strip the brain and AI into their naked forms, so they are not shrouded in mystery. What is revealed by doing this is an opportunity for absolutely everyone to take part in the defining issue of our generation – the impact of AI on the human brain. Maybe it will never happen. Maybe it is already happening. Certainly, it is safer to keep questioning, to remain vigilant and to keep asking questions. Now is the time to be eagle-eyed and spot any emerging cerebral change.

There is a compromise to be had between shaping ourselves to fit the world and shaping the world to fit ourselves.[574] Gradually with AI we may lose the inclination and capacity to engage in critically reflective thought, making us more cognitively and emotionally vulnerable and thus more anxious – and more prone to manipulation from false news, deception and political rhetoric.[575]

To mitigate consequences, the best protection is to activate reflective thinking, introduce questions into decision-making, temper emotional urges, delay gratification, foster moral self-awareness and lead by example – don't follow the crowd.[576] Make a conscious effort to decide if something should be outsourced to AI or not. Protect your brain, using the same natural skills developed when seeking out a good bargain – stay ahead of the curve when making a deal, shop around before investing and know when to walk away. Get into healthy habits, such as:

- **Attention:** Practise paying attention to your own inner belief system and moral code. Ask yourself: Am I prioritising tasks accordingly? Can I present complex issues in a simple way? Can I spot fake data and seek out important trends, correlations and causations?

- **Memory**: Practise new ways of thinking – be creative with concepts to accelerate the uptake of information. Ask yourself: Can I use experiences from other walks of life to help solve this current task? Can I figure out new solutions to make things more successful for myself and for others?
- **Listen and respond:** Practise tailoring messages to different target audiences. Ask yourself: Do I listen and give myself time and space to reflect? Can I put myself in other people's shoes and think from their perspective? Can I think of more meaningful explanations and outcomes?
- **Decision process:** Practise seeking out challenging things to solve. Ask yourself: Do I bring energy to help solve problems? How can I be more decisive and accurate? Am I willing to step-in even at awkward moments? Can I slow down and do I know when to press ahead?
- **Executive functioning skills:** Practise critical thinking, planning, organising and helping others. Ask yourself: Can I seek out new ways to be creative? Can I break down the new challenges into parts and select a route map to the solution? Can I see opportunities beyond the obvious? Can I lead by example? Can I learn to do all this with enthusiasm, connection, satisfaction, coherence, meaning and self-belief? How can I make a positive impact on the world?

In summary, AI is to be celebrated – but ruthlessly and relentlessly also remember potential brain ramifications. The 'big brain revolution' is perhaps closer, and change set to be bolder, than any of us can imagine – or would like to admit.

Acknowledgements

It is impossible to list everyone who has listened during the birth of this book. It has relied upon an ecosystem of close family and friends offering unwavering support and positivity. I only have space to mention a few special people here. They were there on good and bad days and supported me during the early mornings, late nights and far longer than anticipated head-down time frame. Some sayings which became catchphrases during the epic book journey include words from my sister, Dr Heidi Tempest: 'Good things take time.' Marie Curie: 'Nothing in life is to be feared, it is only to be understood.' Dr Leonid Shapiro: 'The world is waiting to be changed for the better.' Professor Stephen Hawking: 'Intelligence is the ability to adapt and change.' Saleem Asaria: 'Be grateful and make every day awesome.' And Dr Ivana Rosenzweig: 'Out of sight is not out of mind.'

Thanks in particular go to: Alina Trabattoni, Rachael Beale and Samira Quasem for reads, edits and referencing. Thanks to Camilla Lillieskold, who designed the book cover, Vinh Tran at Austin Macauley publishers for getting this to print and Tom Wilkins for the book launch.

To those who supported me in the office: Clara Tse, Dr Tim Ringrose, Marc Kitten, Dr Joe Taylor, Claudio Prante, Hugo Starrsjo, Marina Gilic, Dr Haran Jackson, Roma Dixit, Richard Hall, Leopoldo Carbone, Eva Kagan, Rose de Ladoucette, Dr Sam Winward, Patrick Baensch, Dr Helen Berlin, Dr Stewart Southey and Professor Steve Smith.

Plus many others, inclusive of: Professor Sir John Gurdon, Shaa Wasmund MBE, Professor Sahfi Ahmed, Lady Emma Pidding, Lord David Prior, Sophia Ahrel, Molly Nichols, Sarah Ahmed, Professor John Keown, Father Richard Finn, Dr Gavin Jarvis, Dr Paul Goldsmith, Omiros Sarikas, Marcus and JJ Evans, Tim Montgomerie, Robert and Vanda Halfon, Lord Tariq Ahmad, Saddiqa Masud, Dr Karen Sayal, Mike Weatherley, Gill Plimmer, Peter Botting, Dr Nund Rudarakanchana, Sasha Orr, Richard Evans, Dr Ilan Lieberman, Dr Mark Burby, Dr John Waters, Dr Tilak Das, Dr Elizabeth Fistein, Dr Will Watson, Richard Merrin, Steve Mastin, Simon Darling, Hamid Yunis, Sharon Lamb, Stephan Rau, Michael and Prema Pritchett, Barbara Pusca, Major General Michael von Bertele, Dr Jake Taylor-King, Henry Whitfield, Dan Vahdat, Dr Rav Seeruthun, Stephen Jolly, Ben Maddison, Dr Nick Moore and many others! The final thanks goes to my cutest godsons: Fingal Evans and Elias Prante.

References

[1] Cummings, B. *The Book of Common Prayer; The Texts of 1549, 1559, and 1662*. Oxford: Oxford University Press, (2013).

[2] Agerholm, H, "Government should impose screen time limits for children on social media, minister suggests", *The Independent*, (2018 Mar 10). Available from: <https://www.independent.co.uk/news/uk/home-news/children-social-media-online-screen-time-time-limits-matt-hancock-a8249391.html>

[3] Hayes, M, "How to quit your tech: a beginner's guide to divorcing your phone", *The Guardian*, (2018 Jan 13). Available from: <https://www.theguardian.com/technology/2018/jan/13/how-to-quit-your-tech-phone-digital-detox/>

[4] Purcell, K, Rainie, L, Heaps, A and others, "How Teens Do Research in the Digital Wold", *Pew Research Centre* [serial online], (2012 Nov 1). Available from: <http://www.pewinternet.org/2012/11/01/how-teens-do-research-in-the-digital-world/>

[5] Sandee, LaMotte, "MRIs Show Screen Time Linked To Lower Brain Development In Pre-schoolers", *CNN*, (2019). Available from: <https://edition.cnn.com/2019/11/04/health/screen-time-lower-brain-development-preschoolers-wellness/index.html>

[6] Etchells, P, 'No, research does not say that 'iPads and smartphones may damage toddlers' brains'', *The Guardian*, (2015 Feb 2). Available from: <https://www.theguardian.com/science/head-quarters/2015/feb/02/no-research-does-not-say-that-ipads-and-smartphones-may-damage-toddlers-brains/>

[7] Ophir, E, Nass, C., Wagner, A D, "Cognitive Control in Media Multitaskers", Proceedings of the National Academy of Sciences of the United States of America, *National Academy of Sciences*, 106(2009), 15583–87.

[8] Baumgartner, S E, Weeda, W D, Van Der Heijden, L L, and others., "The Relationship Between Media Multitasking and Executive Function in Early Adolescents", *Journal of Early Adolescence*, 34(2014), 1120-44.

[9] Hill, A, "Children struggle to hold pencils due to too much tech, doctors say", *The Guardian*, (2018 Feb 25). Available from:<https://www.theguardian.com/society/2018/feb/25/children-struggle-to-hold-pencils-due-to-too-much-tech-doctors-say/>

[10] Gaudiosi, J, 'How Microsoft Just Changed 'Minecraft'', *Fortune*, (2016 March 1). Available from: <http://fortune.com/2016/03/01/how-microsoft-just-changed-minecraft/>

[11] Carr, N G, *"The Shallows: What the Internet Is Doing to Our Brains"*, (W W Norton & Company, 2010).

[12] *House* [TV], (2004-2012) FOX.

[13] Zeki, S, 'The Neurobiology of Love', *FEBS Letters*, (2007);581(14):2575-79.

[14] Edwards, H., Edwards, D, 'Your primer on how to talk about the 'fourth industrial revolution'', *Quartz,* [serial online]. (2018 Jan 23). Available from: <https://qz.com/1090176/how-to-think-about-job-automation-studies/>

[15] Horton, H, "Amazon Alexa recorded owner's conversation and sent to 'random' contact, couple complains", *The Telegraph*, (2018 May 25). Available from: <https://www.telegraph.co.uk/news/2018/05/25/amazon-alexa-recorded-owners-conversation-sent-random-contact/>

[16] Raven, D, "Naked celebrity pictures leaked before Jennifer Lawrence—From Rihanna to Miley Cyrus 12 stars exposed online", *Mirror*, (2014 Sep 1).

[17] Rideout, V, Robb, M B, "Social Media, Social Life: Teens Reveal Their Experiences", *Common Sense Media,* [serial online]. (2018). Available from: <https://www.commonsensemedia.org/research/social-media-social-life-2018/>

[18] Tjaden, P, Thoennes, N, "Prevalence, Incidence, and Consequences of Violence Against Women: Findings From the National Violence Against Women Survey", *Journal of National Institute of Justice Centers for Disease Control and Prevention.* (1998):1–16.

[19] New Scientist, *How Your Brain Works Inside the Most Complicated Object in the Known Universe*, (John Murray Learning, 2017), Chapter 7.

[20] Diamond, M C, Scheibel, AB, Murphy, GM Jr, and others, "On the brain of a scientist: Albert Einstein", *Experimental Neurology,* 88 (1985), 198-204.

[21] Dicke, U, Roth, G, "Neuronal factors determining high intelligence", *Philos Trans R Soc Lond B Bio Sci,* 371(2016), 20150180.

[22] Private conversation with Dr Joe Taylor, Oxford University, (2019).

[23] Mathews, M S, Linskey, M E, and Binder, D K, "William P van Wagenen and the First Corpus Callosotomies for Epilepsy", *Journal of Neurosurgery,* 108(2008), 608-13.

[24] Gao, X, Li, B, Chu, W, and others, "Alien Hand Syndrome Following Corpus Callosum Infarction: A Case Report and Review of the Literature", *Experimental and Therapeutic Medicine,* 12(2016), 2129–2135.

[25] Killgore, W D S, and Yurgelun-Todd, D A, "The Right-hemisphere and Valence Hypotheses: Could they both be right (and sometimes left)?", *Social Cognitive and Affective Neuroscience*, 2(2007), 240–250.

[26] Price, J, "JK Rowling*", Trailblazers of the Modern World: World Almanac Library.* (2004).

[27] Breazeale, R, "The Role of the Brain in Happiness", *Psychology Today*, [serial online]. (2013 Feb 19). Available from: <https://www.psychologytoday.com/gb/blog/in-the-face-adversity/201302/the-role-the-brain-in-happiness>

[28] Liu, S, Chow, H M, Xu, Y, and others, "Neural correlates of lyrical improvisation: An fMRI Study of Freestyle Rap", *Scientific Reports.* 2(2012), 834.

[29] Hofman MA, 'Size and shape of the cerebral cortex in mammals. II. The cortical volume', *Brain Behaviour Evolution,* 32(1988), 17–26.

[30] Javed, K, Forshing, L, "Neuroanatomy, Cerebral Cortex*", In: StatPearls* [Internet], (2019).

[31] Osilla, EV, Sharma, S, "Physiology, Temperature Regulation*", In:StatPearls* [Internet], (2019).

[32] Heid, M, "Does Thinking Burn Calories? Here's What the Science Says", *Time,* [serial online]. (2018 Sep 19). Available from: <http://time.com/5400025/does-thinking-burn-calories/>

[33] Alhola, P, Polo-Kantola, P, "Sleep deprivation: Impact on cognitive performance", *Neuropsychiatr Disease and Treatment,* 3(2007), 553-567.

[34] Waters, F, Chiu, V, Atkinson, A, Blom, J D, "Severe Sleep Deprivation Causes Hallucinations and a Gradual Progression Toward Psychosis With Increasing Time Awake", *Frontiers in Psychiatry,* 9(2018), 303.

[35] Gable, S L, Hopper, E A, Schooler, J W, "When the Muses Strike: Creative Ideas of Physicists and Writers Routinely Occur During Mind Wandering", *Psychological Science, 30(* 2019), 396-404.

[36] Yonck, R, *The Heart of the Machine. Our Future in a World of Artificial Emotional Intelligence* (Arcade Publishing, 2017).

[37] Jäncke, L, "The plastic human brain", *Restorative Neurology and Neuroscience,* 27(2009), 521-38.

[38] Hebb, D O, *The Organisation of Behavior* (Wiley & Sons, 1949).

[39] How to become a London taxi driver, *Transport for London,* (2018). Available from: <http://content.tfl.gov.uk/knowledgeoflondonprospectus.pdf>

[40] Maguire, E A, Gadian, DG, Johnsrude, I S, and others, "Navigation-related Structural Change in the Hippocampi of Taxi Drivers", *Prox Natl Acad Sci U S A,* 97(2000), 4398-4403.

[41] Bechtle, M, *How to Communicate with Confidence* (Baker Books, 2013).

[42]Fry, H, "We hold people with power to account. Why not algorithms?", *The Guardian,* (2018 Sep 17), Available from: <https://www.theguardian.com/commentisfree/2018/sep/17/power-algorithms-technology-regulate>

[43] Moore, M, 'Driver followed satnav to edge of 100ft drop,' (2009), *Telegraph.* Available from: <https://www.telegraph.co.uk/motoring/news/6197826/Driver-followed-satnav-to-edge-of-100ft-drop.html>

[44] New World Encyclopedia, *Alfred Binet,* (2016) Available from: <http://www.newworldencyclopedia.org/p/index.php?title=Alfred_Binet&oldid=994382>

[45] Sunet, JM, Barlaug, DG and Torjussen, TM, "The end of the Flynn effect? A study of secular trends in mean intelligence test score of Norwegian conscripts during half a century", *Science Direct Intelligence,* 32(2004), 349-362.

[46] New Scientist, *How Your Brain Works Inside the Most Complicated Object in the Known Universe*, (John Murray Learning, 2017), P.67.

[47] Lipsett, A, "We're as good as we can get, says evolution expert", *The Guardian*. (2008 Oct 7). Available from:<https://www.theguardian.com/education/2008/oct/07/research.highereducation>

[48] Benson, E, "Intelligent intelligence testing", *American Psychological Association,* 34.2(2003).

[49] Goleman, D, *Emotional Intelligence: Why it can matter more than IQ*, (Bloomsbury Publishing PLC, 1996).

[50] Woods, D L, Wyma, JM, Yund, E W, and others, "Factors influencing the latency of simple reaction time", *Frontiers in Human Neuroscience*, 9(2015), 131.

[51] Jahanshai M, Brown RG, Marsden CD. "A comparative study of simple and choice reaction time in Parkinson's, Huntington's and cerebellar disease", *Journal of Neurology, Neurosurgery and Psychiatry*, 56(1993), 1169-1177.

[52] Maia PD, Kutz JN, "Reaction time impairments in decision-making networks as a diagnostic marker for traumatic brain injuries and neurological disease", *Journal of Computational Neuroscience,* 42.3(2017), 323-347.

[53] Cornell University Blog, "We have two ears and one mouth so that we can listen twice as much as we speak" (2011 October 19), Available from: <http://blogs.cornell.edu/cuus/2011/10/19/we-have-two-ears-and-one-mouth-so-that-we-can-listen-twice-as-much-as-we-speak/>

[54] Hanes, D A and McCollum, G, "Cognitive-vestibular interactions: A review of patient difficulties and possible mechanisms", *Journal of Vestibular Research*, 16.3(2006), 75-91.

[55] Waldrop MM, "Inside the Moonshot Effort to Finally Figure Out the Brain", *MIT Technology review*, (2017 October 12).

[56] Harris KD, "Cortical computation in mammals and birds", *Proc Natl Acad Sci U S A,* 112.11, (2015), 3184-3185.

[57] Gornall J, "Will we ever understand the human brain?", *World Economic Forum,* (2014 Sept 11).

[58] Mason J, Steenhuysen J, "Obama launches research initiative to study human brain", *Reuters*, (2013 April 2).

[59] Cepelewicz J, "The US Government Launches a $100-Million "Apollo Project of the Brain", *Scientific American,* (2016 March 8).

[60] Human Outcome Project, "Human Connectome Project -Mapping The Human Brain Connectivity" (2019). Available from: <http://www.humanconnectomeproject.org/>

[61] Venter JC, Adams MD, Myers EW, Li PW and others, "The sequence of the human genome", *Science,* 291(2001), 1304–1351.

[62] Marsh, H, "Can man ever build a mind?", *The Financial Times*. (2019 Jan 10). Available from: <https://www.ft.com/content/2e75c04a-0f43-11e9-acdc-4d9976f1533b>

[63] Marsh, H, 'Can man ever build a mind?', *Financial Times*. (January 2019).

[64] Critchlow, H, *Consciousness* (London: Ladybird Books, 2018).

[65] Rocca J, "Galen and the ventricular systems", *Journal of the History of the Neurosciences,* 6.3(1998), 227-39.

[66] Critchlow H, *Consciousness: A Ladybird Expert Book,* (London: Penguin Books, 2018).

[67] Goldman AI, "Theory of Mind", *Oxford Handbook of Philosophy and Cognitive Science,* (Oxford University Press: Oxford, 2012).

[68] Güzeldere G, *The Nature of Consciousness: Philosophical debates,* (Cambridge: MIT Press, n.d.) pp.1-67.

[69] Gennaro, R J, "Consciousness", *Internet Encyclopedia of Philosophy.* (n.d.), Available from: <https://www.iep.utm.edu/consciousness/>

[70] Eliasmith, C, *How to Build a Brain: A Neural Architecture for Biological Cognition,* (Oxford University Press, 2013).

[71] Eliasmith, (2013), see above.

[72] Waymire, J C, "Organisation of Cell Types", *Neuroscience Online Department of Neurobiology and Anatomy, McGovern Medical School,* (n.d.). Available from: <https://nba.uth.tmc.edu/neuroscience/m/s1/chapter08.html>

[73] Lim H A, "Genes, Stem Cells and Regenerative Medicine", *Asia-Pacific Biotech News*, 17.8(2013).

[74] Lally, P, Van Jaarsveld, C H M, Potts, H W W, and others, "How are habits formed: Modelling habit formation in the real world", *European Journal of Social Psychology*, 40.6(2009).

[75] Wooldridge, M, *Artificial Intelligence: Everything you need to know about the coming AI. A Ladybird Expert Book*, (Michael Joseph, 2018).

[76] McCulloch WS, Pitts W, "A Logical Calculus of Ideas Immanent in Nervous Activity", *Bulletin of Mathematical Biophysics*, 5.4(1943), 115–133.

[77] Rosenblatt F, "The perceptron: a probablilistic model for information storage and organisation in the brain", *Psychol rev*, 65.6(1958), 386-408.

[78] Eliasmith C, Stewart TC, Choo X, Bekolay T, DeWolf T, Tang Y, and others, "A large-Scale Model of the Functioning Brain", *Science 338.6111(*2012), 1202-5.

[79] Krogh, A, "What are artificial neural networks?", *Nat Biotechnology,* 26.2(2008), 195-7.

[80] Woodward, S, "Machine Learning*", Cambridge Alumni Magazine*, 85(2018).

[81] Wimmer H, Perner J, "Beliefs about beliefs: Representation and constraining function of wrong beliefs in young children's understanding of deception", *Cognition, 13.1(*1983), 103–128.

[82] Baron-Cohen S, Leslie A M, Frith U, "Does the autistic child have a 'theory of mind'?", *Cognition,* 21.1(1985), 37-46.

[83] Nematzadeh A, Burns K, Grant E, Gopnik A, Griffiths TL, "Evaluating theory of mind in question answering", *Conference on Empirical Methods in Natural Language Processing*, (Hong Kong, China, Nov 3-7, (2019)).

[84] Cueva C, Roberts RE, Spencer T, Rani N, Tempest M, Tobler PN, and others, "Cortisol and testosterone increase financial risk taking and may destabilize markets", *Sci Rep,* 5(2015) 11206.

[85] Coates J M, and Herbert, J, "Endogenous steroids and financial risk taking on a London trading floor", *Proc Natl Acas Sci USA*, 105.16(2018), 6167-6172.

[86] "Stress Hormones In Financial Traders May Trigger 'Risk Aversion' And Contribute To Market Crises," *University of Cambridge*, (2019). Available from: <https://www.cam.ac.uk/research/news/stress-hormones-in-financial-traders-may-trigger-risk-aversion-and-contribute-to-market-crises>

[87] Adams, T, "Testosterone and high finance do not mix: so bring on the women", *The Guardian*, (2011 Jun 19). Available from: <https://www.theguardian.com/world/2011/jun/19/neuroeconomics-women-city-financial-crash>

[88] Tarnow, J MD, "The Thrill of the Chase", *The Tarnow Centre, (n.d.).*

[89] Jabr F, "Gambling on the Brain", *Scientific American,* 309.5(2013), 28-30.

[90] "Watchdog says 'sit up and listen' as study shows rise in child problem gamblers," *University of Cambridge*, (2018 Nov 21). Available from: <https://www.belfasttelegraph.co.uk/news/uk/watchdog-says-sit-up-and-listen-as-study-shows-rise-in-child-problem-gamblers-37550918.html>

[91] "Young People & Gambling 2018 – A research study among 11-16 year olds in Great Britain," *Gambling Commission*, (Nov 2018).

[92] Jabr F, "Gambling on the Brain", *Scientific American,* 309.5(2013), 28-30.

[93] Bechara A, Damasio AR, Damasio H, Anderson SW, "Insensitivity to future consequences following damage to human prefrontal cortex", *Cognition,* 50.1(1994), 7-15.

[94] Windmann S, Kirsch P, Mier D, Stark R, Walter B, Güntürkün O, Vaitl D, "On framing effects in decision making: linking lateral versus medial orbitofrontal cortex activation to choice outcome processing", *J Cogn Neurosci,* 18.7(2006), 1198-211.

[95] Mischel, W. *The Marshmallow Test: Understanding Self-control and How To Master It.* (Bantam Press, 2014).

[96] Mischel, (2014), see above.

[97] Byrom T Dhammpada, *The Sayings of the Buddha (Shambhala Pocket Classics)* (Boulder: Shambhala Publications Inc, 1994).

[98] "My Philosophy of Industry by Henry Ford, Interview conducted by Fay Leone Faurote", *The Forum,* 79.4(1928), 481.

[99] Duncker, K, "'On Problem Solving'", *Psychological Monographs,* 58.5(1945).

[100] Parcell, G., Collison, C, *No More Consultants. We know more than we think* (John Wiley & Sons Ltd, 2009).

[101] Willingham, DT, "Ask the Cognitive Scientist. The Privileged Status of Story", *American Federation of Teachers.* [serial online] (2004). Available from: <https://www.aft.org/periodical/american-educator/summer-2004/ask-cognitive-scientist>

[102] Opitz, B, 'Memory function and the hippocampus', *Front Neural Neuroscience*, 34.5(2014), 1-9.

[103] Chial, H, "DNA sequencing technologies key to the Human Genome Project", *Nature Education,* 1.1(2008), 219.

[104] Alzheimer's Association. "Alzheimer's Disease Facts and Figures", *Alzheimers Dementia*, 8.2(2012), 131-68.

[105] Snowdon, DA, "Aging and Alzheimer's Disease: Lessons From the Nun Study", *Gerontologist, 37.2(*1997), 150-156.

[106] Riley KP, Snowdon DA, Desrosiers MF, Markesbery WR, "Early life linguistic ability, late life cognitive function, and neuropathology: Findings from the Nun Study", *Neurobiology of Aging,* 26.3(2005), 341-7.

[107] Zarrelli, N, "The Neurologists Who Fought Alzheimer's By Studying Nuns' Brains", *Atlas Obscura.* (2019). Available from: <https://www.atlasobscura.com/articles/the-neurologists-who-fought-alzheimers-by-studying-nuns-brains>

[108] Brackley, P, 'Alzheimer's breakthrough from University of Cambridge scientists 'could lead to drug trials in two years'', *Cambridge Independent*, (2018 Sept 30).

[109] Squire, LR, Dede, AJO, "Conscious and Unconscious Memory Systems", *Cold Spring Harb Perspect Biol, 7.3, (*2015).

[110] Molloy M Scientists discover how to 'upload knowledge to your brain'. *The Telegraph,* (2016 March 1).

[111] Berger, TW, Song, D, Chan, RHM, Marmarelis, VZ, LaCoss, J, Wills, J, and others, "A Hippocampal Cognititve Prosthesis: Multi-Input, Multi-Output Nonlinear Modelling and VLSI Implementation", *IEEE Trans Neural Syst Rehabil Eng,* 20.2(2012), 198-211.

[112] Berger, (2012), see above.

[113] Berger, (2012), see above.

[114] Gross, MJ, "The Pentagon Wants to Weaponise the Brain. What Could Go Wrong?", *The Atlantic,* (2018 Nov).

[115] *Chuck,* [TV], NBC, (2007-2012).

[116] *Black Mirror* [TV], BBC, (2011-2019).

[117] *The Matrix* [Film], Dirc. The Wachowskis, (1999), Warner Bros.

[118] "New mind-uploading start-up can only preserve 'fresh' brains", *Cool Hunting*, [serial online] (2018 March 15). Available from: <https://coolhunting.com/tech/nectome-preserves-your-brain/>

[119] Saarni, C, *The Guilford series on social and emotional development. The development of emotional competence*, (New York: Guilford Press, 1999).

[120] Pessoa, L, "A network model of the emotion brain", *Trends Cognitive Sci*, 21.5(2017), 357-371.

[121] Topiwala, K, "Of the brain, by the brain, and for the brain", *Neurology*. (2018).

[122] Carnegie, D, *How to stop worrying and start living,* (Gallery Books, 2004).

[123] Rickles, D, Hawe, P, Shiell, A, "A simple guide to chaos and complexity", *J Epidemiol Community Health,* 61.11(2009), 933-937.

[124] Cattell, RB, *Abilities: Their structure, growth, and action,* (New York: Houghton Mifflin, 1971).

[125] Simon, P, 'Watch the Awkward Moment Prince Charles Said 'Whatever in Love Means' When Asked If He Loved Diana', *People Magazine,* (2017).

[126] Scheve, T, "How many muscles does it take to smile?", *HowStuffWorks.com,* [serial online] (2009 Jun 2). Available from: <https://science.howstuffworks.com/life/inside-the-mind/emotions/muscles-smile.htm>

[127] Ekman, P, "Universal Facial Expressions of Emotions", *California Mental Health Research Digest*, 8.4(1970), 151-158.

[128] Ekman, P, *Basic Emotions. In: Dalgleish T Power M (Eds) Handbook of Cognition and Emotion*, (Sussex: John Wiley & Sons, 1999).

[129] Mulder, P, "Communication Model by Albert Mehrabian", *ToolsHero.* [serial online] (2012). Available from: <https://www.toolshero.com/communication-skills/communication-model-mehrabian/>

[130] Sayette, M, Cohn, J, Wertz, J, Perrott, M, Parrott, D, "A Psychometric Evaluation of the Facial Action Coding System for Assessing Spontaneous Expression", *Journal of Nonverbal Behaviour*, 5(2001), 167-186.

[131] Picard, RW, *Affective Computing. Cambridge*, (MIT Press, 2000).

[132] Tettegah, SY, Gartmeier, M, eds, *A Real-Time Speech Emotion Recognition System and its Application in Online Learning,* (Cambridge: Academic Press, 2016).

[133] The Telegraph, "We can tell if you're fibbing", (2003 Dec 17), Available from: <https://www.telegraph.co.uk/finance/personalfinance/insurance/2871936/We-can-tell-if-youre-fibbing.html>

[134] Kruger J, Epley N, Parker J, Ng ZW. 'Egocentrism Over E-Mail: Can We Communicate as Well as We Think?', *J Pers Soc Psychol* (2005), vol, 89, no. 6, pp. 925-36.

[135] Kruger, (2005), see above.

[136] "Announcing the Oxford Dictionaries "Word" of the Year 2015", *Oxford Dictionaries*, (2015 Nov 17). Available from: <https://www.oxforddictionaries.com/press/news/2016/9/2/WOTY>

[137] Pang, B, Lee, L, "Opinion mining and sentiment analysis", *Foundations and Trends,* 2.1, (2008), 1-135.

[138] Pagolu, VS, Challa, KNR, Panda, G, Majhi, B, "Sentiment Analysis of Twitter Data for Predicting Stock Market Movements", *International conference on Signal Processing, Communication, Power and Embedded System,* (2016 Oct 3)-5.

[139] Kandasamy, N, Garfinkel, SN, Page, L, Hardy, B, Critchley, HD, Gurnell, M, and others, "Interoceptive Ability Predicts Survival on a London Trading Floor", *Scientific Reports,* 6.6(2016), 32986.

[140] Zijderveld, G, "The World's Largest Emotion Database: 5.3 Million Faces and Counting", *Affectiva,* (2017). Available from: <blog.affectiva.com/the-worlds-largest-emotion-database-5.3-million-faces-and-counting>

[141] "Affectiva Automotive AI: Building Emotionally Aware Cars with In-Cabin Sensing", *Affectiva,* (2018). Available from: <blog.affectiva.com/affectiva-automotive-ai-building-emotionally-aware-cars-with-in-cabin-sensing>

[142] Kairos, *Kairos: Serving Businesses with Face Recognition*, (n.d.). Available from: <www.kairos.com>

[143] Knapp, A, "Facial Recognition Company Kairos Acquires Emotion Analysis Company IMRSV", *Forbes,* (2015 Apr 6).

[144] McLoughlin, G, "Limerick start-up Emotion Reader bought by Miami based company in multi-million dollar deal", *Independent.ie,* [serial online] (2018 Jul 13). Available from: <https://www.independent.ie/business/irish/limerick-startup-emotion-reader-bought-by-miami-based-company-in-multimillion-dollar-deal-37115017.html>

[145] Virdee-Chapman, B, "Kairos Acquires Emotion Reader", *Kairos.com.* [serial online] (2018 Jul 12). Available from: <https://www.kairos.com/blog/kairos-acquires-emotionreader>

[146] Klausner, A, "Teen broadcasts her suicide on Facebook Live", *New York Post,* (January 2017).

[147] Tinari, G, "Apple scoops up A.I. startup that analyses users' emotions", *Cult of Mac,* [serial online] (2016 Jan 7). Available from: <https://www.cultofmac.com/405662/apple-buys-emotient/>

[148] Dickens, C, *Great Expectations*, 20th edn (London: Chapman and Hall, 1861).

[149] Oxford dictionary. Available from: <https://en.oxforddictionaries.com/definition/decision>

[150] Edmonds, M, "Is laughter contagious?" *HowStuffWorks.com.* [serial online] (2009 June). Available from: <https://science.howstuffworks.com/life/inside-the-mind/emotions/laughter-contagious.htm>

[151] Kramer, ADI, Guillory, JE, Hancock, JT, "Experimental evidence of massive-scale emotional contagion through social networks", *Proceedings of the National Academy of Sciences*, 111.24(2014), 8788-8790.

[152] Agrawal, A, Gans, J, Goldbarb, A, "Prediction Machines. The Simple Economics of Artificial Intelligence", *Harvard Business Review Press*, (2018). 75.

[153] Frick, W, "3 ways to improve your decision making", *Harvard Business Review*, (2018 Jan 22).

[154] *Educating Rita* [Film], Acorn Pictures, (1983).

[155] Ellenberg, J, *How Not to Be Wrong: The Hidden Maths of Everyday Life,* (London: Penguin Books, 2015).

[156] Tversky, A, Kahneman, D, "Judgment under uncertainty: Heuristics and biases", *Science,* 185(1974), 1124–1131.

[157] Agrawal, A, Gans, J, Goldfarb, A, "Prediction Machines: The Simple Economics of Artificial Intelligence", *Harvard Business Review*, (2018).

[158] Rotman School of Management, "Prediction Machines: The Simple Economics of Artificial Intelligence", *University of Toronto.* [serial online] (April 17, 2018). Available from: <http://www.rotman.utoronto.ca/Connect/MediaCentre/NewsReleases/2018041 7>

[159] Agrawal, A, Gans, J, Goldfarb, A, "Prediction Machines: The Simple Economics of Artificial Intelligence", *Harvard Business Review*, (2018).

[160] Dwyer, C, "12 Common Biases that Affect How We Make Everyday Decisions", *Psychology Today.* [serial online] (2018 Sep 7). Available from: <https://www.psychologytoday.com/gb/blog/thoughts-thinking/201809/12-common-biases-affect-how-we-make-everyday-decisions>

[161] Danziger, S, Levav, J, Avnaim-Pesso, L, "Extraneous factors in judicial decisions", *PNAS*, 108.17(2011), 6889-6892.

[162] Schmitt, GR, Reedt, L, Blackwell, K, "Demographic Differences in Sentencing: An Update to the 2012 Booker Report", *United States Sentencing Commission*, (2017).

[163] Harriot, M, "Money Bail Might Be the Most Racist, Immoral Part of America's Criminal Injustice System", *The Root,* [serial online]. (2018 Dec 20). Available from: <https://www.theroot.com/money-bail-might-be-the-most-racist-immoral-part-of-am-1831241786 >

[164] 'Race and death penalty', *Death Penalty information Center,* [serial online] (2019). Available from: <https://deathpenaltyinfo.org/race-and-death-penalty>

[165] Hasler, BS, Spanlang, B, Slater, M, "Virtual race transformation reverses racial in-group bias", *PLoS One,* 12.4(2017), 0174965.

[166] University of Barcelona, "Study shows the influence of immersive virtual reality on racial bias", *Phys.org,* [serial online] (2017 May 22). Available from: <https://phys.org/news/2017-05-immersive-virtual-reality-racial-bias.html#jCp>

[167] Sweeny, L, "Discrimination in Online Ad Delivery", *arXiv.org.* [serial online], (2013 Jan 28). Available from: <http://dx.doi.org/10.2139/ssrn.2208240>

[168] *Suits* [TV], (2011-2019), USA.

[169] The Canadian Press, "Self-driving cars allowed on Ontario roads, minister says", *CTV News Toronto*, (January 2019).

[170] Chapman FS, 'A study of the influence of custom on the moral judgment,' *Bulletin of the University of Wisconsin* (1908); No. 236.

[171] "Self-Driving Cars: Who To Save, Who To Sacrifice?", *CBC News*, (2019). Available from: <https://ici.radio-canada.ca/info/2019/voitures-autonomes-dilemme-tramway/index-en.html>

[172] *2001:A Space Odyssey* [Film], Dirc. Kubrick, S, (1968) MGM.

[173] *Westworld* [TV], (2016-18), HBO.

[174] Daugherty, PR, Wilson, J, "Fin 24 Book Review-Human and machine interaction in the age of AI", *Fin 24 Book Review*, [serial online] (2018 May 3). Available from: <https://paul-daugherty.com/2018/05/03/fin-24-book-review-human-and-machine-interaction-in-the-age-of-ai/>

[175] Manyika, J, Lund, S, Chui, M, Bughin, J, Woetzel, J, Batra, P, and others, "Jobs lost, jobs gained: What the future of work will mean for jobs, skills, and wages", *McKinsey Global Institute analysis*, [serial online] (2017 Nov). Available from: <https://www.mckinsey.com/featured-insights/future-of-work/jobs-lost-jobs-gained-what-the-future-of-work-will-mean-for-jobs-skills-and-wages>

[176] Choudhury, S R, "Machines will soon be able to learn without being programmed", *CNBC*, (2018 Apr 17). Available from: <https://www.cnbc.com/2018/04/17/machine-learning-investing-in-ai-next-big-thing.html>

[177] Private conversation with Prof. Shafi Ahmed, Colorectal Surgeon and Industry Expert, (2019).

[178] Timm, A, "A note from our CEO: Root is now in 20 states", *Root Insurance Co,* [serial online] (2018 Aug14). Available from: < https://www.joinroot.com/blog/root-is-now-in-20-states/>

[179] Lohr, S, "From Agriculture to Art – the A.I. Wave Sweeps In", *The New York Times,* (2018 Oct 21).

[180] Cialdini, R, *Pre-Suasion: A Revolutionary Way to Influence and Persuade*, (Penguin Random House Books, 2016).

[181] English, A, "Understanding Bounded Rationality and Satisficing", *Medium*, (2016 Jun 3). Available from: <https://medium.com/homeland-security/understanding-bounded-rationality-and-satisficing-175e787955d6>

[182] Thaler, R H, and Sunstein, C. R, *Nudge: Improving Decisions About Health, Wealth and Happiness,* (Yale University Press, 2008).

[183] Newell, B, "'Nudging' people towards changing behaviour: what works and why (not)?", *The Conversation,* (2014 June 5). Available from:

<http://theconversation.com/nudging-people-towards-changing-behaviour-what-works-and-why-not-27576>

[184] 'Barack Obama's Feb. 5 Speech', *The New York Times,* (2008 Feb 5).

[185] Zolfagharifard, E, "Major UK companies preparing to microchip employees", *The Telegraph,* (2018 Nov 10).

[186] Zolfagharifard, (2018), see above.

[187] Thaler, R H, and Sunstein, C. R, *Nudge: Improving Decisions About Health, Wealth and Happiness,* (Yale University Press, 2008).

[188] Draycott, J, "Severed Limbs and Wooden Feet: How the Ancients Invented Prosthetics", *The Conversation,* [serial online] (2017 Mar 17). Available from: <https://theconversation.com/severed-limbs-and-wooden-feet-how-the-ancients-invented-prosthetics-77741>

[189] Wollastone, V, "The prosthetic that simulates TOUCH: Nerve endings wired to sensors create the 'feeling' of a real limb", *Daily Mail Online*, [serial online] (2015 Jun 8). Available from: <https://www.dailymail.co.uk/sciencetech/article-3115225/The-prosthetic-simulates-TOUCH-Nerve-endings-wired-sensors-creates-feeling-real-limb.html>

[190] Nathan, S, "Future prosthetic: towards the bionic human", *theengineer.co.uk,* [serial online] (2018 Jan). Available from: <https://www.theengineer.co.uk/future-prosthetic/>

[191] Nathan, (2019), see above.

[192] Nathan, (2019), see above.

[193] Gieson, EV, "Electrical Prescriptions (ElectRx)", *Darpa,* Available from: <https://www.darpa.mil/program/electrical-prescriptions?>

[194] Park, A, "Why It's Time to Take Electrified Medicine Seriously", *Time,* (2019). Available from: <https://time.com/5709245/bioelectronic-medicine-treatments/>

[195] Nathan, S, "Future prosthetic: towards the bionic human", *theengineer.co.uk,* [serial online], (2018 Jan). Available from: <https://www.theengineer.co.uk/future-prosthetic/>

[196] Neuro Assessment & Development Center, *Executive Functioning.* [serial online] Available from: <https://www.neurodevelop.com/executive_functioning>

[197] Diamond, A, "Executive functions", *Annual Review Psychology,* 64(2013), 135-68.

[198] Graham, M*., Nuturing Children From Trauma to Growth Using Attachment Theory, Psycholoanalysis and Neurobiology*, (Routledge, 2019), p.114.

[199] Graham, (2019), see above.

[200] University of Wisconsin-Madison, "Psychopaths' brains show differences in structure and function", *School of Medicine and Public Health University of Wisconsin-Madison*, [serial online] (2017 Jul 11).

[201] Moskowitz, C, "Criminal Minds Are Different From Yours, Brain Scans Reveal", *Live Science,* [serial online] (2011 Mar 4). Available from: <https://www.livescience.com/13083-criminals-brain-neuroscience-ethics.html>

[202] Decety, J, "The Neurodevelopment of Empathy in Humans", *Developmental Neuroscience,* 32.4(2010), 257-267.

[203] Neylan, TC, "Frontal lobe function: Mr. Phineas Gage's famous injury", *Journal of Neuropsychiatry Clinical Neuroscience,* 11.2(1992), 280-1.

[204] Goel, V, Dolan, RJ, "Reciprocal neural response within lateral and ventral medial prefrontal cortex during hot and cold reasoning", *Neuroimage,* 20.4(2003), 2314-21.

[205] Steimke, R, Nomi, JS, Calhoun, VD, Stelzel, C, Paschke, LM, Gaschler, R, and others., "Salience network dynamics underlying successful resistance of temptation", *Social Cognitive and Affective Neuroscience,* 12.12(2017), 1928-1939.

[206] Séguin, JR, Arseneault, L, Tremblay, RE, "The contribution of 'Cool' and 'Hot' components of executive function to problem solving in adolescence: Implications for developmental psychopathology", *Cognitive Development,* 22(2007), 530–543.

[207] Nigg, JT, "Response inhibition and disruptive behaviors: toward a multiprocess conception of etiological heterogeneity for ADHD combined type and conduct disorder early-onset type", *Annals of the New York Academy of Sciences,* 1008(2003), 170-82.

[208] Bechara, A, Damasio, A, "The somatic marker hypothesis: A neural theory of economic decision", *Games and Economic Behavior*, 52(2005), 336-372.

[209] Brock, LL, Rimm-Kaufman, SE, Nathanson, L, Grimm, KJ, "The contributions of 'hot' and 'cool' executive function to children's academic achievement, learning-related behaviors, and engagement in kindergarten", *Early Childhood Research Quarterly*, 24.3(2009), 337–349.

[210] Kahneman, D, *Thinking, Fast and Slow*, Reprint edn, (London: Penguin Books, 2012).

[211] Wilson-Mendenhall, CD, Barrett, LF, Barsalou, LW, "Neural Evidence that Human Emotions Share Core Affective Properties", *Psychological Science*, 24.6(2013), 947-956.

[212] Riskin, J, "Eighteenth-Century Wetware", Web.Stanford.Edu, (2013). Available from: <https://web.stanford.edu/dept/HPS/representations1.pdf>

[213] Rao, S, Chen, S, Ava, A, LaRocca, Christiansen, M, Senko, A, Shi, C, and others, "Remotely Controlled Chemomagnetic Modulation Of Targeted Neural Circuits", *Nature Nanotechnology*, 14 (2019), 967-973.

[214] Dolhun, R, "New Deep Brain Stimulation (DBS) System Approved for Parkinson's", *The Michael J. Fox Foundation For Parkinson's Research Foxfeed Blog*, [serial online] (2017 Dec 15). Available from:

<https://www.michaeljfox.org/foundation/news-detail.php?new-deep-brain-stimulation-dbs-system-approved-for-parkinson>

[215] Dolhun, (2017), see above.

[216] Epilepsy Society, *Seizure Types,* (2019). Available from: <https://www.epilepsysociety.org.uk/seizure-types#.Xbw7J3d2uUk>

[217] Epilepsy Society, (2019), see above.

[218] Gonçalves, J, Bicker, J, Gouveia, F, Liberal, J, Oliveira, R, Alves, G, and others., "Nose-To-Brain Delivery Of Levetiracetam After Intranasal Administration To Mice", *International Journal Of Pharmaceutics*, 564 (2019), 329-339.

[219] Science Daily, "Electronic Device Implanted In The Brain Could Stop Seizures", 2019. Available from: <https://www.sciencedaily.com/releases/2018/08/180829143824.htm>

[220] Science Daily, (2019), see above.

[221] SciTech daily, *Researchers Control Seizures In Epileptic Mice Using Brain Cells*, (2019). Available from: <https://scitechdaily.com/researchers-control-seizures-in-epileptic-mice-using-brain-cells/>

[222] Antal, A, Boros, K, Poreisz, C, Chaieb, L, Terney, D, Paulus, W, "Comparatively weak after-effects of transcranial altering current stimulation (tACS) on cortical excitability in humans", *Brain Stimuli,* 1.2(2008) 97-105.

[223] Chaieb, L, Paulus, W, Antal A, "Evaluating aftereffects of short-duration transcranial random noise stimulation on cortical excitability", *Neural Plasticity,* (2011), 105927.

[224] Moliadze, V, Atalay, D, Antal, A, Paulus, W, "Close to threshold transcranial electrical stimulation preferentially activates inhibitory networks before switching to excitation with higher intensities", *Brain Stimulation,* 5.4(2012), 505-11.

[225] Wach, C, Krause, V, Moliadze, V, Paulus, W, Schnitzler, A, Pollok, B, "Effects of 10 Hz and 20 Hz transcranial alternating current stimulation (tACS) on motor functions and motor cortical excitability", *Behavioural Brain Research*, 241(2013), 1–6.

[226] Clark, VP, Coffman, BA, Mayer, AR, Weisend, MP, Lane, TD, Calhoun, VD, and others, "TDCS guided using fMRI significantly accelerates learning to identify concealed objects", *Neuroimage*, 59.1(2012), 117-28.

[227] Nitsche, MA, Paulus, W, "Sustained excitability elevations induced by transcranial DC motor cortex stimulation in humans", *Neurology*, 57.10(2001), 1899-901.

[228] Coffman, BA, Clark, VP, Parasuraman, R, "Battery powered thought: enhancement of attention, learning, and memory in healthy adults using transcranial direct current stimulation", *Neuroimage,* 85(2014), 895–908.

[229] Cona, G, Treccani, B, Umiltà, CA, "Is cognitive control automatic? New insights from transcranial magnetic stimulation", *Psychonomic Bulletin & Review,* 23.5(2016), 1624-1630.

[230] 'Brainpatch.Ai', *Brainpatch*, (2019). Available from: <http://www.brainpatch.ai>

[231] Cona, G, Treccani, B, Umiltà, CA, "Is cognitive control automatic? New insights from transcranial magnetic stimulation*", Psychonomic Bulletin & Review*, 23.5(2016), 1624-1630.

[232] Tucker, P, "The Military Is Building Brain Chips to Treat PTSD", *The Atlantic,* (2014 May 29).

[233] Knapton, S, "Paraplegic man standing and moving legs again as scientists rewire spine", *The Telegraph,* (2017 Oct 27).

[234] D De Graaf, M, "Groundbreaking brain implant reverses 'locked-in' syndrome: Mother-of-three with ALS can talk again after revolutionary procedure", *Mail Online*, [serial online] (2016 Nov 14). Available from: <https://www.dailymail.co.uk/health/article-3936314/Groundbreaking-brain-implant-REVERSES-locked-syndrome-Mother-three-ALS-talk-revolutionary-procedure.html>

[235] Vansteensel, MJ, Pels, EGM, Bleichner, MG, Branco, MP, "Fully Implanted Brain-Computer Interface in a Locked-In Patient with ALS", *New England Journal of Medicine,* 375(2016), 2060-2066.

[236] James Cameron, *The Terminator*, (Pacific Western Productions, and Cinema, 1984), [Film].

[237] "What consumers really think about AI: A Global Study", *Pegasystems*, (2017). Available from: < https://www.pega.com/ai-survey>

[238] Cellan-Jones, Rory, 'Stephen Hawking warns artificial intelligence could end mankind', *BBC News*, (2014, Dec).

[239] Musk, Elon, "China, Russia, soon all countries w strong computer science. Competition for AI superiority at national level most likely cause of WW3 imo", *Twitter @elonmusk,* (2014 September 4).

[240] ''Whoever leads in AI will rule the world': Putin to Russian children on Knowledge Day', *RT International*, (2017 September 1).

[241] Mcarthur, T, Lam-Mcarthur, J, Fontaine, L*., Oxford English Dictionary,* 2nd edn (Oxford University Press, 2018).

[242] Christian, B, Griffiths, T. "Algorithms to Live by. The Computer Science of Human Decisions", (William Collins, 2016).

[243] Griffiths, (2016), see above.

[244] Private conversation with Dr. Ahmad Assaf, Beamery, (2019).

[245] Turing, A M, "Computing Machinery and Intelligence", *Mind*, 59.236(1950), 433-460.

[246] Von Ahn, L, Blum, M, Hopper, NJ, Langford, J, "CAPTCHA: Using Hard AI Problems for Security", *Eurocrypt,* (2003).

[247] Staff of the Senate Committee on Commerce, Science, and Transportation, "A review of the data broker industry: Collection, Use, and Sale of Consumer Data for Marketing Purposes", (2013, Dec). Available from: <http://educationnewyork.com/files/rockefeller_databroker.pdf>

[248] Wolfie C, "Corportate Surveillance in Everyday Life*", Cracked Labs*, (June 2017). Available from: <https://crackedlabs.org/en/corporate-surveillance>

[249] Fry, H, *Hello World How to be human in the age of the machine*, (Doubleday, 2018).

[250] Humby, C., Hunt, T., and Phillips, T, *Scoring Points: How Tesco is Winning Customer Loyalty*, (Kogan Page Publishers, 2003).

[251] Humby, C, (2003), see above.

[252] Maurer, T, *Cybermercenaries The State, hackers and Power*, (Cambridge University Press, 2017).

[253] Youyou, W, Kosinski, M, Stillwell, D, "Computer-based personality judgements are more accurate than those made by humans", *Proceedings of the National Academy of Science,* (2017).

[254] "Protecting Yourself From The Consequences Of Anthem's Data Breach", *Nytimes.Com*, (2019). <https://www.nytimes.com/2015/02/06/business/protecting-yourself-from-the-consequences-of-anthems-data-breach.html>

[255] Eckert, S, Andreas, D, ''Dark Data' DEFCON Conference', *YouTube*, (2017 Oct. 20). Available from: <https://www.youtube.com/watch?v=1nvYGi7-Lxo>

[256] Hern, Alex, ''Anonymous' Browsing Data Can Be Easily Exposed, Researchers Reveal', *The Guardian*, (2017). Available from: <https://www.theguardian.com/technology/2017/aug/01/data-browsing-habits-brokers>

[257] Hern, (2017), see above.

[258] Abine Inc., *DeleteMe,* (2019). Available from: <https://deleteme.com/>

[259] "The World's Most Valuable Resource Is No Longer Oil, But Data", *The Economist*, (2019). Available from: <https://www.economist.com/leaders/2017/05/06/the-worlds-most-valuable-resource-is-no-longer-oil-but-data>

[260] Gantz, J, Reinsel, D, and Rydning, J, 'Data Age 2025: The Evolution of Data to Life-Critical.' *International Data Corporation*, (April 2017).

[261] Lynch, Shana. 'Andrew Ng: Why AI Is the New Electricity', *Stanford Business*, (March 2017).

[262] Tegmark, M, "Life 3.0: Being Human in the Age of Artificial Intelligence", *Allen Lane*, (2017).

[263] New York University, "AI Now", *AI Now Institute,* (2019). Available from: <https://ainowinstitute.org/>

[264] Minsberg, T, "Read This. Then Put Away Your Phone", *The New York Times*, (2019 March 1). Available from: <https://www.nytimes.com/2019/03/01/business/addictive-technology.html>

[265] Kimball, S, "Zuckerberg Backs Stronger Internet Privacy and Election Laws: 'We need a more active role for governments'', *CNBC*, (2019 Mar 30). Available from: <https://www.cnbc.com/2019/03/30/mark-zuckerberg-calls-

for-tighter-internet-regulations-we-need-a-more-active-role-for-governments.html>

[266] Moor, J, "The Dartmouth College Artificial Intelligence Conference: The Next Fifty years", *AI Magazine,* 27.4(2006), 87-9.

[267] Kaplan, J, *Artificial Intelligence: What Everyone Needs to Know*, (Oxford University Press, October 2016).

[268] Kaplan, (2016), see above.

[269] Crevier, D *AI: The Tumultuous Search for Artificial Intelligence*,[Ebook], (Basic books, 1993).

[270] Crevier, (1993), see above.

[271] Crevier, (1993), see above.

[272] Crevier, (1993), see above.

[273] Crevier, (1993), see above.

[274] Waxman, OB, "The Number of Ways You Can Put Together 6 LEGO Bricks Will Astound You", *TIME*, (July 2015).

[275] Moore, G, "Cramming more components onto integrated circuits", *Electronics Magazine*, 38.8(1965), 114-117.

[276] Seirawan, Y, Simon, HA, Munakata, T, "The implications of Kasparov vs. Deep Blue", *Communications of the ACM,* 40.8(1997).

[277] Hsu, F, Anantharaman, T, Campbell, M, Nowatzyk, A, "A Grandmaster Chess Machine", *Scientific American*, (1990).

[278] Ferrucci, D, Levas, A, Bagchi, S, Gondek, D, Mueller, ET, "Watson: Beyond Jeopardy!", *Artificial Intelligence,* 199(2003), 93–105.

[279] BBC News Technology, *IBM's Watson supercomputer crowned Jeopardy king*, (2011). Available from: < https://www.bbc.co.uk/news/technology-12491688>

[280] Confucius, *The Analects*, trans. By Lau, D.C., (Penguin Classics, September 1979).

[281] Gibbs, S, "Google Acquires UK AI start up Deep Mind", *The Guardian*, (2014 Jan).

[282] Gibbs, S, (2014), see above.

[283] "From AI to protein folding: Our Breakthrough runners-up", *Science*, (2016 Dec).

[284] Metz, C, "In two moves, AlphaGo and Lee Sedol redefined the future", *Wired*, (2016 Mar).

[285] Metz, C, "Google's AlphaGo continues dominance with second win in China", *Wired*, (2017 May).

[286] Spratt, EL, "Creation, curation, and classification: Mario Klingemann and Emily L. Spratt in conversation", *XRDS* 24.3(2018).

[287] "Artificial Intelligence and the Art of Mario Klingemann", *Sothebys*, (2019). Available from: <https://www.sothebys.com/en/articles/artificial-intelligence-and-the-art-of-mario-klingemann>

[288] Sutton, B, "Artwork Created By AI Sells For £40,000 At Sotheby's", *Artsy*, (2019). Available from: <https://www.artsy.net/news/artsy-editorial-artwork-created-ai-sold-40-000-sothebys-failing-generate-fervor-propelled-ai-work-sell-40-times-estimate-year>

[289] Miller, A, 'Can machines be more creative than humans?', *The Guardian Technology*, (2019 Mar).

[290] "U.S. Card Fraud Losses Could Exceed $12B By 2020", *Forbes.Com*, (2019). Available from: <https://www.forbes.com/sites/rogeraitken/2016/10/26/us-card-fraud-losses-could-exceed-12bn-by-2020/#26c28244d243>

[291] Wiggers, Kyle, "Ebay's AI Can Identify 40% Of Credit Card Fraud Cases With 'High Precision", *Venturebeat,* (2019). Available from: <https://venturebeat.com/2018/11/07/ebays-ai-can-identify-40-of-credit-card-fraud-cases-with-high-precision/>

[292] Nakamoto, S, "Bitcoin: A Peer-to-Peer Electronic Cash System", (2008). Available from: <https://bitcoin.org/en/bitcoin-paper>

[293] Laurence, T, "Blockchain For Dummies*", John Wiley & Sons*, (2017).

[294] United States Securities and Exchange Commission, "Form 10-Q", *Sec.Gov*, (1934). Available from: <https://www.sec.gov/Archives/edgar/data/1018724/000101872418000159/amzn-20180930x10q.htm>

[295] U.S. Food and Drug Administration, "Donna-Bea Tillman", *Accessdata.Fda.Gov*, (2019). Available from: <https://www.accessdata.fda.gov/cdrh_docs/pdf18/DEN180044.pdf>

[296] Apple, *Institutions that support health records on iPhone,* [online] (2019). Available from: <https://support.apple.com/en-us/ HT208647>

[297] Cloud Healthcare Pledge, *itic.org,* [online] (2018). Available from:<https://www.itic.org/publicpolicy/CloudHealthcarePledge.pf>

[298] "NIH Funding Bolsters Rare Diseases Research Collaborations", *National Institutes Of Health (NIH)*, (2019). Available from: <https://www.nih.gov/news-events/news-releases/nih-funding-bolsters-rare-diseases-research-collaborations>

[299] U.S. Food and Drug Administration, *Approved Cellular and Gene Therapy Products*, [online] (2019). Available from: <https://www.fda.gov/biologicsbloodvaccines/cellulargenetherapyproducts/approvedproducts/default.htm>

[300] Mojica FJ, Rodriguez-Valera F, 'The discovery of CRISPR in archaea and bacteria', *FEBS J* (2016), vol. 283, no.17, pp. 3162-69.

[301] Ribeil, J, and others, "Gene Therapy in a Patient with Sickle Cell Disease", *New England Journal of Medicine*, 376.9(2017), 848-855. Available from: <doi:10.1056/NEJMoa1609677>

[302] Cyranoski, D, Ledford, H, "International outcry over genome-edited baby claim", *Nature,* 563(2018), 607-608.

[303] Klein, A, Le Page, M, "World's first gene-edited babies announced", *New Scientist*, 240(2018). Available from: <doi:10.1016/s0262-4079(18)32191-2>

[304] Private conversation with Professor Stephen Smith, Scientific Clinician and former lead of the UK's first Academic Health Sciences Centre at Imperial College Healthcare NHS Trust, (2019).

[305] United States Securities and Exchange Commission, "Form 8-K", *Sec.Gov*, (2019). Available from: <https://www.sec.gov/Archives/edgar/data/1288776/000119312509133284/d8k.htm>

[306] Moosavi, A, Ardekani, AM, "Role of Epigenetics in Biology and Human Diseases", *Iranian Biomedical Journal,* 20.5(2016), 246-58.

[307] Moosavi, (2016), see above.

[308] Alegría-Torres, Alejandro, J, Baccarelli, A, Bollati, V, "Epigenetics And Lifestyle", (2019).

[309] Francis, RC, *Epigenetics: How Environment Shapes Our Genes,* (W. W. Norton & Company, 2012).

[310] "The Science", *Chronomics, Available from:< https://www.chronomics.com/>*

[311] Burgess, A, *The Executive Guide to Artificial Intelligence: How to identify and implement applications for AI in your organisation, (*Palgrave Macmillan, 2018).

[312] Quora, "How Would You Explain Deep Learning To An 8 Year Old?", (2019). Available from: <https://www.quora.com/How-would-you-explain-deep-learning-to-an-8-year-old>

[313] Quora, (2019), see above.

[314] Quora, (2019), see above.

[315] Domingos, P, *The Master Algorithm: How the Quest for the Ultimate Learning Machine Will Remake Our World,* (Basic Books, 2015).

[316] Mr 'LII Bayes, "An Essay towards Solving a Problem in the Doctrine of Chances, By the Late Rev. Mr Bayes, F R S Communicated by Mr. Price, in a Letter to John Canton, A M F R S", *Philosophical Transactions of the Royal Society of London*, 53(1763), 370–418. Available from: <doi:10.1098/rstl.1763.0053>

[317] "MCM Methods," *University of Sheffield*, Available from: <https://www.sheffield.ac.uk/polopoly_fs/1.60510!/file/MCMC.pdf >

[318] "Ibm's IBM's Watson is better at diagnosing cancer than human doctors," *Wired, (2013). Available from:* <https://www.wired.co.uk/article/ibm-watson-medical-doctor>

[319] *The Hitchhiker's Guide to the Galaxy, Dir.* Jennings, G, (2005), Bueno Vista Pictures.

[320] "Amelia is More Than a Bot," *IPsoft*. Available from: *<https://www.ipsoft.com/amelia/>*

[321] "Of beer and diapers, and other sale-boosting tricks," *NUS,* (2018). Available from: <https://www.comp.nus.edu.sg/news/features/2793-2018-goh-khim-yong-heng-cheng-suang/>

[322] MIT Technology Review, "Inside the Moonshot Effort to Finally Figure Out the Brain", *Medium*, (2019). Available from: <https://medium.com/mit-technology-review/inside-the-moonshot-effort-to-finally-figure-out-the-brain-39f95c31b780>

[323] Kahn, C, "From Images To Actions: Opportunities For Artificial Intelligence In Radiology", *Pubs.Rsna.Org*, (2019). Available from: <https://pubs.rsna.org/doi/full/10.1148/radiol.2017171734?mobileUi=0&>

[324] Kahn, (2019), see above.

[325] Waldrop, M, "Inside the Moonshot Effort to Finally Figure Out the Brain", *MIT Technology Review*, (2017 Oct).

[326] Topol, E J, "High-performance medicine: The Convergence of Human and Artificial Intelligence", *Nature Medicine*, 25.1(2019), 44-56. Available from: <doi:10.1038/s41591-018-0300-7>

[327] Topol, (2019), see above.

[328] Rjupurkar, P, Irvin, J, and others, "CheXNet: Radiologist-Level Pneumonia Detection on Chest X-Rays with Deep Learning," (2017). Available from: <https://stanfordmlgroup.github.io/projects/chexnet/>

[329] "Home", *Kheiron*. Available from: <https://www.kheironmed.com>

[330] Kolata, G, "Colonoscopies Miss Many Cancers, Study Finds", *New York Times*, (2008).

[331] Mori, Y, and others, "Real-Time Use of Artificial Intelligence in Identification of Diminutive Polyps During Colonoscopy", *Annals of Internal Medicine*, 169.6(2018), 357–366. Available from: <doi:10.7326/M18-0249>

[332] Holme, Ø., Aabakken, L, "Making Colonoscopy Smarter with Standardised Computer-Aided Diagnosis", *Annals of Internal Medicine*, 169.6(2018), 409–410. Available from: <doi:10.7326/M18-1901>

[333] Gulshan and others, "Development and Validation of a Deep Learning Algorithm for Detection of Diabetic Retinopathy in Retinal Fundus Photographs", *Jamma Network,* 316.22(2016), 2402-2410. Available from: < doi:10.1001/jama.2016.17216>

[334] Poplin, R, and others, "Prediction of Cardiovascular Rick Factors from Retinal Fundus Photographs via Deep Learning", *Nature Biomedical Engineering,* 2(2018), 158-164.

[335] De Fauw, J, and others, "Clinically Applicable Deep Learning for Diagnosis and Referral in Retinal Disease", *Nature Medicine,* 24.9(2018), 1342–1350. Available from: <doi: 10.1038/s41591-018-0107-6>

[336] Willems, J, and others, "The Diagnostic Performance of Computer Programs for the Interpretation of Electrocardiograms", *New England Journal of Medicine*, 325.25(1991), 1767–1773.

[337] Willems, (1991), see above.

[338] "KardiaMobile", *Alive Cor,* Available from: <*https://www.alivecor.com/kardiamobile*>

[339] iRhythm Technologies, Inc, *Uninterrupted Ambulatory Cardiac Monitoring,* (2019). Available from: <https://www.irhythmtech.com>

[340] Avati and others, 'Improving Palliative Care with Deep Learning,' Cornell University, (2017 Nov).

[341] Mukhergee, S, 'This cat sensed death, what if computers could to?', *The New York Times,* (2019 Jan). Available from: <https://www.nytimes.com/2018/01/03/magazine/the-dying-algorithm.html >

[342] 'Tempus Launches New Mobile App to Make Clinical and Geonomic Data more Accessible to Physicians at the Point of Care', *Associated Press*, (2018 Sept 19).

[343] Medtronic, *Clinical protocol-driven weaning tools,* (n.d.). Available from: <https://www.medtronic.com/covidien/en-gb/clinical-solutions/weaning-management/improving-weaning-management.html>

[344] Smith, A, "New interactive service set to tackle misinformation and non-adherence", *PharmaTimes*, [serial online] (2019 April 25). Available from: <http://www.pharmatimes.com/news/new_interactive_service_set_to_tackle_misinformation_and_non-adherence_1285578>

[345] McFadden, C, 'These 7 AI-Powered Doctor Phone Apps Could Be the Future of Healthcare.' *Interesting Engineering.* (2019 Jan 24). Available from: <https://interestingengineering.com/these-7-ai-powered-doctor-phone-apps-could-be-the-future-of-healthcare>

[346] "How A Robot Passed China's Medical Licensing Exam", *South China Morning Post*, (2019). Available from :<https://www.scmp.com/news/china/society/article/2120724/how-robot-passed-chinas-medical-licensing-exam>

[347] "Google Buys Fitbit for $2.1 Billion", *The Verge*, (2019). Available from: <https://www.theverge.com/2019/11/1/20943318/google-fitbit-acquisition-fitness-tracker-announcement>

[348] Private conversation with Dan Vahdat, Co-Founder of Medopad, (2018).

[349] Zhang, Li-Li, S. Duff Canning, and Xiao-Ping Wang, "Freezing of Gait in Parkinsonism and its Potential Drug Treatment", *Curr Neuropharmacol,* (2019).

[350] Bilsand, E., and others, '*Plasmodium* dihydrofolate reductase is a second enzyme target for the antimalarial action of triclosan.' *Scientific Reports*, vol. 8, (2018 Jan).

[351] Bilsand, E (2018), see above.

[352] Butcher, M, 'Benevolent Starts AI Collaboration with AstraZeneca to Accelerate Drug Discovery', *Techcrunch*, (May 2019). Available from: <https://techcrunch.com/2019/05/01/benevolentai-starts-ai-collaboration-with-astrazeneca-to-accelerate-drug-discovery/>

[353] Butcher, (2019), see above.

[354] "AstraZeneca Starts Artificial Intelligence Collaboration to Accelerate Drug Discovery," *AstraZeneca Media,* (2019 Apr 30). Available from: <https://www.astrazeneca.com/media-centre/press-releases/2019/astrazeneca-starts-artificial-intelligence-collaboration-to-accelerate-drug-discovery-30042019.html>

[355] "How to unlock innovation with deep tech", *BCG,* Available from: <https://www.bcg.com/en-gb/featured-insights/how-to/invest-in-deep-tech-startups.aspx>

[356] Mahatma Gandhi Quotes, *BrainyMedia Inc*, (2019). Available from: <https://www.brainyquote.com/quotes/mahatma_gandhi_109078>

[357] Telepathy. *Encyclopedia.com* [serial online] (2019 May). Available from: <https://www.encyclopedia.com/humanities/dictionaries-thesauruses-pictures-and-press-releases/telepathy>

[358] Attrill, A, *Cyberpsychology*, (Oxford University Press 2015).

[359] Parsons TD, *Cyberpsychology and the brain. The Interaction of Neuroscience and Affective Computing. Cambridge,* (Cambridge University Press, 2017).

[360] Cole SR and Voytek B, 'Brain Oscillations and the Importance of Waveform Shape', *Trends Cign Sci,* (2017);21(2):137-149.

[361] 'What are brainwaves?', *Brainworks – Train your mind,* [serial online] (2019 June 2). Available from: <https://brainworksneurotherapy.com/what-are-brainwaves>

[362] Brown M, Marmor M, Vaegan, Zrenner E, Brigell M, Bach M, 'ISCEV Standard for Clinical Electro-oculography (EOG)', *Documenta Opthalmologica,* (2006);113(3):205-212.

[363] Vidal M, Bulling A, Gellersen H, "Analysing EOG Signal Features for Discrimination of Eye Movements with Wearable Devices," *New York: ACM*; (2011).

[364] Vilarejo, M, Zapirain, G and others, "A Stress Sensor Based on Galvanic Skin Response (GSR) Controlled by ZigBee," *Sensors,* (2012). Available from: < https://www.ncbi.nlm.nih.gov/pmc/articles/PMC3386730/>

[365] Mills K. 'The basics of electromyography', *J Neural Neurosurgery Psychiatry* (2005);76(2):ii32-ii35.

[366] Baillet S, 'Magnetoencephalography for brain electrophysiology and imaging', *Nature Neuroscience*, (2017); 20:327-339.

[367] "Engineers Develop A Pill For Long-Term Drug Release: New Tablet Attaches To Lining Of The GI Tract, Resists Being Pulled Away", *Science daily*, (2019). Available from:<https://www.sciencedaily.com/releases/2016/04/160406124633.htm>

[368] Parsons TD, '*Cyberpsychology and the brain. The Interaction of Neuroscience and Affective Computing*', (Cambridge University Press; 2017).

[369] Jiang, L, et al, 'BrainNet: A Multi-Person Brain-to-Brain Interface for Direct Collaboration Between Brains*', arXiv.org*, (2018, Sept):1809.08632.

[370] Adam Gazzaley, A, and Larry D Rosen, *The Distracted Mind: Ancient Brains in a High-Tech World,* (The MIT Press, 2016), pp. 206.

[371] Visser, Susanna N, and more, 'Trends in the Parent-Report of Health Care Provider-Diagnosed and Medicated Attention-Deficit/Hyperactivity Disorder: United States, 2003–2011', *JAACAP,* vol. 53, no. 1, (2014, Jan), pp. 34-46.

[372] Qian, X, et al. 'Brain-computer-interface-based intervention re-normalises brain functional network topology in children with attention deficit/hyperactivity disorder', *Translational Psychiatry*, vol. 8, no. 149, (2018 Aug).

[373] Brooks, M, "Video Game 'Rewires' ADHD Brain to Improve Attention", *Medscape* (2018). Available from: <https://www.medscape.com/viewarticle/900994>

[374] "EEG test to help understand and treat schizophrenia," *BioSpace,* (2014). Available from: <https://www.biospace.com/article/around-the-web/eeg-test-to-help-understand-and-treat-schizophrenia-university-of-california-san-diego-ucsd-study-/>

[375] Kaplan, Jerry, *Artificial Intelligence: What Everyone Needs to Know*, (Oxford University Press, 2016 Oct), pp. 35.

[376] Yonck, Richard, *Heart of the Machine: Our Future in a World of Artificial Emotional Intelligence*, (Arcade Publishing, 2017, March), pp. 143.

[377] Bergstrom JR, Duda S, Hawkins D, McGill M, 'Physiological Response Measurements. In: Eye Tracking in User Experience Design,' 1st ed. *Elsevier*; (2014). p 81-108.

[378] "Home-Mindstrong Health", *Mindstrong Health*, (2019) <https://mindstronghealth.com>

[379] 'Future of Preventative Behavioural Healthcare Powered by Machine Learning', *Technology and Operations Management: Harvard Business School,* [serial online] (2018 Nov 13). Available from: <https://rctom.hbs.org/submission/the-future-of-preventative-behavioral-healthcare-powered-by-machine-learning/>

[380] Metz, R, "The Smartphone App That Can Tell You're Depressed Before You Know It Yourself", *MIT Technology Review*, (2018 Oct). Available from: <https://www.technologyreview.com/s/612266/the-smartphone-app-that-can-tell-youre-depressed-before-you-know-it-yourself/>

[381] Metz R, (2018 Oct), see above.

[382] 'Dementia Statistics: Numbers of people with dementia.' *Alzheimer's Disease International*. [serial online]. Available from: <https://www.alz.co.uk/research/statistics>

[383] "Artificial Intelligence: How to get it right", *NHS*, (2019). Available from: <https://www.nhsx.nhs.uk/assets/NHSX_AI_report.pdf>

[384] Tanaka H, et al, 'Detecting Dementia Through Interactive Computer Avatars', *IEEE Journal of Translational Engineering in Health and Medicine*, vol. 5, (2017, Sept), pp. 1-11.

[385] Farooq, I, 'Computer avatars are now able to detect dementia', *European Pharmaceutical Review*, (2018 Sept).

[386] Orwell, G. *Nineteen Eighty-Four,* (London: Secker and Warburg, 1949).

[387] Knight, Will, 'The Dark Secret at the Heart of AI', *MIT Technology Review*, (2017, April).

[388] Bonsor K and Johnson R, 'How Facial Recognition Systems Work', *HowStuffWorks,* [serial online]. Available from: <https://electronics.howstuffworks.com/gadgets/high-tech-gadgets/facial-recognition1.htm>

[389] David White, Richard I. Kemp, Rob Jenkins, Michael Matheson and A. Mike Burton, ''Passport errors' errors in face matching'', *PLOSOne*, (2014 Aug).

[390] Fry, Hannah, *Hello World: How to be Human in the Age of the Machine*, (Doubleday, 2018).

[391] "About Us", *FDNA.* Available from: <http://fdna.com/about-us/>

[392] Garbade MJ, 'A Simple Introduction to Natural Language Processing', *Medium.* [serial online] (2018 Oct 15). Available from: <https://becominghuman.ai/a-simple-introduction-to-natural-language-processing-ea66a1747b32>

[393] Hoy MB. Alexa, Siri, Cortana, and More, 'An Introduction to Voice Assistants', *Medical Reference Services Quarterly,* (2018); 37(1):81–88.

[394] Hughes, O, 'Oxehealth secures 'world first' accreditation for optical vital signs tech', *Digitalhealth*, (2018 Oct 2). Available from: <https://www.digitalhealth.net/2018/10/oxehealth-secures-world-first-accreditation-for-optical-vital-signs-tech/>

[395] Bodkin, Henry, 'New remote pulse sensors promise a good night's sleep at last for NHS hospital patients', *The Telegraph*, (2018 Sept).

[396] Private conversation with Hugh Lloyd-Jukes, Oxehealth, (2019).

[397] Haskins, C, 'Dozens of Cities Have Secretly Experimented With Predictive Policing Software:Motherboard', *Tech by Vice.* (2019 Feb 6). Available from: < https://www.vice.com/en_us/article/d3m7jq/dozens-of-cities-have-secretly-experimented-with-predictive-policing-software>

[398] Baraniuk, C, 'Exclusive: UK police wants AI to stop violent crime before it happens', *New Scientist*, (2018 Nov).

[399] Minority Report [Film] Dirc. Spielberg, S, (2002), 20TH Century Fox.

[400] "Tokyo's Perseusbot is the Real-Life Robocop", *Inquisitr.Com*, (2019). Available from: <https://www.inquisitr.com/5188815/tokyos-perseusbot-is-the-real-life-robocop/>

[401] 'AI powered robot to be trialed in Japanese train station,'(2019). Available from:<https://channels.theinnovationenterprise.com/articles/ai-powered-robot-to-be-trialed-in-japanese-train-station>

[402] Knight, Will, "Why Everyone Benefits If We Emphasize The Human Side Of The Technology", *MIT Technology Review*, (2019). Available

from:<https://www.technologyreview.com/s/609060/put-humans-at-the-center-of-ai/>

[403] Von Neuman, J, and Morgenstern, O, *Theory of Games and Economic Behaviour*, (Princeton University Press, 1944).

[404] *The Princess Bride* [Film], dirc. Jennings, G, (Harcourt Brace Jovanovich, 1973).

[405] *Casino Royale* [Film], dirc. Campbell, M, (2006), Sony Pictures.

[406] Krishnan, M, Mishcke, J, and Remes, J, 'Is the Solow Paradox Back?', *Mckinsey Quarterly*, (2018 June).

[407] Vinge, Vernor, "The Coming Technological Singularity: How to Survive in the Post-Human Era', *NASA Conference Publication 10129*, (1993), pp. 11–22.

[408] Nick Hay, "The stamp collecting device," (2007). Available from: <http://www.singinst.org/blog/2007/06/11/thestamp-collecting-device>

[409] Good, Irving J, 'Speculations concerning the first ultra intelligent machine', *Advances in Computers*, vol. 6, (1966), pp. 31-88.

[410] "Artificial Intelligence: Construction Technology's Next Frontier", *Mckinsey & Company*, (2019). Available from: <https://www.mckinsey.com/industries/capital-projects-and-infrastructure/our-insights/artificial-intelligence-construction-technologys-next-frontier>

[411] Kulp, Scott A., and Benjamin H. Strauss, "New Elevation Data Triple Estimates Of Global Vulnerability To Sea-Level Rise And Coastal Flooding", *Nature Communications*, (2019).

[412] "The Last Invention We Will Ever Make", *Medium*, (2019). Available from: <https://medium.com/ai-revolution/the-last-invention-we-will-ever-make-4bf0026fd03c>

[413] Fromm, Eric, *The Sane Society*, (Rinehart & Company, 1955).

[414] Birks et al, 'Robotic Seals as Therapeutic Tools in Aged Care Facility: A Qualitative Study', *Journal of aging research* (2016).

[415] Jøranson, N., et al, 'Effects on Symptoms of Agitation and Depression in Persons with Dementia Participating in Robot-Assisted Activity: A Cluster-Randomised Controlled Trial', *Journal of the American Medical Directors Association,* vol. 16, no. 10, (2015, Oct), pp. 867-873.

[416] *New Dog-Like Robot From Boston Dynamics Can Open Doors*, [Video], *YouTube*, (2018).

[417] Picard, R, *Affective Computing,* (The MIT Press, 1997).

[418] Picard, (1997), see above.

[419] Brave, S, et al. 'Computers that care: Investigating the effects of orientation of emotion exhibited by an embodied computer agent', *International Journal of Human-Computer Studies*, vol. 62, (2005, Feb) pp. 161-178.

[420] Picard, R. W, *What does it mean for a computer to 'have' emotions? Emotions in Humans and Artifacts*, (MIT Press, 2013).

[421] Muir, D., et al, 'Assessing the psycho-social impact of computers, brain research, and behaviourism: The von Neumann effect', *Sociological Forum*, vol. 3, (1988), pp. 606-612, doi:10.1007/bf01115417.

[422] Reeves, B, and Nass, C, *The Media Equation: How people treat computers, television, and new media like real people and places,* (Cambridge University Press, 1996).

[423] McEneaney, J, et al, 'Agency Effects in Human–Computer Interaction*', International Journal of Human-Computer Interaction*, vol. 29, no. 12, (2013 Apr), pp.798-813.

[424] Edwards J. Some, 'Soldiers Are So Attached To Their Battle Robots They Hold Funerals For Them When They 'Die'', *Business Insider*, [serial online] (2013 Sep 18). Available from:< https://www.businessinsider.com/some-soldiers-are-so-attached-to-their-battle-robots-they-hold-funerals-for-them-when-they-die-2013-9?r=US&IR=T>

[425] Saracho, O, "Theory of mind: children's understanding of mental states", *Early Child Development and Care*, (2014);184(6):949-961.

[426] McLeod, S, 'Bowlby's Attachment Theory', *Simplypsychology,* (2017 Feb 05). Available from: <https://www.simplypsychology.org/bowlby.html>

[427] Keyes, & K. A. Moore, *Well-being: Positive development across the life course* (pp. 191-204), (Erlbaum Associates Publishers, 2016).

[428] Taylor, Chloe. 'SoftBank alumni launches robot companion designed to love humans', *CNBC*, (2018, Dec). Available from: <https://www.cnbc.com/2018/12/18/softbank-alumni-launches-robot-companion-designed-to-love-humans.html>

[429] "Lovot Is The First Robot I Can See Myself Getting Emotionally Attached To", *The Verge*, (2019). Available from:<https://www.theverge.com/2019/1/10/18176002/lovot-groovex-robot-emotional-attachment-ces-2019>

[430] Smith C, "Robot 'teacher' to help children with autism developed by scientists", *Imperial College London News*, [serial online] (2017 Feb 2). Available from: <https://www.imperial.ac.uk/news/177318/robot-teacher-help-children-with-autism/>

[431] Jha, A, 'The robot teaching autistic children how to communicate', *ITV News*, (2017 Feb 16). Available from: <https://www.itv.com/news/2017-02-16/the-robot-teaching-autistic-children-how-to-communicate/>

[432] "Your kid's new reading buddy could be a robot", *UChicago Medicine,* (2018). Available from:<http://healthlibrary.uchospitals.edu/content/daily-news-feed-v1/your-kids-new-reading-buddy-could-be-a-robot/>

[433] Michaelis, J, and Mutlu, B, 'Reading socially: Transforming the in-home reading experience with a learning-companion robot', *Science Robotics*, vol. 3, no. 21, (2018, Aug).

[434] Hart, B, and Risley, T.R, 'The Early Catastrophe: The 30 Million Word Gap by Age 3', *American Educator*, (2003), pp. 4-9.

[435] Hart, (2003), see above.

[436] Simon, Matt, 'How Rude Humanoid Robots Can Mess with Your Head', *Wired Magazine*, (2018, Aug).

[437] Griffin, Andrew, "Fortnite Battle Royale Exposes Children to Scams that Could Also Endanger Parents, Warn Experts", [Print] (2018 July 9).

[438] Griffin, (2018), see above.

[439] "Sophia - Hanson Robotics", *Hanson Robotics*, (2019). Available from: <https://www.hansonrobotics.com/sophia/>

[440] Stone, Zara, 'Everything You Need to Know About Sophia's Robot Love', *Forbes*, (2018, Aug). Available from: <https://www.forbes.com/sites/zarastone/2018/08/09/everything-you-need-to-know-about-sophias-robot-love/#6efbcb3615ad>

[441] Weisberger, Mindy, "Life-like 'Sophia' Robot Granted Citizenship To Saudi Arabia", (2019). Available from:<https://www.livescience.com/60815-saudi-arabia-citizen-robot.html>

[442] Field, T and Reite, M, *Psychobiology of Attachment and Separation* (New York Academic Press, 1985).

[443] "Triangulation 242 Sphero," *Twit Tv* [TV] (2019). Available from:<https://twit.tv/shows/triangulation/episodes/242>

[444] Breznican, "A Star Wars: BB-8 gender revealed for Force Awakens droid," *Entertainment Weekly.* (2015 Nov 13). Available from: <https://ew.com/article/2015/11/13/bb-8-gender-star-wars/>

[445] Danaher, J and more, *Robot Sex: Social and Ethical Implications,* (The MIT Press, November 2017).

[446] Kendall P. Blobular, "Doll combines hugs and phone calls to help reduce stress", *Japan Today.* [serial online] (2013 Oct 20), Available from:<https://japantoday.com/category/features/lifestyle/blobular-doll-combines-hugs-and-phone-calls-to-he>

[447] Patrick Lin, Keith Abney, George A Bekey, *Robot ethics: the ethical and social implications of robotics*, (MIT Press, 2014).

[448] Danaher, J and more, *Robot Sex: Social and Ethical Implications* (The MIT Press, November 2017), p. 97.

[449] 'Woman reveals love for robot, wants to marry it', *Daily Mail,* (2016). Available from: <http://www.dailymail.co.uk/femail/article-4060440/Woman-reveals-love-ROBOT-wants-marry-it.html>

[450] Danaher, J and more, *Robot Sex: Social and Ethical Implications,* (The MIT Press, November 2017).

[451] Kidd C. 'Introducing the Mabu Personal Healthcare Companion', *Catalia Health*, (2015 June 12). Available from: <https://www.cataliahealth.com/introducing-the-mabu-personal-healthcare-companion/>

[452] Kidd, (2015), see above.

453 Kidd, (2015), see above.

454 Lipshaw JM, "The Epistemology of the Financial Crisis: Complexity, Causation, Law and Judgement", *Southern California Interdisciplinary Law Journal,* (2009), 19(2):299-351.

455 "Subliminal", *English Oxford Living Dictionaries,* (2019). Available from: < https://www.oxfordlearnersdictionaries.com/definition/english/subliminal>

456 Craighead WE, Nemeroff CB, *The Concise Corsini Encyclopaedia of Psychology and Behavioral Science,* (Hoboken: John Wiley & Sons, 2004).

457 McClelland, David C, "Human Motivation", (1988). Available from: https://doi.org/10.1017/cbo9781139878289.

458 McClelland, David C, (1988), see above.

459 Sanders MD, Warrington EK, Marshall J. Wieskrantz L, "Blindisight': Vision in a Field Defect", *The Lancet* (1974);303 (7860):707-708.

460 Takahashi K, *The Effect of Subliminal Messages and Suggestions on Memory: Isolating the Placebo Effect*, (Florida State University Libraries, 2008).

461 Vicary J.M, "The circular test of bias in personal interview surveys," *Public Opinion,*(1955);19:215–218.

462 'Does subliminal advertising actually work?', *BBC News: Magazine*, [serial online] (2015 Jan 20). Available from: <https://www.bbc.co.uk/news/magazine-30878843>

463 BBC, (2015), see above.

464 "When (And Why) Was Subliminal Messaging Banned?" *Subliminal Messaging* [serial online]. Available from: < https://www.subliminal-messaging.com/when-and-why-was-subliminal-messaging-banned/>

465 Friedman WJ, "Federal Communications Commission," *FCC News.* [serial online] (2001 Mar 9). Available from: <https://transition.fcc.gov/Speeches/Tristani/Statements/2001/stgt123.html>

466 "Hours of video uploaded to YouTube every minute as of July 2015", *Statista.* [serial online] (2015 Jul). Available from: <https://www.statista.com/statistics/259477/hours-of-video-uploaded-to-youtube-every-minute/>

467 "Impact of media use on children and youth", *Paediatric Child Health.* (2003);8(5):301-306.

468 "NHS Cervical Screening Programme: South Region, Cervical Screening Policy 2015", *NHS England,* V1 (2015).

469 Galston WA, 'Why the government must help shape the future of AI. Brookings,' (2018 Sept13). Available from: <https://www.brookings.edu/research/why-the-government-must-help-shape-the-future-of-ai/>

470 Wilson B, *Subliminal Seduction*, (Key Prentice-Hall, 1973).

[471] S. Dingfelder, "The Science of Political Advertising", *APA*, (2012). Available from: <https://www.apa.org/monitor/2012/04/advertising >

[472] Hibbard K, Hegarty P Blots, "A history of the Rorschach ink blot test in Britain," *J Hist Behav Sci,* (2016); 52(2):146-66.

[473] "Rorschach Technique," *Minddisorders,* 2019. Available from: <http://www.minddisorders.com/Py-Z/Rorschach-technique.html>

[474]Stibil, Jeff, "Subliminal messaging you advantage business and life," *Usa Today*, (2019). Available from: <https://eu.usatoday.com/story/money/columnist/2018/03/27/how-use-subliminal-messaging-your-advantage-business-and-life/454784002/>

[475] Her, (2013) [Film], dr. Spike Jones, *Annapurna Pictures.*

[476] Nield D, 'Microsoft's New 'Holoportation' Tech Lets You Jump Into Someone Else's Reality. Science alert', (2016 Apr 1). Available from: < https://www.sciencealert.com/microsoft-s-new-holoportation-tech-lets-you-jump-into-someone-else-s-reality>

[477] Nield, (2006), see above.

[478]'Bound Volume Hansard – Debate 444(130)', *parliament.uk* [serial online] (Mar 22 2006). Available from:<https://publications.parliament.uk/pa/cm200506/cmhansrd/vo060322/debtext/60322-06.htm>

[479] Jones D, "Left or right-wing? Brain's disgust response tells all", *New Scientist*, (Oct 30. 2013).

[480] Jones D, (2013), see above.

[481] "National Election Studies (NES) - SAGE Research Methods", *Methods.Sagepub.Com*, (2019). Available from: <https://methods.sagepub.com/reference/encyclopedia-of-survey-research-methods/n317.xml>

[482] Chemi, Eric, "Facts Matter Most in Convincing Voters", *CNBC,* (2019). Available from: <https://www.cnbc.com/2015/10/16/t-facts-matter-most-in-convincing-voters.html>

[483] Western, Drew, *The Political Brain: The Role of Emotion in Deciding the Fate of thee Nation,*(Public Affairs, 2008).

[484] Western, (2008), see above.

[485] Mettler, Katie, 'Obama Yes We Can, thank Michelle for that', (2019). Available from: <https://www.washingtonpost.com/news/morning-mix/wp/2017/01/11/obamas-yes-we-can-thank-michelle-for-that/>

[486] Knutson KM, Wood JN, Spampinato MV, Grafman J, 'Politics on the Brain: An fMRI Investigation', *Soc Neuroscience,* (2006);1(1):25-40.

[487] Western, Drew, *The Political Brain: The Role of Emotion in Deciding the Fate of thee Nation,'* (Public Affairs, 2008).

[488] Tiles JE, 'The Combat of Passion and Reason', *Philosophy* (1977);52(201):321-330.

[489] Rosenberg M, Confessore N, Cadwalladr, 'How Trump Consultants Exploited the Facebook Data of Millions', *The New York Times,* (2018 Mar 17).

[490] "Bloomberg J Does Trump's 'Weaponised AI Propaganda Machine' Hold Water?", *Forbes*, (2017 Mar 5).

[491] 'What The 5 Major Personality Traits Could Reveal About You', *Psychology Today*, (2019). Available from: <https://www.psychologytoday.com/us/blog/what-mentally-strong-people-dont-do/201605/what-the-5-major-personality-traits-could-reveal>

[492] Sissons B, "Which personality test is more accurate, the Big 5 personality test or the Myers-Briggs test?", *Quora*, (2019 Aug 7). Available from: <https://www.quora.com/Which-personality-test-is-more-accurate-the-Big-5-personality-test-or-the-Myers-Briggs-test>

[493] "The Big Five Personality Traits Model and Test," *Mind Tools.* Available from: <https://www.mindtools.com/pages/article/newCDV_22.htm>

[494] Polonski VW, "How artificial intelligence conquered democracy", *The Independent*. (2017 Aug. 15).

[495] "Democracy's Wisdom,"*Depts.Washington.Edu*, (2019). Available from: <http://depts.washington.edu/uwch/documents/articles/2013%20Democracys%20Wisdom.pdf>

[496] "NPR Choice Page", *Npr.Org*, (2019). Available from: <https://www.npr.org/sections/13.7/2018/03/12/592868569/no-man-is-an-island-the-wisdom-of-deliberating-crowds?t=1572799906007>

[497] Stasser, G., & Titus, W, "Pooling of unshared information in group decision making: Biased information sampling during discussion", *Journal of Personality and Social Psychology*, (1985): 148:1467–1478.

[498] Fisher, B. A*, Small group decision making: Communication and the group process,* (McGraw-Hill Education, 1974).

[499] *The Wizard of Oz* [Film], Dirc. Fleming.V (1939), MGM.

[500] "Secrets Of The Wizard Of Oz", *BBC News*, (2019). Available from:<http://news.bbc.co.uk/1/hi/magazine/7933175.stm>

[501] Robitzski, Dan, "A Quarter Of Europeans Trust AI More Than Politicians", *Futurism*, (2019). Available from: <https://futurism.com/europeans-trust-ai-politicians>

[502] "AI-Politicians: A Revolution In Politics", *Medium*, (2019). Available from: <https://medium.com/politics-ai/ai-politicians-a-revolution-in-politics-11a7e4ce90b0>

[503] Medium, (2019), see above.

[504] Wagner, Meg, "This Virtual Politician Wants To Run For Office", *CNN*, (2019). Available from: <https://edition.cnn.com/2017/11/23/tech/first-virtual-politician-trnd/index.html>

[505] "AI-Politicians: A Revolution In Politics", *Medium*, (2019). Available from: <https://medium.com/politics-ai/ai-politicians-a-revolution-in-politics-11a7e4ce90b0>

[506] Milmo C, 'After 50 years, KitKat takes a break from the slogan that made its name', *The Independent* (2004).

[507] Walker T, 'How Hillary Clinton lost to Donald Trump', *The Independent,* (2016 Nov 9).

[508] Frank, Robert, 'Jeff Bezos is now the richest man in modern history', *CNBC*, (July 2018).

[509] Wingfield, N, and Bowles, N, 'Jeff Bozos, Mr. Amazon, Steps Out', *The New York Times*, (January 2018).

[510] Partners & Collaborators, *Machine Intelligence Garage*. Available from: <https://www.migarage.ai/partners-and-collaborators/>

[511] "About Amazon Staff Prime Air," *The Amazon blog – Dayone*, [serial online] Available from: <https://www.aboutamazon.co.uk/innovation/prime-air>

[512] Tillman M. "What is Amazon Go, where is it, and how does it work?" *Pocket-lint.* [serial online] (2019 Feb 18). Available from: <https://www.pocketlint.com/phones/news/amazon/139650-what-is-amazon-go-where-is-it-and-how-does-it-work>

[513] Farrell, Sean, 'Amazon Go checkout-free stores look set to come to UK.' *The Guardian*, (December 2016).

[514] "Netflix's History: From DVD Rentals To Streaming Success", *Bbc.Co.Uk*, (2019). Available from: <http://www.bbc.co.uk/newsbeat/article/42787047/netflixs-history-from-dvd-rentals-to-streaming-success>

[515] Bond S, "Netflix nears 100m subscriber milestone", *The Financial Times*, (2017).

[516] Smith, John R, 'IBM Research Takes Watson to Hollywood with the First "Cognitive Film Trailer", *IMB Research*, (August 2016).

[517] Mattioli, Heather, "Mcdonald's Buys Israeli Digital Start-up Dynamic Yield", *WSJ*, (2019). Available from: <https://www.wsj.com/articles/mcdonalds-nears-deal-to-buy-israeli-digital-startup-dynamic-yield-11553552124>

[518] "Google Search Statistics," *Internet Live Stats.* [serial online]. Available from: <https://www.internetlivestats.com/google-search-statistics>

[519] "How google uses Information from sites or apps that use our services", *Google*, Available from: <https://policies.google.com/technologies/partner-sites?hl=en-US>

[520] Google, (n.d), see above.

[521] Shewan D, "How Much Does Google Ads Cost", *WordStream*, (2019 Jun 9). Available from: <https://www.wordstream.com/blog/ws/2015/05/21/how-much-does-adwords-cost>

[522] Berger, J, *Contagious. Why Things Catch On.* Reprint Ed. (New York: Simon & Schuster; 2016).

[523] "The History Of Uber - Uber's Timeline - Uber Newsroom US", *Uber Newsroom*, (2019). Available from: <https://www.uber.com/newsroom/history/>

[524] Martin, Nicole, "Uber Charges More If They Think You're Willing To Pay More", *Forbes*, (2019). Available from: <https://www.forbes.com/sites/nicolemartin1/2019/03/30/uber-charges-more-if-they-think-youre-willing-to-pay-more/#d91cabf73654>

[525] 'Narcissus (Greek Mythology)', *Encyclopaedia Britannica.* Available from: <https://www.britannica.com/topic/Narcissus-Greek-mythology>

[526] Ferrari PF, Bonini L, Fogassi. "From monkey mirror neurons to primate behaviours: possible 'direct' and 'indirect' pathways", *Philosophical Transactions B*, (2009); 364(1528):2311-2323.

[527] Kuo L, "World's first AI news anchor unveiled in China", *The Guardian,* (2018 Nov 9).

[528] Kuo, (2018), see above.

[529] "China Luxury Report 2019", *McKinsey & Company*, (2019).

[530] Tzu, Sun, *The Art of War*, (Giles, Lionel, trans., Pax Librorum, 2009).

[531] "What is NASA's Asteroid Redirect Mission?", *NASA.gov,* (2017). Available from: <https://www.nasa.gov/content/what-is-nasa-s-asteroid-redirect-mission>

[532] Beiser, Vince, 'The Robot Assault on Fukushima', *Wired Magazine*, (April 2018).

[533] Cabreira TM, Brisolara LB, Ferreriara Jr. PR, 'Survey on Coverage Path Planning with Unmanned Aerial Vehicles', *Drones*, (2019);3(1):4.

[534] Barrie A, "Bee-sized bots set to dominate future battles for cities", *Fox News*, (2018 Oct 26). Available from: <https://www.foxnews.com/tech/bee-sized-bots-set-to-dominate-future-battles-for-cities>

[535] "Department Of Defense Announces Successful Micro-Drone Demonstration", *U.S. Department Of Defense*, (2019). Available from: <https://www.defense.gov/Newsroom/Releases/Release/Article/1044811/department-of-defense-announces-successful-micro-drone-demonstration>

[536] Martin, Timothy, 'How North Korea's Hackers Became Dangerously Good', *The Wall Street Journal*, (2018 Apr).

[537] Sir Morse, A, "Investigation: WannaCry cyber attack and the NHS", *National Audit Office*, (April 2018).

[538] Field M, "WannaCry cyber attack cost the NHS £92m as 19,000 appointments cancelled", *The Telegraph,* (2018 Oct 11).

[539] "US and UK blame North Korea for Wanna cry cyberattack", *DW*, (2017 Dec 19). Available from: <https://www.dw.com/en/us-and-uk-blame-north-korea-for-wannacry-cyberattack/a-41852493-0>

[540] Petroff A, Larson S, "Another big malware attack ripples across the world", *CNN Tech*, [serial online] (2017 Jun 28). Available from: <https://money.cnn.com/2017/06/27/technology/hacking-petya-europe-ukraine-wpp-rosneft/index.html>

[541] Hern, Alex, 'Hackers publish private photos from cosmetic surgery clinic', *The Guardian*, (May 2017).

[542] Hern, Alex, 'Stolen nude photos and hacked defibrillators: is this the future of ransomware?', *The Guardian*, (August 2017).

[543] "Hackers Publish Info Of 25,000 Lithuanian Cosmetic Surgery Patients", *Data Leaks, Breaches & Hacks*, (2019). Available from: <https://www.dataleaklawyers.co.uk/blog/hackers-publish-info-25000-lithuanian-cosmetic-surgery-patients>

[544] "Company Overview", *Darktrace.Com*, (2019). Available from: <https://www.darktrace.com/en/overview/>

[545] Kai W Wucherpfennig, Eric S Huseby, and more, "Structural Biology of the T-cell Receptor: Insights into Receptor Assembly, Ligand Recognition, and Initiation of Signaling", *Cold Spring Harbor Perspective Biol*ogy. (2010 Apr).

[546] Sir Bacon, F, *Meditationes Sacrae*, (1597).

[547] Ellul, J, *Propaganda: The Formation of Men's Attitudes*, (1962).

[548] Doward J, Gibbs A, 'Did Cambridge Analytica influence the Brexit vote and the US election?', *The Guardian,* (2017 Mar 4).

[549] "The Cambridge Analytica Files | The Guardian", *The Guardian*, (2019). Available from: <https://www.theguardian.com/news/series/cambridge-analytica-files>

[550] Shen, Xinmei, "Skynet, China's Massive Video Surveillance Network", *Abacus*, (2018). Available from : <https://www.abacusnews.com/who-what/skynet-chinas-massive-video-surveillance-network/article/2166938>

[551] Botsman, Rachel, 'Big data meets Big Brother as China moves to rate its citizens', *Wired Magazine*, [Print] (October 2017).

[552] Xiaoxiao L. Ant, "Financial Subsidiary Starts Offering Individual Credit Scores", *Caixin*, [serial online] (2015 Mar 2). Available from: <https://caixinglobal.com/2015-03-02/101012655.html>

[553] Burton G, 'Chinese citizens with poor 'social credit rating' to be barred from public transport', *The Inquirer*, [serial online] (2018 Mar 19). Available from: <https://www.theinquirer.net/inquirer/news/3028737/chinese-citizens-with-poor-social-credit-rating-to-be-barred-from-public-transport>

[554] Kennedy B, 'The Scary Concerns China's Credit Scores are raising', *CNBC*, [Serial Online]. Available from: <https://www.cbsnews.com/news/the-scary-concerns-chinas-credit-scores-are-raising/>

[555] "South Korea Aims High on AI, Pumps $2 Billion Into R&D", *Medium*, [serial online]. (2018 May 16.). Available from:

<https://medium.com/syncedreview/south-korea-aims-high-on-ai-pumps-2-billion-into-r-d-de8e5c0c8ac5>

[556] Kania E, "China May Soon Surpass America on the Artificial Intelligence Battlefield." *The National Interest.* [serial online] (2017 Feb 21). Available from: <https://nationalinterest.org/feature/china-may-soon-surpass-america-the-artificial-intelligence-19524>

[557] Vernon, Jamie, "Understanding The Butterfly Effect", *American Scientist,* (2019). Available from: <https://www.americanscientist.org/article/understanding-the-butterfly-effect>

[558] Lorenz, Edward N, 'Deterministic Nonperiodic Flow', *Journal of the Atmospheric Sciences,* vol. 20, no.2, (1963), pp. 130141,Chapter 17.

[559] Schwab, Klaus, *The Fourth Industrial Revolution,* (World Economic Forum, 2016).

[560] Wong, Andrew, 'The 'father of A.I' urges humans not to fear the technology', *CNBC News,* (May 2018).

[561] Dickens, Charles, *The Life and Adventures of Martin Chuzzlewit,* (1843), Chapter 10.

[562] Heit, Helmut, 'There are no facts…Nietzsche as Predecessor of Post-Truth?', *Studia Philosophica Estonica,* (2018):11(1): 44–63.

[563] Turing, A M, 'Computing Machinery and Intelligence.' *Mind,* vol. 59, no. 236, (October 1950), pp. 433-460.

[564] Stellan Ohlsson, Aaron Urasky, "Verbal IQ Of A Four-Year Old Achieved By An AI System", *Citeseerx.Ist.Psu.Edu.* (2019). Available from: <http://citeseerx.ist.psu.edu/viewdoc/summary?doi=10.1.1.386.6705>

[565] J. Friedland and B.M.Cole, 'From Homo-Economicus to Homo-Virtus: A System-Theoretic Model for Raising Moral Self-Awareness', *Journal of Business Ethics,* 155, no 1, (March 2019): 191-2015.

[566] 'AI Can Help Us Live More Deliberately', *MIT Sloan Management Review.* (2019) [Print].

[567] Guerrini, Federico, 'Chinese Schools Track Students with 'Intelligent Uniforms', *Forbes.* (2018, Dec).

[568] Vara, Vauhini, 'We Will Literally Predict Their Life Outcomes - Backchannel', *WIRED,* (2019). Available from: <https://www.wired.com/2016/05/we-will-literally-predict-their-life-outcomes/>

[569] Goddard C, 'More Than Just Teddy Bears. Psychology Today', [serial online] (2014 Jul 15). Available from: <https://www.psychologytoday.com/gb/blog/the-guest-room/201407/more-just-teddy-bears>

[570] 'The Artificial Intelligence Clinician learns optimal treatment strategies for sepsis in intensive care', *Nature Medicine,* 24:1716–1720, (2018). Available from:<https://www.nature.com/articles/s41591-018-0213-5>

[571] 'The Top 12 Health Chatbots', *The Medical Futurist*, [serial online] (2018 May 29). Available from: < https://medicalfuturist.com/top-12-health-chatbots>

[572] Stone Z, 'Your AI Physical Therapist Will Make You Better, Faster', *Forbes*. [serial online] (2019 Mar 6). Available from: <https://www.forbes.com/sites/zarastone/2019/03/06/your-ai-physical-therapist-will-make-you-better faster/#29772e44bf7e>

[573] Shi Z, Li CX, 'How AI is changing how we do business: the father of contemporary AI gives his views', *China Daily*, [serial online] (2017 Jun 23). Available from: < http://africa.chinadaily.com.cn/opinion/2017-06/23/content_29863158.htm>

[574] Wollheim, R, *The Thread of Life,* (New Haven, CT: Yale University Press, 1984)

[575] G. Lukianokk and J. Haidt, '*The Coddling of the American Mind: How Good Intentions and Bad Ideas are Setting Up a Generation of Failure*', (New York: Penguin Random House, 2018).

[576] A.Gopalas, 'Marketplace Sentiments', *Journal of Consumer Research* 41, no.4 (Dec. 1, 2014: 995-1014).